BY JAMES SCHUYLER

POEMS
Freely Espousing (1969)
The Crystal Lithium (1972)
Hymn to Life (1974)
The Morning of the Poem (1980)
A Few Days (1985)
Selected Poems (1988)
Collected Poems (1993)

NOVELS
Alfred and Guinevere (1958)
A Nest of Ninnies (with John Ashbery, 1976)
What's for Dinner? (1978)

PROSE AND POEMS
The Home Book (edited by Trevor Winkfield, 1977)

COLLECTED POEMS

JAMES

SCHUYLER

COLLECTED

POEMS

THE NOONDAY PRESS

FARRAR, STRAUS AND GIROUX

NEW YORK

Copyright © 1993 by the Estate of James Schuyler
Printed in the United States of America
Published in Canada by HarperCollinsCanadaLtd
Designed by Cynthia Krupat
First published in 1993 by Farrar, Straus and Giroux
This edition first published in 1995 by The Noonday Press
Third printing, 1998

Library of Congress Cataloging-in-Publication Data
Schuyler, James.
[Poems. Selections]
Collected poems / James Schuyler.—1st ed.
p.   cm.
Includes index.
I. Title.
PS3569.C56A17   1993   811'.54—dc20   92-40977   CIP

CONTENTS

from The Home Book 1951–1970 (1977)

The Crystal Lithium (1972)

SOUTHAMPTON AND NEW YORK

Hymn to Life (1974)

The Morning of the Poem (1980)

A Few Days (1985)

Last Poems

EDITORS' NOTE

When James Schuyler died on April 12, 1991, he was assembling recent poems for a new collection which he hoped to publish the following year. Many of these poems were read by him publicly toward the end of his life. Some were published in magazines and journals. As we read through this loosely formed manuscript, we became aware that though it was not large enough to warrant publication as a separate book, it was important that the poems be published as his last work, something, we feel, he would have wished.

Our thought was to include them with the complete texts of his previous books of poems, several long out of print, in a *Collected Poems*.

We are indebted to Jonathan Galassi, Schuyler's editor at Farrar, Straus and Giroux, for his help and counsel at every stage of the preparation of this book, though, of course, we bear the responsibility for the choices made.

Tom Carey
Raymond Foye
Darragh Park

New York City
Spring 1993

FREELY

ESPOUSING

(1 9 6 9)

FOR ANNE AND FAIRFIELD PORTER

Freely Espousing

a commingling sky

        a semi-tropic night
        that cast the blackest shadow
        of the easily torn, untrembling banana leaf

or Quebec! what a horrible city
so Steubenville is better?
        the sinking sensation
when someone drowns thinking, "This can't be happening to me!"
the profit of excavating the battlefield where Hannibal whomped the
    Romans
the sinuous beauty of words like allergy
the tonic resonance of
pill when used as in
"she is a pill"
on the other hand I am not going to espouse any short stories in which
    lawn mowers clack.
No, it is absolutely forbidden
for words to echo the act described; or try to. Except very directly
as in
bong. And tickle. Oh it is inescapable kiss.
Marriages of the atmosphere
are worth celebrating
        where Tudor City
catches the sky or the glass side
of a building lit up at night in fog
"What is that gold-green tetrahedron down the river?"
"You are experiencing a new sensation."

        if the touch-me-nots
        are not in bloom
        neither are the chrysanthemums

the bales of pink cotton candy
in the slanting light
        are ornamental cherry trees.
        The greens around them, and
        the browns, the grays, are the park.

It's. Hmm. No.
>Their scallop shell of quiet
>is the S.S. *United States*.
>It is not so quiet and they
>are a medium-size couple who
>when they fold each other up
>well, thrill. That's their story.

February

A chimney, breathing a little smoke.
The sun, I can't see
making a bit of pink
I can't quite see in the blue.
The pink of five tulips
at five p.m. on the day before March first.
The green of the tulip stems and leaves
like something I can't remember,
finding a jack-in-the-pulpit
a long time ago and far away.
Why it was December then
and the sun was on the sea
by the temples we'd gone to see.
One green wave moved in the violet sea
like the UN Building on big evenings,
green and wet
while the sky turns violet.
A few almond trees
had a few flowers, like a few snowflakes
out of the blue looking pink in the light.
A gray hush
in which the boxy trucks roll up Second Avenue
into the sky. They're just
going over the hill.
The green leaves of the tulips on my desk
like grass light on flesh,
and a green-copper steeple
and streaks of cloud beginning to glow.

I can't get over
how it all works in together
like a woman who just came to her window
and stands there filling it
jogging her baby in her arms.
She's so far off. Is it the light
that makes the baby pink?
I can see the little fists
and the rocking-horse motion of her breasts.
It's getting grayer and gold and chilly.
Two dog-size lions face each other
at the corners of a roof.
It's the yellow dust inside the tulips.
It's the shape of a tulip.
It's the water in the drinking glass the tulips are in.
It's a day like any other.

With Frank and George at Lexington

Polly Red Top Thermos is with us
and my 75-pound Flip-It pen
no lighter than our heads
on the rocks
among the shrinking snow.

Is this lichen, this stuff here?
And these leaves,
are they oak leaves,
and what can I read
in char, such as: black branch
were you a dogwood tree?
I feel it was, though.

The snow has footsteps in it
like wet cement; a cowlick
is in a tuft of last year's grass;
cars fly by like bees; and so on.

Freely Espousing

A big quill hat bends an evergreen
introspectively down.

It feels good here.

A Reunion

Week after week glided away in the St.
Clare mansion . . .
HARRIET BEECHER STOWE

You will like their upstairs
papered with wrappers off Blue Goose oranges.
You will like their grandmother.
They keep up her grave.
You may get to like them.

Quick, Henry, the Flit!

The rain is raining all around
Chevy Chase, Maryland
my Maryland, and Granny
by no strange coincidence
is reading aloud "The Ballad of Chevy Chase"
out of *Journeys Through Bookland*.

We are en route to *Ivanhoe*.
Rebecca, you are lovely as yellow ivory,
while as for you, the ugly one, ugh.

Now we are in Paris, Virginia,
where the only place to piss
in private is a full bucket in a sodden room.
The mock orange bush is in fruit.
We are en route to Old Point Comfort.

Where the gray and booming surf
("Make him put his clothes on:
his lips are blue") shoots ashore
a giant skewer. A telephone pole.
My those long, big, pointed
wooden things are dangerous.

And Granny? Granny is mighty sore.
Somebody used her personal towel.
So am I. It is raining
on the Fourth of July. No rockets.
Slap. Drat the mosquitoes.

A New Yorker

I

The way eyes turn
to fly away from winter
among the many famous tables
the oldest and finest names
M. and Mme. Jean Fribourg and others
the best Paris has to offer.
Beloved showplace,
the great artists treasure many qualities
even as you read this.
Tiny sea horse, starfish, shells and sand,
soft light flannel woven in England,
the scenic route to Rio,
tomorrow you may be anywhere in Europe.
Ingeniously arranged, a small compact bundle which fits into the
                                                    smallest corner
a special pride
more and more and more
instinctive as a bird's flight south,
a lovely ritual
captured in artistic patterns.
Don't weep over onions.
Join our treasure hunt.

Don't forget,
many wait a lifetime.

II

In the countryside around Perugia
a hallowed snifter
brings lastingness to loveliness,
mirror-finished in deep wine,
gem in the sun.
Rings of rare gems
exhilarating as a wind
at the Blue Hill Buffet, in Blue Hill, Maine,
will not see their smiles,
the accepted shape.
Closer than you think
there's romance:
leaves of diamonds
sparkling with gaiety,
witches disguised as beautiful maidens,
the larger types of private room accommodations.

Walter Scott

Assured by many
unacceptable to the public
numerous difficulties
journals, notes and letters
formed of the sentiments
the slightest view

Death of his Father.—His Mother.—

Whene'er thou seest a sailor floating lie;
Lay on his poor remains a pious hand;

She is a handsome woman, has black eyes
she supposed it was January in London as well as there
he is perfectly mad, he makes very neat straw mats

study is the delight and soul of man
regard it not, my dear sister

The cave of pain

Violets are carefully enfolded in the letter
the choicest pictures of Murillo
I first met with him at Cadiz, he afterwards returned
they sailed in the same ship to Buenos Aires
I have also written by the Porcupine

I saw, for the first time, Walter Scott
speaking of the incessant rain

Greetings from the Chateau

for David Noakes

Why did Massenet compose *Thaïs?*
Why was there spiteful silence in the prune orchard?
He rests his arms on the pond balustrade.
He has bread in his hands.
Pianos sing in the palace,
the Empress bathes, the Emperor
climbs short flights of library steps
to take down a world's smallest atlas.

Alas. It is very hot and the carp
flew off into the wood, Rosa's bull
boarded up in the Square. "Dinner.
Champagne at five. My letters answered.
Remember to mend the tape recorder."

In the palace, the double-bodied sphinxes
stare at the geometry of the gardens
delighting another dusk, and the canal to the sky.

Royals

Called dog men,
they go out and have encounters.
Their blue eyes pick up and discharge
the green of their jackets, or ties.
Men with clear-green eyes unnerve angels.

Or perhaps they are unnerving as angels.
It is certain they are not angels.
They may be of another order,
between us and heaven like the atmosphere
between us and the sky, appointed
to clarify deathbed facts.
Unable to talk with us,
they know about us and argue about the facts
and the motives we may not know ourselves.
Their arguing might be clarifying
to those who know them whom they do not know
as they know us who do not know them.
We see them of course,
talk with them and even touch them,
are struck by their glances.
We show them our secret, however ill-kept.
They tell us nothing about themselves.
They seem to tell everything,
what they are is obvious when we see them.
We accept as facts our conjectures about them
we were not aware we had made.
They help make real our conjectures.

They live in rooms around town
and perhaps are what we become for a part of life
without knowing afterward.
This is no stranger than their rooms,
the inside of a cloud of red dust (it is, however, a room),
a room grown with lichens with a moon in it,
or wherever we pass them, or a roof.

"The Elizabethans Called It Dying"

Beyond Nagel's Funeral Parlor
          ("Your cousin says you filled her station wagon up;
            I didn't say it your cousin said it")
and (is it a perpetual wake they have
or just a popular parlor?)
                the novelty ice cream cake and soda shop
                the boys hang out in front of
                until they're eighteen then move across the street
in front of the saloon   Munich beer on draught
not forgetting the big church with the doleful bells
cheerily summoning housewives to early Mass
          ("The good thing about religion is
            it gives a man a sense of his place in the universe")
to Carl Schurz Park
kept reasonably free of la-di-da
after all the Mayor lives in it
in the huge glare of the electric sign on Doctors' Hospital
that says HOSPITAL
what are they trying to do, solicit trade in Queens?
or is that Welfare Island?
the river races upstream, neap tide turned
past the posh apartments
          did you ever sit back and try to remember
          whether particular paving stones were hex- or octagons?
          seen once at night and presumably memorized
                sloshing around in the rain
your eyes lips and nostrils
vary a distinct and unique shape—
          why it's The Raindrop Prelude!
home—
          not to be in love with you
I can't remember what it was like
          it must've been lousy

March Here

Wet
    the tide out
DONALD'S GARAGE
                        neon sign
left on all night
        a red pulse
    pale
under the skin
        throbs
                    when you turn your head
    light
        tall in the sky
walks over towers
                the hard-running river
    in your neck
    the steady pulse
    gently beats
                        damp
            from your bath
            your body
exhales a soft wet smell
                    of March

Fabergé

"I keep my diamond necklace in a pond of sparkling water for invisibility.

"My rubies in Algae Pond are like an alligator's adenoids.

"My opals—the evening cloud slipped in my pocket and I felt it and vice versa.

"Out of all the cabs I didn't take (a bit of a saver) I paved a street with gold. It was quite a short street, sort of a dollhouse cul-de-sac.

"And there are a lot of other pretties I could tell about—ivory horses carved inside bone dice; coral monkeys too tiny to touch; a piece of jade so big you might mistake it for the tundra and a length of

chalcedony as long as the Alcan Highway which is the Alcan Highway.
It is solidified liquid chalcedony.

"Here, just for you, is a rose made out of a real rose and the
dewdrop nestled in a rosy petal that has the delicate five-o'clock-shadow
fuzz—blue—is not a tear. I have nothing to cry about now I have you."

A White City

My thoughts turn south
a white city
we will wake in one another's arms.
I wake
and hear the steampipe knock
like a metal heart
and find it has snowed.

December

Il va neiger dans quelques jours
FRANCIS JAMMES

The giant Norway spruce from Podunk, its lower branches bound,
this morning was reared into place at Rockefeller Center.
I thought I saw a cold blue dusty light sough in its boughs
the way other years the wind thrashing at the giant ornaments
recalled other years and Christmas trees more homey.
Each December! I always think I hate "the over-commercialized event"
and then bells ring, or tiny light bulbs wink above the entrance
to Bonwit Teller or Katherine going on five wants to look at all
the empty sample gift-wrapped boxes up Fifth Avenue in swank shops
and how can I help falling in love? A calm secret exultation
of the spirit that tastes like Sealtest eggnog, made from milk solids,
Vanillin, artificial rum flavoring; a milky impulse to kiss and be friends
It's like what George and I were talking about, the East West
Coast divide: Californians need to do a thing to enjoy it.
A smile in the street may be loads! you don't have to undress everybody.
                    "You didn't *visit* the Alps?"

Freely Espousing

"No, but I saw from the train they were black
and streaked with snow."
Having and giving but also catching glimpses
hints that are revelations: to have been so happy is a promise
and if it isn't kept that doesn't matter. It may snow
falling softly on lashes of eyes you love and a cold cheek
grow warm next to your own in hushed dark familial December.

Ilford Rose Book

Thank you for your letter
and its extenuations. "He
said to tell them it is they
not he who said
a drawing can be illustrationy."
Another night. The grass
yellower. And the elms close in.
Flaming gray to the west
a blinding shadow. Dusty Easter
eggs, an ashtray no one
will wash, Dad
with all his buttons on
back in the watch fob days.

Rachmaninoff's Third

for Frank O'Hara

a moment and
              over and with
the picking strings
              Horowitz enters
accurate and fully
              singing
we're younger
              than we ever were
no matter what's better

                    dreams can't swell greater, truer
a horse
        shivers his mane
the white underthroat
                    darkly reflected
a storm banks up
                    in uncoiling celluloid
exorbitant intimacy
                    I hope you're listening
to your city station
                    8 million people
living in harmony
                    enjoy the benefits
of democracy
                    why not live a little?
We'll shoot the rapids
                    on Rogue River
before they build that dam

Money Musk

for Janice Koch

Hamlin Garland rose up from the Oklahoma powwow and declared with
            spirit,
"I will write *The Red Pioneer*. President 'Teddy' Roosevelt shall hear,
I mean, Great Chief, read, of the travail of Polished-Stone-Age
            Aboriginals adapting to the White Man's way.
            How."
Meantime, Henry B. Fuller strolled by Lake Michigan. He was glad *The
            Cliff-Dwellers* was well behind him.
"Henry," Hamlin Garland arrived with William Dean Howells and said,
            "you ought to write a Wisconsin novel."
Henry B. Fuller chuckled. Like a wind from the plains, Willa Cather
            passed
troubled by whether a blue shadow painting could be truly restful.
Theodore Dreiser suspected the cabal.
Rose of Dutcher's Coolly, singing in the firelight of the only fireplace
in Nashonoc, singing about Tod Claymore and his daughter, the old old
            song of Miss Marple and her knitting

and Dr. Gideon Fell in his shovel hat, and older still,
how you and Nellie Gray lay abed day after day in the bug-festooned
        garret of the Boucle d'Or
doped by hunger, singing *Sherlock Holmes and Dr. Watson,* mutedly,
        owing to your great great hunger.
They had not imagined back in Topeka what it is like to have to buy
        every blest bite to eat
much less not having the wherewithal to buy a bite. Paris.
The light lies long in Dutcher's Coolly. The Wisconsin Elwoods
        removed—years and years—
to Indiana. It is a dream of the great Midwest: and what about the twenty
        silent years,
crushing America? Don't you think it made people happy, when they
        loved Pike's Peak
and it was not just a dessert? or candy bar? When West meant more
        than drowning, full of cocaine?
"You speak true, Hamlin Garland," Red Wing declared, "though to
        small purpose and with less effect."

A Man in Blue

Under the French horns of a November afternoon
a man in blue is raking leaves
with a wide wooden rake (whose teeth are pegs
or rather, dowels). Next door
boys play soccer: "You got to start
over!" sort of. A round attic window
in a radiant gray house waits like a kettledrum.
"You got to start . . ." The Brahmsian day
lapses from waltz to march. The grass,
rough-cropped as Bruno Walter's hair,
is stretched, strewn and humped beneath a sycamore
wide and high as an idea of heaven
in which Brahms turns his face like a bearded thumb
and says, "There is something I must tell you!"
to Bruno Walter. "In the first movement
of my Second, think of it as a family
planning where to go next summer

in terms of other summers. A material ecstasy,
subdued, recollective." Bruno Walter
in a funny jacket with a turned-up collar
says, "Let me sing it for you."
He waves his hands and through the vocalese-shaped spaces
of naked elms he draws a copper beech
ignited with a few late leaves. He bluely glazes
a rhododendron "a sea of leaves" against gold grass.
There is a snapping from the brightwork
of parked and rolling cars.
There almost has to be a heaven! so there could be
a place for Bruno Walter
who never needed the cry of a baton.
Immortality—
in a small, dusty, rather gritty, somewhat scratchy
Magnavox from which a forte
drops like a used Brillo Pad?
Frayed. But it's hard to think of the sky as a thick glass floor
with thick-soled Viennese boots tromping about on it.
It's a whole lot harder thinking of Brahms
in something soft, white and flowing.
"Life," he cries (here, in the last movement),
"is something more than beer and skittles!"
"And the something more
is a whole lot better than beer and skittles,"
says Bruno Walter,
darkly, under the sod. I don't suppose it seems so dark
to a root. Who are these men in evening coats?
What are these thumps?
Where is Brahms?
And Bruno Walter?
Ensconced in resonant plump easy chairs
covered with scuffed brown leather
in a pungent autumn that blends leaf smoke
(sycamore, tobacco, other),
their nobility wound in a finale
like this calico cat
asleep, curled up in a breadbasket,
on a sideboard where the sun falls.

Sestina

A translation of Dante's
Al poco giorno . . .

I have reached, alas, the long shadow
and short day of whitening hills
when color is lost in the grass.
My longing, all the same, keeps green
it is so hooked in the hard stone
that speaks and hears like a woman.

In that same way this new woman
stands as cold as snow in shadow,
less touched than if she had been stone
by the sweet time that warms the hills
and brings them back from white to green,
dressing them in flowers and grass.

Who, when she wreathes her hair with grass,
thinks of any other woman?
The golden waves so mix with green
that Love himself seeks its shadow
that has me fixed between small hills
more strongly than cemented stone.

More potent than a precious stone,
her beauty wounds, and healing grass
cannot help; across plains and hills
I fled this radiant woman.
From her light I found no shadow
of mountain, wall, or living green.

I have seen her pass, dressed in green,
and thought the sight would make a stone
love, as I, even her shadow.
And I have walked with her on grass,
speaking like a lovesick woman,
enclosed within the highest hills.

But streams will flow back to their hills
before this branch, sappy and green,

catches fire (as does a woman)
from me, who would bed down on stone
and gladly for his food crop grass
just to see her gown cast shadow.

The heavy shadow cast by hills
this woman's light can change to green,
as one might hide a stone in grass.

An Almanac

Shops take down their awnings;
women go south;
few street lamp leaners;
children run with leaves running at their backs.
In cedar chests sheers and seersuckers displace flannels and wools.

Sere leaves of the Scotch marigolds;
crystals of earth melt;
the thorn apple shows its thorns;
a dog tracks the kitchen porch;
wino-hobos attempt surrender to warm asylums.

Caged mink claw;
gulls become pigeons;
snow bends the snow fence.
Heavy food;
rumbling snowplows.

Seats in the examination hall are staggered.
The stars gleam like ice;
a fragment of bone;
in the woods matted leaves;
a yellowish shoot.
A lost key is found;
storm windows are stacked on the beams of the garage.

Freely Espousing

Thinness

I

(like, *Her Cardboard Lover*)
not mist, smoke or atmosphere
a weakness in the light
why I do believe the sun is trying
really making an effort
                (today you could eat it
                and not burn your lips)
to switch on spring
and following flurries

II

I like this cool drawn-outness
like a city without any men or women
who've all gone into the country
because it's the day of the year
when everyone goes into the country

Someone proclaimed it once
so everyone keeps on going.
Meantime, the sick, the slothful, the bemused
make the most of town and its unusual
silent state, no trip hammers, no gas buggies
no old Indian woman selling wild flowers

III

February, your arms are so long
for such a short month
your hair is so fine
it drifts across your eyes
and I feel one barely visible strand
when we kiss: gracile, you are not
like March, boisterous and butch

IV

February expects others to be nicer
than it is itself: knowing this
about itself makes it a nice month.
You have a pretty good character, February.

V

The pallid light and the weak shadows
cold in the shadows and cool in the light
the February river reflecting nothing
alight like tarnished foil—the gulls
are as dirty as peigons—and it's high
time for crocuses, bloodroots, hepaticas
and other nascent what-have-yous

Hudson Ferry

April what an ice-cold promise
I saw a cherry almost in bloom today
one of five magnolias opened all its buds
wide and pointing at the sun
going down in front of City Hall

they cleaned it. It looks new.
Why can't they stop cleaning things
and sweep the streets. Like the April weather
you can't talk about the weather
it's like saying my lady's damask cheek

look at the smoke blazing over Jersey
the flats are on fire it's like a flushed cheek
and nearer a smokestack blows a dense dark blue
smoke is hot it looks cold trailing like hair
the bite-me kind springy or flung about

you can't get at a sunset naming colors
the depth the change the charge deep out of deep
the flaring upward what it nails on houses
the smoke swiftly pouring at the stack
hangs lazy wide and scarce dispersed

look at Esta, Isador and Alvin bright
rosy-gilded with wind-burnished cheeks
laughing and chatting in the wind

above the slap and river hoots
and there's Miss Strong Arm, toting her torch

it's another city going back
the moon one night past its full
writes signs vanishing hypnotically
downtown the towers block massively
at the rail a man who rests his hands

looks heroic: he works at night: going from or to?
I don't know I hardly know why I'm on the river
late at night. It's a bore, waiting for a train
reading a tabloid. The City Hall all clean
gleams like silver like the magnolias in the moonlight

Flashes

Dark day
              hard, swarming
                      west
                              the Chrysler Building
silver, soluble
                                      south
          not a hole
                  a depth
                          brightening
          almost to pinkness
                  smoke
                              spreading, climbing
                              moving back on itself
hanging dissolving forming going renewing
                  mixed with cloud
          steams
                  and darks
      a bird
                  snapped by
                              it's raining
just in one spot

                    flashes
     in puddles
                on a tar roof

April and Its Forsythia

It's snowing on the unpedimented lions. On ventilator hoods
white triangles. It evens up wrinkled tar roofs,
smooths out rough concrete coping, showing the shape
of a wall side between coping top and roof. The census
taker was just here. She had on transparent overshoes, coat and
hat: are clothes less secret? Less snowlike?
Snow isn't secret, showing further aspects, how small
cast lions would look if they grew maned, tame yet whitely
fierce; how the center of the sidewalk is always a path
steps tend to, as across a plain, through a wood; how cars
swing out heavily and big at a corner, turning voluminously
as a fleshy dancer. That census taker. I'm the head of a household.
I am also my household. Not bad. It's still snowing, down
and across: when cloth gets old and stretched, a twill
may have a gusty, snowy movement. Rough on poor rats
who work in it, must go out in it: it's dirty cold wet slush
underfoot, you hear it under wheels: swoosh, and slop
when they stop. Mr. Merzeg, the super, loves it. Used to drop
to 30 below the nine months he spent in Siberia. Wow. There
they really get snow! Not just wet feathers, like New York.
What variety snow falls with and has: this kind lays like wet sheets
or soaked opaque blotting paper: where a surface makes
a natural puddle, its own melting darkens it, as though it had lain
all winter and the thaw is come. Is this change in weather in early April
just what the sugarbush needed, upstate and further up, New Hampshire,
     Vermont?
Maple syrup production is off, the *Times* says, due to the vogue for
     maple furniture.
Willingly or not, you can't give your Cape Cod cobbler's table
with a lamp attachment above a ship's-type wheel back to its grove.
Now it falls on two diagonals, except it's more: the depth dimension
of air. Ugh. The head of this household is going out in it.

Willingly or not, I'll check up on Central Park
where branches of sunshine were in bloom on Monday.

Roof Garden

tubs of . . .
            memory
for a moment
        won't supply a name
                    not portulacas
                                (". . . she had on her
                                new dressmaker dress and
                                spectator pumps . . .")
petunias
        tubs of pink petunias
a gray roof
        black when it's hot
light grays today
                    green tubs of punctured glow
                            before a glowing wall
all the walls reflecting light
at six on a summer evening
                        the petunias shimmer in a breeze
a long, long time ago
                    petunias
adorable, sticky flower

May 24th or So

Among white lilac trusses, green-gold spaces of sunlit grass.
The shade side of a clothes pole, dark innards of a light-violet shell.
Everything trembles
everything shakes
in the great sifter:
bud scales, pollen, all the Maytime trash

whose sprinkles are clocks that tell
the time of the dandelion take-over generation,
never quite coming to pass.
A man passes
in calendula-colored socks.
A robin passes

               zip

                   thud

punctuating the typescript of today with a comma on the too-close cut
                                             grass.
Then erases it for a full stop in a lilac.
in Y's and V's and W's
an elm ascends
smoothly as an Otis Elevator.
Other trademarks blur in the gone-over forsythia hedge.
A table and a chair, carved chunkily in the lawn,
are the colors of an oystershell as though beneath the sod were chalk
                                             not sand.

Why it seems awfully far
from the green hell of August
and the winter rictus,
dashed off, like the easiest thing

Penobscot

Open water facing Bradbury snags fog in its spruce.
Eagle has a meadow down its spine;
Compass, a cave; Scrag, five trees.
On Dirigo apples hang down into raspberries;
nearby, a lilac. Many remember
its old name, Butter, though Little Spruce Head
only one man still calls Frenchman's.
Birch-pale Beach has a chapel,
Bear has sheep. On others:
seals, butter-and-eggs, cellar holes.
From here we see them all, and more,
and the Camden Hills, Mount Desert, Blue Hill, Deer Isle

and ocean facing Isle au Haut
where the breakers roll stones to cannon balls.

Today

The bay today breaks
in ripples of applause.
The wind whistles.
Spruce and bright-leaved birch
at the edge
are flat yet plump
as letters with "see enclosures."
A gull mews, the mailboat toots,
the wind rises and pours with a noise like water
and spills black jazz
from spiked brown seed cups of red columbine.
The wind takes with it
a wrack of voices: "the who?"
and unintelligible shapes of phrases
or one scrape: hickory on cement.
Across the bay today
a white house smaller than a thumbnail moon
shines like the light
it shows at night, a star
or sun of kerosene.
The barn swallows from the eaves
are up to something, maybe
showing their fledglings how to do it, scything
an insect harvest from the air.
Round and brown as rabbit droppings,
seed pods of blue-eyed grass
bobble and split along the seams:
so big for so small a flower.
A sailboat scuds,
a poplar tugs at roots
in soil a scurf on rock.
Everything chuckles and creaks
sighs in satisfaction

reddens and ripens in tough gusts of coolness
and the sun smites

Sorting, wrapping, packing, stuffing

dirty socks in dirty sneakers
capless tubes of unguents among brushes and septic Band-Aids
adhesive flowers into spongy books
when the great bronze bell
sounds its great bronze bong
it will find a lifetime jar of Yuban Instant in my right hand,
in my left, Coleman's Mustard.
But how do you pack a blue fire escape—even if the man
got off it out of the 97 degree sun
and blizzards, then sullied snow that left
disclosing no car where one was. Excuse me, druggist,
can you take this blue fire escape out of my eye?
        (no, no one is going to ask anyone to take anything
        out of a heart, not even a tear with a hambone in it.
        All there is
        is blood and thump).

Now the blue fire escape
is packed, and it is
already tomorrow O little brown bat guano
of course it is still today
with the bay crinkling at the edges
of a tomorrow when Creeping Charlie and Stinking Willie flourish
                        under glass on the moon.
Imagine going to the sun for the winter
if it's like Miami
Or getting an earth burn
Or

better we should slip into this Ice Age remnant granite boulder
and grab a snooze
it is too much like packing
on Saturn

                  Freely Espousing

where they have poison ivy like we have Himalayas
poisonous only to planets

                give us a gingham smile
red white and checkered
Help

        the blue fire escape!
it's coming unpacked all over the floor like a Milky Way
lighting the north
an aurora borealis of neckties

                      Knize
                      Sulka
                      Au Chardon d'Ecosse

stuff wrap cram snap
        "Hello Lincoln?
        I want to store
        a blue fire escape."

How pretty, rising from the long Memorial Pool
among toy boats all day and stars all night
glittering and cold as Santa Claus

                "See you at The Petunia Pump.
                More later."

The time is getting out of hand
              splash splash
cut down the books
to fit an Oshkosh nutshell
            My Heart Is like a Green Canoe
            The World Is a Long Engagement Party
            The Great Divorce Has Been Annulled
            Romance of Serge Eisenstein
            Immanuel Kant, Boy Detective
            Emma Kant, Mother of Men
            Judy Kant, R.N.
The spruce have stopped shrinking
they never began and great hunks of the world will fit

Seeking

for old New England
in old trials: to each conviction
what percentile of unapprehended
drunks, lustful lookers, sleights-of-finger?
Unless the convicted
were innocent as witches. There is that
about old New England.
People understand each other better than that
usually, though, no matter how they testify
guardedly on the phone: "It's not just
that she's lazy, has round heels and sews
Paris labels in Klein's clothes":
as the bird feigning lameness
draws to itself yet more to the nest the attention it seeks to thwart.
Here is its nest, in this old New England
woodpile: three robin's-egg-blue
robin's eggs: ergo: that lame bird was a big healthy robin
though it dropped dead at your feet. That's
just DDT. The romance
of certain old clothes
may be merely olfactory. Still, there must've been a lot of
watched pots under stovepipe hats
("Seen Walcott's new 'Pilgrim' beaver?")
and a stranger from Spain
found the freedom to kiss
and play kissing games a
little hard to take. Later,
liked it. Real old New Englanders: viz. Juanita
Walcott y Gomez, Blue Juanita
corrupted to *Blue Juniata*. That was later, and farther west
where the wild rice lightly rattled into canoes
and the better people came from the East
humming, "By the Rude Bridge"
and, "Flower from the Caerulean Wall." You can't get far enough
from old New England (humming, "The Lowell Factory Girl Song")
since you can't get any nearer.
This hair bracelet won't tell us much
(a late, Hispano-Dutch, connection: somewhere along the line

Freely Espousing

the Juanita link pops up
in Gomez Walcott y van Aau)
nor this portrait of old Judge Lindsey Wooley
"The scourge of the Passamaquody,"
a collateral of Blue Juanita's. Say, who are these bug-big
old New Englanders pursuing and pursued by
red men the height of a red mite? The sun is white
on clapboards in green Wiscasset
and in a cellar hole
dusky tulips
incline their heads.
       "Maine isn't old New England!"
Maine is Maine I can hardly remember
when it was still Massachusetts
or where Emma Eames lived (Bath)
or the birthplace of Maxine Elliott (Rockland)
or Edna St. Vincent Millay on her island (Matinicus)
or Robert Tristram Coffin humming "Forever Is Not Far"
     (wonder where he fits in the
"Judge and Mrs. Wooley v. A. Tristram-Gomez take pleasure" picture?
You remember, her daughter by hubby no. 1, Lindsey Coffin: Frani
the girl with the labels. She married a bohunk from Scranton:
Mlokosewitsch.
(Paeonia Mlokosewitschii!
large globular
perfect complement
jade-green of leaves and pink petioles
of unusual distinction
      indeed. Mlokosewitsch
       you live on
honored in old New England
       like Epilobium anguistifolium
Great Rose Willow Herb or common fireweed
   in early August
        summoning fall
Remember to slam the parentheses behind you
) bang and) bang and)) double bang
(to be on the safe side).
Here are seven lucky stones
     OOOOOOo
found in old New England. And a snail shell @

                         the common Nash
                         the stately Reo
          dumped in old New England bays
                         metal reefs
                         instant housing
          for fishy prey of predator fish.
          "Conservation," says the bulletin of Our Lady of the Sea,
          "is true charity." The wood church looking out
          over wrinkle-rocked Stonington
          its doors wide open to all the thanksgivers who can't crowd in
          for the contract the Crotch Island Quarry got
          for the granite to build the Memorial
          after a year long layoff. Old New Englanders
          (with names like Haskell and Cacciacavallo)
          eating an island out of the sea
          like the wonderful fish and terrible food
          at Glad's Lunch

Crocus Night

The fire had struggled from my hand
SUSAN COOLIDGE

The heavy umbrellas
aren't worth their weight.
Doors swing and slam
checked by gusts. A whisperer
has a friendly reek.
A hell broth!
and hollows among clouds.
Then the moon goes crocus.

Milk

Milk used to come in tall glass, heavy and uncrystalline as frozen melted
snow. It rose direct and thick as horse-chestnut tree trunks that do not
spread out upon the ground even a little: a shaft of white drink narrowing

at the cream and rounded off in a thick-lipped grin. Empty and unrinsed, a diluted milk ghost entrapped and dulled light and vision.

Then things got a little worse: squared, high-shouldered and rounded off in the wrong places, a milk replica of a handmade Danish wooden milk bat. But that was only the beginning. Things got worse than that.

Milk came in waxed paper that swelled and spilled and oozed flat pieces of milk. It had a little lid that didn't close properly or resisted when pulled so that when it did give way milk jumped out.

Things are getting better now. Milk is bigger—half-a-gallon, at least— in thin milky plastic with a handle, a jug founded on an oblong. Pick it up and the milk moves, rising enthusiastically in the neck as it shifts its center of weight. Heavy as a breast, but lighter, shaping itself without much changing shape: like bringing home the milk in a bandana, a neckerchief or a scarf, strong as canvas water wings whose strength was only felt dragged under water.

On the highway this morning at the go-round, about where you leave New Hampshire, there had been an accident. Milk was sloshed on the gray-blue-black so much like a sheet of early winter ice you drove over it slowly, no matter what the temperature of the weather that eddied in through the shatterproof glass gills. There were milk-skins all around, the way dessert plates look after everyone has left the table in the Concord grape season. Only bigger, unpigmented though pretty opaque, not squashed but no less empty.

Trembling, milk is coming into its own.

Going

In the month when the Kamchatka bugbane
finally turns its strung-out hard pellets white
and a sudden drench flattens the fugitive
meadow saffron to tissue-paper scraps
and winds follow that crack and bend without breaking
the woody stems of chrysanthemums so the good of not disbudding

shows in lower smaller flights of metallic pungency,
a clear zenith looks lightly dusted and fades to nothing
at the skyline, shadows float up to lighted surfaces
as though they and only they kept on the leaves
that hide their color in a glassy shine.
A garnering squirrel makes a frantic chatter at a posse of cats
that sit and stare while their coats thicken. Days
are shorter, more limpid, are like a kiss
neither dry nor wet nor on the lips
that sends a light shock in rings
through all the surface of the skin. Early, in the middle
of the afternoon, the light slants
into rooms that face southwest: into this room
across a bookcase so the dead-brown gold-stamped
spines look to be those to take down now:
Hodge and His Masters, The Cereals in America.
If a leaf of gold were beaten to transparency,
and all that here roots and extrudes were tarnished silver
and blackened bronze—bumped and brushed against
here and there into high lights—
were seen through it by the wind-flickered quick-setting sun,
October would look no different than it looks

The Master of the Golden Glow

An irregular rattle (shutters) and
a ferule tapped
on a blackboard—or where you come from
do they say chalkboard?—anyway it's not any sort of pointer
it's a sash facing west
wood and glass drummed on by autumn tatters.
Say, who are you
anyway? "I think we may have met before.
God knows I've heard enough about you."
That largest maple—
half its leaves an undreamt of butter:
if only safflower oil
were the color of its name

the way olive oil is. "Why,
don't you *like* butter?"
The doctor's youngest son
paddles the canoe while he (the doctor) casts
for mud-flavored carp in the long brackish pond:
Agawam, meaning lake. Lake Pond,
Pond Lake, Lake Lake, Pond Pond,
its short waves jumping up and down
in one place with surplus energy to spend.
Somewhere, out of the wind,
the wind collects a ripe debris.
"I'll tell you who I am: someone
you never met
though on a train you studied a boil on my neck
or bumped into me
leaving a late late party
                                    'Sorry'
or saw throwing bones in the ocean
for an inexhaustible retriever."
The wind drops. The sky darkens
to an unfathomable gray
and through hardware cloth one
leaf is seen to fall
describing the helixes of conch-shell cores
gathered in summer, thrown out in autumn.
More litter, less clutter.

Stun

If you've ever been in a car
that was hit by a train
whang
(a tearing like metal shears)
flip   spin
                    "Why I'm perfectly OK!"
this streaming blood
a euphoric sweat of thanksgiving
and later

a hunk of scrap iron
just there on the turnpike
for no reason
flies up and
whang
it goes on your new underneath
well, it's like you were thrown
grabbed by the scruff of the neck
head over heels right into Proust's steamy cup
just another crumb
of scalloped cookie
odious and total memory
                              (of the cells, no doubt)
in prickle-green, speed-lashed
Massachusetts

"Earth's Holocaust"

It's time again.
Tear up the violets
and plant something more difficult to grow.
Everything a little cleaner, a little more ugly:
cast cement tubs of malevolent ageratums,
and: "Your grandmother baked
and froze that pie. We saved it
for a special occasion." Codicils
don't add up to much when there's nothing to leave:
a bedroom, stretching from Portland
to Richmond stunningly furnished in
French-motel provincial. On the brighter side
plastic seaweed has proved
an unqualified success. As have ready-glued scrapbooks
which if out of style
still epitomize. In this one
is your first matchbook cover,
an advertisement with a misprint,
a pair of bronze baby shoes,
a tinted enlargement of a tintype.

Freely Espousing

Twins on the upswing: there are more people.
A regular Shriners' parade of funerals.
But there are not less people.
There are more people
of all sorts, conditions and flavors.
Getting to shake each
by the hand takes time.
Not more though
than abstracting the grain of dust
from each raindrop. Starfish
have no sense of time, at all.

Poem

How about an oak leaf
if you had to be a leaf?
Suppose you had your life to live over
knowing what you know?
Suppose you had plenty money

"Get away from me you little fool."

Evening of a day in early March,
you are like the smell of drains
in a restaurant where paté maison
is a slab of cold meat loaf
damp and wooly. You lack charm.

3/23/66

It's funny early spring weather, mild and washy
the color of a head cold.
The air rushes. Branches
are going nowhere, like the ocean,
spring salt unstopping sinuses. Winter salt doesn't.

36

Everything just sitting around: a barn without eaves,
a dumpy cottage set catty-corner
on its lot, a field with a horse in it.
A plane goes over, leaving its wake,
an awakening snore. A truck
passes, perceived as a quick shuffle
of solitaire cards. And the poor old humpy lawn
is tufted with Irish eyebrows of onion grass.
A chill on the nape smells frowsty
the spring no more awake
than a first morning stretch
and no more asleep. Growing
and going, in sight and sound, as the fire last night
looked out at us reading *Great Expectations* aloud
and fled up the chimney.

Industrial Archaeology

Early May (a late spring) a field
of clover and rust where jungles
in June will hide a perilous adit:
many fall, none recover. So much
for West Virginia. A tangle of string,
clamps and catches: a "Braquette"
a name not long to be known to fame. (If you
have to ask, you can't have it.) Ingenuity
so recent in our history
naturally there is a marginal plethora.
Still, Yankee know-how plants
tomatoes in metal sleeves (old king-
size juice cans) attractive
of beneficent electricity. So much
thought of in Emmaus, Pennsylvania.
(Why didn't you ask?
It entailed no risk.) "From your drawing
your find appears a piece
of a stamping machine. It is of no value
other than sentimental." Old wooden

colander, mirror-winged vanity table,
disposable aerosol-cologne dispenser,
magnesium chain ladder, bottled good-luck
sprig, green-wax stem, circuitry,
unique patented mechanism, in Connecticut
even grass fights for its life. Also
wild blue tar-loving chicory
the negative expression of a wish.

Now and then

for Kenward Elmslie

Up from the valley
now and then a chain saw rising to a shriek, subsiding to a buzz
"Someone" is "cutting in his wood lot" another day
shows they are not
someone is two men clearing shoulders
of a narrow high-crowned road
stacked poles were lately saplings
the leaves on the slash gone limp, unstarched, unsized
one man with one fierce eye and where the other should be
an ill-knit cicatrix
men who don't make much aren't much
for spending what they do
on glass eyes, tooth-straightening devices ("a mouth
like the back of a switchboard"), nose jobs, dewenning operations
a country look prevails
and a vestigial fear of the evil eye lurks
". . . my skin creeps . . ."
                    Out of Adamant Co-op
men in "overhauls" step into evening rising
in long-shadowed bluish haze to gold and pink
by Sodom Lake (was it that any Bible name
was an OK name?) and boys stare unabashed
and unaggressive not what the man on the bus fled
from his one day job talking excitedly about
"teen-age Puerto Rican tail-bait" and
"You can *have* New York!" Some present
you'd rather have wouldn't you an apple tree

that climbed up into keels over
sad, and too bad, the best apples on Apple Hill
still, it can be propped or budded on new stock or just
that it once was there
                              Driving past, driving down, driving over
along the Winooski
through the home of Granite City Real Ice Cream
The Monument Capitol
buildings of rusticated granite marred
to our eyes by etched polished granite remodeled downstairs
may be found by a future happily heterodox
"There's a touch of autumn—
                         there's another touch of autumn"
and the dark tranquility of hemlocks encroaching on untilled fields
"You can't make a living
plowing stones" subsistence
farming is well out of style: "You can't call it living
without the margin"
coveted obsolescence!
a margin like that on this page
a paper luxury "Collectors"
the lady in the antique shop said "are snapping up
silver" "Since we're off the silver standard?" "Why,
maybe so" Perhaps
six 1827 Salem coin-silver spoons for $18
or what about
"Have you *The Pearl of Orr's Island?*"
"*That's* a book I'd want to read myself.
I'm from here but live in Florida.
Winters are too hard: 40 below.
You don't feel it though
like zero in Boston. I'll take St. Johnsbury any day
over Boston."
                    Over St. Johnsbury the clouds shift in curds
and a street goes steeply down
into Frenchtown by the railroad station
into which anachronistically comes
a real train: yesterday's torment of dust-exhaling plush
on the backs of bare knees today's nostalgia
but not much. Curls cut out of wood, brick
of a certain cut and color, a hopped-up cripple

on a hill above his pond, a slattern
frowning at the early-closed state liquor store,
an attic window like a wink,
The Scale Co., St. Johnsbury has everything
                    Not this high hill a road
going in undergrowth leads up to
by walls of flat cleared-field stones
so many and so long a time to take
so much labor so long ago and so soon
to be going back, a host to hardhack
and blueberry baby steps
first fallings from a sky
in which the wind is moving furniture
the upholstery of summer coming all unstitched
the air full of flying kapok
and resolutions: "remember to fetch the ax
whack back pine intrusions"
from the road turning down to a lower field
and across the roughest one the County keeps
a woman and a boy come up
on heavy horses. "Morning!
Had frost
last night at Adamant.
Might have a killing frost
tonight." Quick and clear as the water
where cress grows the cold
breaks on the hills to the soft crash
of a waterfall beyond
a beaver pond
and slides on
flinging imaginary fragments of cat's ice
from its edges to flash
a bright reality in the night sky and it—
the cold—stands, a rising pool, about
Sloven's farmhouse and he dreams
of dynamite. A bog sucks
at his foundations. Somewhere a deer
breaks branches. The trees
say *Wesson. Mazola*
replies a frog.
                    It doesn't happen though the cold

40

that is not that night. It happens all right
not then when the white baneberry
leans secretively where a road forks
met with surprise: "Why here it is:
the most beautiful thing." The spirit
of Gelett Burgess sets Mother Nature
gabbing. "*That's* my Actea pachypoda, dear, we
call it Doll's-Eyes." Got up as smart
as ever in muck and dank she belches
—" 'Scuse: just a touch of gas"—
swamp maple flames and ambles over and plunks
down on a dead rubber tire
to contemplate smashed glass and a rusty tin
and "some of my choicer bits: that
I call Doctor's Dentures. These
are Little Smellies." Not
the sort you look to meet so near
gold-domed, out of scale Montpelier
a large-windowed kind of empty public bigness
so little to show, so much
to take pride in rather more than on the way to Stowe
a pyrocrafted maple board in a Gyp-o-teria
IF MORE MEN WERE SELF STARTERS
FEWER WIVES WOULD HAVE TO CRANK.
Welcome to the chair lift and cement chalet.
                                        Days
of unambiguous morning when dawn
peels back like a petal to disclose blue depths
deep beyond all comprehending and tall field growth bends
with a crushing weight of water cut
into sac-shaped portions, each less than a carat
and which streak an early walker's trouser legs
"You're soaked!" crossing on a door
the spill to where Nodding Ladies' Tresses
pallidly braid their fragrance and the woods
emit their hum. Days
when the pond holds on its steel one cloud
in which thin drowned trees stand
spare shapes of winter when summer
is just loosening to fall and bits of ribbon
from an electric typewriter patch a screen.

Freely Espousing

Croquet days, scissors-and-paste nights
after dinner on the better sort of ham
and coffee strong enough to float a goose egg.
Are those geese, that V, flying so early?
Can it be so late? in the green state
needles, leaves, fronds, blades, lichens and moss create
                    Can it be so soon before the long white
refrozen in frost on frost
on all twigs again will flash
cross cutting star streaks—the atoms
dance—on a treacherous night
in headlights?

                "Horrible Cold Night
Remain at Home"

                "Clear and Beautiful
Remain at Home"

Buried at Springs

There is a hornet in the room
and one of us will have to go
out the window into the late
August midafternoon sun. I
won. There is a certain challenge
in being humane to hornets
but not much. A launch draws
two lines of wake behind it
on the bay like a delta
with a melted base. Sandy
billows, or so they look,
of feathery ripe heads of grass,
an acid-yellow kind of
goldenrod glowing or glowering
in shade. Rocks with rags
of shadow, washed dust clouts
that will never bleach.

It is not like this at all.
The rapid running of the
lapping water a hollow knock
of someone shipping oars:
it's eleven years since
Frank sat at this desk and
saw and heard it all
the incessant water the
immutable crickets only
not the same: new needles
on the spruce, new seaweed
on the low-tide rocks
other grass and other water
even the great gold lichen
on a granite boulder
even the boulder quite
literally is not the same

II

A day subtle and suppressed
in mounds of juniper enfolding
scratchy pockets of shadow
while bigness—rocks, trees, a stump—
stands shadowless in an overcast
of ripe grass. There is nothing
but shade, like the boggy depths
of a stand of spruce, its resonance
just the thin scream
of mosquitoes ascending.
Boats are light lumps on the bay
stretching past erased islands
to ocean and the terrible tumble
and London ("rain persisting")
and Paris ("changing to rain").
Delicate day, setting the bright
of a young spruce against the cold
of an old one hung with unripe cones
each exuding at its tip
gum, pungent, clear as a tear,
a day tarnished and fractured
as the quartz in the rocks

Freely Espousing

of a dulled and distant point,
a day like a gull passing
with a slow flapping of wings
in a kind of lope, without
breeze enough to shake loose
the last of the fireweed flowers,
a faintly clammy day, like wet silk
stained by one dead branch
the harsh russet of dried blood.

Salute

Past is past, and if one
remembers what one meant
to do and never did, is
not to have thought to do
enough? Like that gather-
ing of one of each I
planned, to gather one
of each kind of clover,
daisy, paintbrush that
grew in that field
the cabin stood in and
study them one afternoon
before they wilted. Past
is past. I salute
that various field.

FROM

THE

HOME BOOK

1951–1970

(1977)

A Grave

While we who wished to help stood helplessly by,
a stranger, whom we neither knew nor loved (saw,
simply, as one of our kind), sank from sight,
drowning, gave up what we value most, our life.

If then between the shifting ocean and sky,
in whose two blacknesses he had seemed the flaw,
had been driven and drawn, tearing night from night
to show us his death's beyond, and ours, a knife!

which did not happen. His agony,
we who stood and watched the threatened promise kept,
could not share, even in fearful sympathy.
Searchlights moved upon the uninjured ocean.
Now he was part of that lighted blackness, slept
in what the screw of our ship set in motion.

Poem

I do not always understand what you say.
Once, when you said, across, you meant along.
What is, is by its nature, on display.

Words' meanings count, aside from what they weigh:
poetry, like music, is not just song.
I do not always understand what you say.

You would hate, when with me, to meet by day
What at night you met and did not think wrong.
What is, is by its nature, on display.

I sense a heaviness in your light play,
a wish to stand out, admired, from the throng.
I do not always understand what you say.

The Home Book 1951–1970

I am as shy as you. Try as we may,
only by practice will our talks prolong.
What is, is by its nature, on display.

We talk together in a common way.
Art, like death, is brief; life and friendship long.
I do not always understand what you say.
What is, is by its nature, on display.

At the Beach

On the Fourth of July at the beach,
the kids from the next cottage
lit sparklers. As fast as they
ran, they seemed from our porch
not to run fast at all. (Spark
stars wavering, the detonating
waves, a hot sky, little wind.)
We sat on the porch in the dark
after the last sparklers, each
speaking in turn till the wind
rose, then went in ourselves.

Self-Pity Is a Kind of Lying, Too

It's
snowing defective
vision days and
X-
mas is coming, like
a plow. And in the
meat the snow. Strange.
It all reminds me
of an old lady I
once saw shivering

naked beside a black
polluted stream. You
felt terrible—but
the train didn't
stop—so. And the
white which is
some other color or
its absence—it
spins on itself
and so do the *Who*
at Leeds I'm playing
to drown the carols
blatting from the
Presbyterian church
steeple which is
the same as fight-
ing fire with oil.
Naked people—old,
cold—one day we'll
just have snow
to wear too.

A Picnic Cantata

I

I feel funny today
but you know what they say:
falls to the floor,
comes to the door.

Who is it you think
might come to the door?
Not the laundry man,
it isn't Monday.
Not the meter reader,
they don't work on Sunday.
Not my cleaning lady,
it isn't Friday.
It might be a mailman

with a special letter,
or a flower shop boy
bringing flowers
from I wonder who?

Or it might be a friend.
It is Sunday.

It is Sunday,
but it's awfully early
for Sunday callers.

Knock, knock.
Who's there?
Open the door.
Open the door who?
Open the door and see.
Good morning, dear,
good morning you,
we thought it might be nice
if you and she
came with me
and we went Sunday driving.

We could make a lunch
and eat a picnic
outside in the sun.

A spring picnic
what a lovely idea
the day is ideal.
What shall we take?
All kinds of things
that are nice to eat.

In the picnic basket I want to find
a roll of lemon rind,
steak and chips,
a T-bone fish,
Milady's Blintzes with white wine sauce
and a pound of Child's creamoginized chocolates.

Four washable plates
and four cloth forks

and lots of napkins.
Napkins are the best part of a picnic.

We can't go on a picnic
without ketchup and a car.
Have you got a car?

You are in my car.

So we are.

Reach me a road map
and I'll map a route.
I love mapping routes
on road maps.
Which route are we on?

Z 3

Let's see.
We ought to be
on 3 B.
Turn left
at 11 F,
stay on that
til you see a hill shaped like a hat.
We can eat our lunch at Hat Hill Park.

My favorite park, named for Henry Hat.
Read what it says about him on the map.

          II
In our search for order
the way is dangerous.
To help us he brought us
master masons of Chartres.

He bent to no tyrant,
he never relented.
Among them all and among us
his free spirit may find it good,
more shared, more deeply understood.
Man is no longer the servant
nor the victim of many minds.

He doesn't sound like the sort of person
                        you might find
eating a picnic lunch on a Sunday in a park.

Fried chicken and champagne.

Maple syrup and wheats.

Are you hungry already?

I was hungry at the start.

Well here we are.

Are we here already?

We are at
Hat Hill Park.

In sun and shade
on picnic tables
lunches are laid
where cowboys ride
a teeter-totter.

Hot dogs sizzle
on pointed sticks,
root beer fizzes
in paper cups,
and napkins fly.

Good old country air. You can't beat it.
Out upon the air ride kites

blown, it seems, from rooms in clouds,
their trailing tails of knotted wings of cloth
switching the highest leaves.
Then the draught fails
and the kites fall.

Up into the air rise cries
born, it seems, like milkweed seed
that float on the most lightly stirring air
miles from their field and pod.
Then the wind drops
and sounds are lost.

I read in a big-little nature book
that the best way to make a fire
is out of wood.
You get the wood.

There are five kinds of pie.
Which kind will you prefer?

I will surely die
if I eat any pie,
but I can't resist
a slice of cherry.

How flaky the crust,
how moist the filling.

Now we have eaten
who will amuse us?

I will ask your stars
what is in store.
Your stars today
have much to say.

III
Happy birthday Taurus!
The recent weeks

should have been
good ones for you.

Work hard during
the coming year.
The returns should be
the best in some years.

During the summer
take care in July
and use diplomacy:
there may be plenty
of trouble around.

Happy birthday Gemini!
This can be a big point
in a peak year for you.
You always have so many
things you want to do.
Quick on the uptake,
you don't waste time.
You will have a chance
to indulge in good times.
You need to get in there,
get around and be seen.
In the early fall
you may have to readjust.
But on the whole
the year is yours to push.

IV

The Sunday paper is full of news.
Here is a letter, sad as a blues.

I have a heart problem, writes E Q.

I knew this other man was married
and had a little boy.
He knew I was married
and mother of three.
But we went out together

and discovered
we had many things in common.

Before we realized it
we had to see each other
at least every other day.
We found a kind of love
we'd never known before.
I had to leave him to
come back to my husband.
I felt it only fair to
be honest with my husband.

My husband and I are planning
on moving to this town.
The other man lives there.
I know that we can never
be free to marry
each other
because of the children.
Do you think it
would be a wise move?

V

I never miss the garden section.
It describes heaven to perfection.

Exquisite as a Java sunset,
graceful as a Polynesian dance,
these huge beauties
larger than a dinner plate
burst into bloom
ninety days after planting.

Bali island red
Samoa pink coral
sands of Tahiti white
greenhouse beauty outdoors
larger than a silver dollar.

Stately colorful Darwins
touched with green,

glistening ebony black and maroon,
tulips in balanced color,
flame pink, shaded rose,
glowing orange, shaded yellow,
big plump top-quality bulbs:
all the exotic brilliance
of the colorful tropical birds.

VI

How quick we came
from where we were.
The day is over
before it began.

The food is eaten,
the drinks are drunk,
evening arrives
too late to have lunch.

Rinse the thermos
and burn the trash,
wrap the silver
in waxed paper.

This left-over pie
will keep to eat
for after supper
at least a week.

Oh dear, look here,
we forgot all about
the radishes
and the relish.

The car is packed,
have you got your hat?
Where is the map
and my driving glasses?
I hope the road
won't be too crowded.

Is the evening star
Venus or Mars?
I see it set
in the peel of the moon,
a bit of ice
in an ice-tea sky.

Look at the outline
of the city.
No wonder our lives
have their ups and downs.

How well you drive,
and thank you, dears,
I loved the picnic,
it was loads of fun.
We must do it
again, real soon.

Good-bye, toodle-oo, so long, good-bye.

Grand Duo

An improvisation for Arthur Gold and Robert Fizdale

the Seine
    "transcend, be real"
        she vanished
        "like a light"

    •

Timeless, tireless, sketched, soft

            cleft mountains
            clothed in wolves and conifers
            breathe on clockwork towns
a river enters
petrified sponge
        perilously water falls

      under weeping skies
      rift by a kiss

   •

Rain lashed the windows of a careening train.
  Tunnels,
boulders, crevasses. Vapors and clouds parted on
  blue.

   •

Art is formality, courtesy, passion, control, practice,
  rehearsing the unrehearsed
             art is no is
                melodiously
                repeated endlessly
                varies naturally
Sweet basic monotone
                heavens of gray
                melt away
green on the blue land   all things awash in jewel and
  beverage colors

   •

Your fingers on keys
sentiments drawn unanxiously
by hyper-accuracy
           Austria! lederhosen, spas and beer
           cookies and the dragon of Klagenfurt
    Music! Schubert! Song!
       a bird declining the verb to be
Florence teaching a child to sing
           nightingale
in German so around sung silence
           nightingales in silence sing

   •

Schubert put his spectacles on
He wrote, *Grand Duo*. Probably,
a four-hand version of a lost symphony. Anyone
may hear it only if you play it.
               Life

                    methodical
                    unquenchable
          (meadows dress themselves in green and daisies
          kine fodder. A smiling boy points out the
               way to town)
                    in rainbows
               after rain, in rain, letters, a recipe

Summers in town are unnatural.
So is the beach. The sun
flushes the cheek of a peach.
                    A gesture in the air
                    unhectoring as a smile
                         "be quick   prolong"
Rapt in a hoked-up coda dream
tumultuous applause   of piano history
     the first forte was played on an instrument
built out of wood that marched back from Dunsinane

                    Schubert

Franz Schubert

Things to Do

Balance checkbook.
Rid lawn of onion grass.
"this patented device"
"this herbicide"
"Sir, We find none of these
killers truly satisfactory. Hand weed
for onion grass." Give
old clothes away, "such as you
yourself would willingly wear."
Impasse. Walk three miles
a day beginning tomorrow.
Alphabetize.

The Home Book 1951–1970

Purchase nose-hair shears.
Answer letters.
Elicit others.
Write Maxine.
Move to Maine.
Give up NoCal.
See more movies.
Practice long-distance dialing.
Ditto gymnastics:
The Beast with Two Backs
and, The Fan.
Complain to laundry
any laundry. Ask for borrowed books back.
Return
junk mail to sender
marked, Return to Sender.
Condole. Congratulate.
". . . this sudden shock . . ."
". . . this swift surprise . . ."
Send. Keep. Give. Destroy.
Brush rub polish burn
mend scratch foil evert
emulate surpass. Remember
"to write three-act play"
and lead "a full and active life."

Dreams

you can't remember, giving a day
a taste, like baking soda—
"It always repeats on me"
"I've dreamt that dream before"
—the morning after, or nastily sweet,
slightly, as low-calorie pop,
or bitter as boiled coffee
or simply receding: "Was that a burp?"
or a low-flying jet.
The said to be boring things

dreams, weather, a bus trip
are so fascinating. "In this dream
I was on a railway—a train—
on a gray day but with blue blobs
            ("Do you dream in color?"
            "Well . . . you knew they were blue . . .")
when a kid threw a rock
and glass flew all over
the conductor: "that was no dream
it really happened."
"You mean dreams don't really happen?"
"Don't ask me. Ask Bishop Berkeley."
He never told his dreams
with a few exceptions, like the one
throwing socks at the ceiling
and when they stuck knew they were mine.
Of course it matters sometimes
a lot to whom a dream is told:
"And there I was at the top
of the palm," her eyes glistened
he a little pale, "swaying and swaying
and the lion roared and roared . . ."
Next week, he had a new secretary
an older woman, a little sot
in her ways. Still, aggressor
and aggressed against, in dreams
in which the dead awaken
horrifyingly, or is it a way
of keeping them alive a little longer
and only sometimes? The horror
wears away like weathered paint,
a screen door slams and there
you stand, young and engaging
again. "I can't escape
the feeling that I saw you"
which once was true.
Or there you are, frowning
a little on the landing
with your clothing disarranged.
Only it's you but isn't you
it's oof: dreams are rather boring

to tell about, especially the stirred
up faintly feverish from too many covers
or too little air kind.
Still, you were there,
in a dream awakening
if not laughing, smiling.

Joint

Veal and mushrooms, wine, a too pungent salad
—like eating anaesthetic—
I do not believe in the legends of food,
I believe in the food.
It is not what carrots are like,
it is the carrots.

The wildwood aisle in church has chapels
of mussels and carrots under arches,
of breasty beets with dirt in their hair,
are lit by strings of lemons
and by fat votive candles in stubby glasses,
smoke and shine of leaves and glass.

"I think we rich should get down on our knees
and thank God we have money."

How the seafood smells, and eels,
how they taste (fried) and lie
in their tank like striated muscle.
Burlap bags of rice
that try to stand, not kneel,
sit open-mouthed and spill
splendor in grains between cobbles.
These sacks will go empty, folded like clothes,
to the country and come back in cart-loads
of frisky cabbage
and of tomatoes, red and gold.
Wine runs in gutters,

sour as sweat, sweet as melons
holding seeds like thoughts
or with seeds in their flesh, like sensations.

Lucky who have to eat
and drink, such as stimulating coffee,
slower than water,
that coats the cup if good and strong.

Jelly Jelly

Summer apples, showy and sugary, mealy and touchy
a finger bruise on the thin skin
brown and silently reproachful as your wife's black eye.

But if September apples ripen
and the sun coats the sights with crinkling sheets
of cold while the waves come yapping
something about "wine dark"
evening primroses in clefts of rocks they lap
in a space labeled, "August 27th, 1965
pay on demand," why then it is
September
when pebbles turn, shedding a summer snow
of salt, palely glowing in the first fall beaches.

The wind is pendant-breasted as a naked Swede.
A frosted fox grape shows
where a bird shat as it ate.
Blackberry canes arch and obtrude big nipples.
And the chaste tree blooms.

Back before I made the egg test
I thought the world as flat and very like an elderberry umbel
full of round juicy people winking and waving,
crying "Hi!" and "Meet you in the jelly!"
or "Under the lid of an elderberry pie."

Sonnet

August, tasting of ripe grapes and afternoon sleep,
sharpening, like the smell of boxwood, the grass blades
that yellow an uncut hill a heavier green
while the trees lean in folds and the rose of Sharon blooms
and blooms at each twig and branch tip like a toy tree,
setting a sleepy cat on an after-lunch table
among uncleared plates, white-and-black like the coolness
of the oilcloth in warm shade: withhold from these days
the rain that made the succulence of which you reek
in haze that hides the furthest view and seems like smoke
seeking, before it is time, the ripening leaves
bronze in your pollen-dusty air that films the sky
and, as the light fades, burns blue, that the hot moon may,
bathing its light in water, find its white coolness.

Voyage autour de mes cartes postales

"A man of words and not of deeds
Is like a garden full of weeds"

Travelling widdershins: The Shelf.
No. The postcards on and above the shelf.
A lurking pale-gray Irish castle by a pebbly river.
A cuboid castle, like something torn down at Battery Park.
A perfect castle for the message on the back:
           Letter will follow.
It came a long long time ago
two weeks at least. Autumn chat
among the glasses: "I wanted to write but . . .
           much of a mad whirl____
           sick____ (tourista____ (other____
           caught up in mural____ (Destruction of Coole)
           sleeping &/or drinking____
           hadn't squat____
           didn't know Erse for____

other_____
                    check one & complete
ah, a button card. A long lashed "20's" chap, slick-haired,
blue bow-tied, puffy sleeved, tweezed, lips a thin red gash,
his right thumb hooked in his belt,
left arm up, wrist in and resting on his waist
holding *The Red Book*
eyes winsomely askance asking, "Ain't I cute?"
He wears six mermaid pearls.
Those at the wrists completely hide his cuffs.
Not so the Indian above
enjoining a bison: "Turn not away your head
                    O brown and curly!"
They stand before two teepees and in the sky
fly two sides of a nickel.
Look softly! for above the teepees
among curtains and flowers
sits a saintly Spanish child
her eyes uplifted to the lobby of The Brown Palace
six balconies under glass,
green glass over the flags, palms, vitrines and fat furniture
without people. Hard times at the old Brown Palace?
Or "dim, subacqueous delights"?
Working down the next stud
from seven hand-tinted children posed as
wading, swimming, rowing, diving
GREETINGS FROM LINCOLNVILLE CENTER, MAINE.
GREETINGS TO YOU, TOO. How cold they must be
Maine being what it is, how well they feign!
past the ice-cream-pantsed-and-blazered man
who plucks a banjo
for a fluffy flapper pointing with a pointed shoe
'neath the world's most silk-shaded bridge lamp
to
The Death of Chatterton the glory of the Tate.
"At last, the luxury of poverty"
to quote.
The little garret with
   "   "   window with
a   "   plant
with just one bloom

peering unidentifiably at sad blue London.
The poor dead boy
has had his hair in the henna lately
great rings and strings of it
on the thin little pillow propped on a fat bolster.
One hand on the floor, in easy elegance
one hand on his rib cage, "   "   "
his primrose-lined grape-
juice velvet coat
tossed on a chair,
his face is greeny-white, a phial has fallen on the floor.
Beside an open chest, a snow of torn-up poems.
Cold light falls down upon the bed
composing the painting on his left and upper hip
androgynously swelling in gentian kneepants.
A hint of ambiguity, perhaps,
like Duse as L'Aiglon? Or a bathetic minimizing:
"He's sleeping—but *his face is greeny-white!*
What is that snow? that phial? why is he lying
on the bed one shoe on? O
Chatterton, what have you done?
The very blossoms turn away."
Chatterton, that marvelous boy,
whoever it is it isn't you.
The little scene compels, though not a tear.
A swift whisk up the next stud
of religious bits: a face from an annunciation,
a bit of gaudy Gaudi flamed
like Niagara Falls with colored lights
a Rest on the *Flight to Egypt*
(Jesus eats grapes, St. Joseph
hits something with a stick)
on past (next stud: gallery five)
The Wedding Cake House, plain as a pie plate
sheathed in Gothic tracery and spires,
at last to where the heart is happiest,
Cupid and Psyche, gray as a biscuit
kneaded by sooty hands (I ate that biscuit),
gut to gut
her arms and one of his around
thick and hearty, his other arm raised
to hold a garland above her head

and disclose that interesting flank,
a pit no longer, where underarm meets chest.
The nipple of a soup-bowl breast points up
and across hefty dragonfly wings
that rise with a tumescent weight.
Down his back, across his rump, between their thighs
flows an amazing bit of cloth
or is it an effluvia that rises
condensed into a steam like cloth?
Two *putti* at hip level pound each other.
Another strains as he lifts her leg,
her foot free, just, of the ground,
in aid of entry. Entwined like trees,
This photo of a deliberate swift terra-cotta cyclone
on the back is called

> Cupid and Psyche
> Clodion (1738–1814)
> The Frick Collection, New York

but on the pedestal can just be read

> The Embrace
> Claude Michel Clodion

Embrace indeed, Clodion!
Seventy-six years of it (one hopes you had)
seems a fair share. Passionate, virginal postcard
to whom shall I scribble you?

Four Poems

for Frank O'Hara

It's 4:30 in Cambridge

and I have a slight headache
on one side only just
enough for a drink.

What a long time since I wrote a poem.

I want to go to Florida
and sit in a shack on the beach
and feel my teeth ache.

The Home Book 1951–1970

"There goes another one," Joan said,
"who can't get it up." But she's
a sweet girl really under the bags
under her eyes. Oh shit (to quote).

Cambridge, I like you very much
to my great surprise. Oh shit (excuse
me, Frank, for stealing your stuff).

Anyway what I really like best
I guess is just driving in a car
the turnpikes are simply grand
and so BORING I have always liked
capital letters and words like
really and very
very very much. I mean I really
adore them. But (I mean BUT
oh hell) will I ever get it up
for him, and what would come of it
oh shit.

It's nice here thinking about all the men
who have one name in common

Between these lines I write your name
in the name of each hair on your chest
(you were so pleased when they came)

And they did come, all curling together
like wisps of clouds over Cambridge
Really it will be so much FUN
when we go to Mexico   Italy   the Canary Islands,
   the Danish baths
and that place in Vienna
and the one
the rich man invited somebody to
where is it in Bali

The plants here are very green
at cocktail time in Cambridge
and I am very sick really of all

the little concrete words such
as names of colors and effectively
used as in Art Reviews

Darling I write your name
between these lines
Very and Really: oh shit
even my spunk has soot on it
like the snow

I adore you! Let's go to Florida.

And Jon Wiener's poems
well they're really grand

I'll bring you one
printed on rubber

It's quarter of five
and the Fucking Tree has birds in its hair.

Mass. Ave., Cambridge, Mass.

The Wizard Pink Wick Deodorizer is capped
and the vapor teats of a cloud are over
the gold lantern and the blue lantern
of a white steeple in this flat brick city
you might like. And there goes the whistle
for a silver noon. It's odd, having an emotion
so much bigger than yourself, as though
the world were silk I could fold and bring
with me in an Amelia Earhart Weekend Bag.

"*. . . this dog's life . . .*"—VERLAINE

We must observe the amenities
even if we are going nuts.
So heat the coffee
and it is time

The Home Book 1951–1970

to get the lock changed.
There is rain on the panes
like the notes of a pianoforte
on the phonograph: it is age and pain
I hate, and death. The rain
falls like the sour strains
of the violins into which the notes
of the pianoforte settle grittily.
Can one really plan to live more spontaneously?
So far as I can tell, some dogs
lead better lives than others.

Frank! Frank!

Afternoon of indecision
in a turgid season
when birds come north can't I see it's time I went south?

But suppose my heart tore in two
like tearing up the only copy of a poem
while night whipped by the train?

suppose
suppose

my sky, my green rooftree, my chimney pots
how much I admire how others cultivate their possessions

and you, white primrose who bloom in the cold

I need an image of my mixed emotion
and all I can think of is Cambridge
flowing around the bends of the Charles
while its water speeds under the sculls

it doesn't matter that much
it's only my life so I'll pack
my dirty shirts, shorts and socks

Goodbye Cambridge,
Goodbye Charles

will you wait for me?

out of my heart flies a smile
that slowly revolves on its tip like a gull
over Cambridge, over the Charles

green bank, goodbye

A Head

A dead boy living among men as a man
called an angel
by me, for want of a word,
spaniel-eyed: wet, with bits
of gold deep in the eyeballs
hidden, like a mysterious ingredient
(c'est là, le mystère)
fringed with black and with black,
thick-grown, delicately thumb-smudged eyebrows
and brown cast on the face
so the lips are an earth red
and the rings or pouches under the eyes
are dark, and all the blue
there is hovers in the hollows
under the ridges of the cheekbones
as, in fall haze, earth,
broken into clods, casts shadows on itself:

except what, in the small hours, shows
the razor's path, its wide swaths
along the cheeks and down below
the strong and bluntly heart-shaped chin
where the taut flesh loosens and softens,
heaviest at the corners of the mouth
turning petulantly down from the fold

The Home Book 1951–1970

that lifts the upper lip and points
to the divider of the nostrils.

This so-called angel
who steps back into the shadows of an empty door
and staggers on short flights of stairs
is filled with a kind of death
that feeds on little things:
fulfilled plans that no longer suit the hour,
appetites that sicken and are not slaked
(such as for milk-shakes),
lost or stolen handkerchieves,
invisible contagion
(such as the common cold).

Within this head where thought repeats
itself like a loud clock, lived
the gray and green of parks before spring
and water on a sidewalk between banks of snow,
a skylit room whose windows were paintings
of windows with views of trees
converging in the park all parks imply;
in that head a million butterflies
took flight like paper streamers and bits of paper
a draught lifts at a parade.

Then they went away.
They went away in a dance-step
to the tune of *Poor Butterfly*
played on a wind-up phonograph
of red mahogany stuck with bits
of gold: right stele for him.

When night comes and lights come on
after the colors fade in the sky,
may he minister as he can to whom he may,
himself or other, give what grace
all the little deaths he stands for,
to me, have left him. He is an angel
for his beauty. So what
if it fades and dies?

Looking Forward to See Jane Real Soon

May drew in its breath and smelled June's roses
when Jane put roses on the sill. The sky,
in blue for elms, planted its lightest kiss,
the kind called a butterfly, on bricks fresh
from their kiln as the roses from their bush.
Summer went by in green, then two new leaves
stood on the avocado stem. The sky
darkened the color of Jane's eyes and snow
wrote her name in white. Such wet snow, that stuck
to the underside of curled iron and stone.
Jane, among fresh lilacs in her room, watched
December, in brown with furs, turn on lights
until the city trembled like a tree
in which wind moves. And it was all for her.

Dorabella's Naples Watercolor

Lamped in a postered arch, her settecento name
unpastes secret matrimonies. Gino Caflisch chocolates
nears. Tell where, where.

The sky's orangerie slushes coffee ice. Apostles
excite a loitered noon. Piazza della Borsa shrugs the
niched white statues.

Dorabella, your sisters? What tree in the palace?
I don't know: which tree. Mothers and children expiate
Persephone's stair.

Liquefaction, gasoline. Debasing an oleograph, a
baby burns. No nose portends: *lire* for the dead, mistress.
Operatic espadrilles: blue.

Capri, Ischia, Pompeii. Dorabella breaks a marble
bull's head, purses, buys striped socks. An inkwell hits
the tiles. Splash. Oh.

Dorabella, your sisters? One sings, one botanizes.
I love tweed with silk, pizza, mechanical organs. Ships
undo me. Squeezed by

thieves, whores, rifled, rippled, the tram
takes home a bright penny, my good luck, and drops
black grapes on Naples.

A Poem

Tags of songs, like salvaged buttons
off vanished dresses, a date
Thursday a week at eight, some guilt
for a cab she not only could not afford but:
pretty immoment matter
greets Dorabella's mounting
or are they subtracting moments. "Surely
should be otherwise, should stop, be
thought about, have other quality
than surprise. When was I last surprised?"
Now more a lilac in rain than a crocus
between her office and some gin, Dorabella
herself encounters numerously,
a not so bad looker for a tied and dyed,
a moustached nun of dubious inner life,
a character actress of no talent and less means,
a swami-smitten dowager needling a dull chauffeur,
or a hurrying woman smoothing gloves.

"What would it be like
to change, sharply as a traffic light?"

Dorabella makes a face
at life, and hurries.

THE
CRYSTAL
LITHIUM
(1 9 7 2)

FOR BOB

Empathy and New Year

*A notion like that of empathy inspires
great distrust in us, because it connotes
a further dose of irrationalism and
mysticism.*
LÉVI-STRAUSS

Whitman took the cars
all the way from Camden
and when he got here
or rather there, said,
"Quit quoting," and took the next
back, through the Jersey meadows
which were that then. But
what if it is all "Maya,
illusion?" I
doubt it, though. Men are not
so inventive. Or
few are. Not knowing
a name for something proves nothing. Right
now it isn't raining, snowing, sleeting, slushing,
yet it is
doing something. As a matter of fact
it is raining snow. Snow
from cold clouds
that melts as it strikes.
To look out a window is to sense
wet feet. Now to infuse
the garage with a subjective state
and can't make it seem to
even if it is a little like
What the Dentist Saw
a dark gullet with gleams and red.
"You come to me at midnight"
and say, "I can smell that after

Christmas letdown coming like a hound."
And clarify, "I can smell it
just like a hound does."
So it came. It's a shame
expectations are
so often to be counted on.

New Year is nearly here
and who, knowing himself, would
endanger his desires
resolving them
in a formula? After a while
even a wish flashing by
as a thought provokes a
knock on wood so often
a little dish-like place
worn in this desk just holds
a lucky stone inherited
from an unlucky man. Nineteen-sixty-
eight: what a lovely name
to give a year. Even better
than the dogs': Wert
(". . . bird thou never . . .")
and Woofy. Personally
I am going to call
the New Year, Mutt.
Flattering it
will get you nowhere.

II

Awake at four and heard
a snowplow not rumble—
a huge beast
at its chow and wondered
is it 1968 or 1969?
for a bit. 1968 had
such a familiar sound.
Got coffee and started
reading Darwin: so modest,
so innocent, so pleased at
the surprise that *he*

should grow up to be *him*. How
grand to begin a new
year with a new writer
you really love. A snow
shovel scrapes: it's
twelve hours later
and the sun that came
so late is almost gone:
a few pink minutes and
yet the days get
longer. Coming from the
movies last night snow
had fallen in almost
still air and lay
on all, so all twigs
were emboldened to
make big disclosures.
It felt warm, warm
that is for cold
the way it does
when snow falls without
wind. "A snow picture," you
said, under the clung-to
elms, "worth painting." I
said, "The weather operator
said, 'Turning tomorrow
to bitter cold.' " "Then
the wind will veer round
to the north and blow
all of it down." Maybe I
thought it will get cold
some other way. You
as usual were right.
It did and has. Night
and snow and the threads of life
for once seen as they are,
in ropes like roots.

Poem

for Trevor Winkfield
December 26, 1970

The wind tears up the sun
and scatters it in snow.
The sky smiles and out
of its mouth drifts free
a milk tooth which of itself
glides under the pillow
of a cloud. The Tooth Fairy
knows where to look and when
to lock away the leaves
long since packed up and
left: "I'm southbound." Not
now, though this funny
fluffy winter rain coasts
down and coats the grass
dry and white, a corn meal
shampoo. "Brush it in,
brush it out." Easier
said than done. Things
take the time they take:
leaves leaving, winter
and its flakes, not less
though shorter lived.

In January

after Ibn Sahl

The yard has sopped into its green-grizzled self its new year
    whiteness.

A dog stirs the noon-blue dark with a running shadow and dirt
    smells cold and doggy

As though the one thing never seen were its frozen coupling
    with the air that brings the flowers of grasses.

And a leafless beech stands wrinkled, gray and sexless—all bone
and loosened sinew—in silver glory

And the sun falls on all one side of it in a running glance, a
licking gaze, an eye-kiss

And ancient silver struck by gold emerges mossy, pinkly
lichened where the sun fondles it

And starlings of anthracite march into the east with rapid jerky
steps pecking at their shadows

Blue

for Yvonne Jacquette

beautiful New
York sky harder
so much than
soft walls you
see here around
it shadowy lamp
lighted plaster
smoothed by a hand
wielded trowel and
roller painted
by hand: Puerto
Rican blue pressed
tin ceiling sky
up into and on
which a white cup
(more of a mug)
falls, falls up-
ward and crack
splits into
two glazed
clay clouds

Spring

snow thick and wet, porous
as foam rubber yet
crystals, an early Easter sugar.
Twigs
aflush.
A crocus
startled or stunned
(or so it looks: crocus
thoughts are few) reclines
on wet crumble
a puddle of leas. It
isn't winter and it isn't spring
yes it is the sun
sets where it should and
the east
glows
rose. No
Willow.

In earliest morning

an orange devours
the crusts of clouds and you,
getting up, put on
your daily life
grown somewhat shabby, worn
but comfortable, like old jeans: at the least,
familiar. Water
boils, coffee
scents the air
and level light plunges
among the layering boughs of a balsam fir
and enflames its trunk.
Other trees are scratched
lightly on the west.

A purposeful mutt
makes dark marks
in blue dew. The day
offers so much, holds
so little or is it
simply you who
asking too much take
too little? It is
merely morning
so always marvelously
gratuitous and undemanding,
freighted with messages
and meaning: such
as, day
is different from the night
for some; see
the south dazzle
in an effulgence
thrown out by an ocean;
a myriad iridescence
of green;
the shape
of the cold egg
you break
and with a fork
again break
and stir and pour
into a pan, where it lightly hisses.
The sediment
in your mind sinks
as something rises
in it, a thought
perhaps, like a tree when it
is just two green
crumpled bits of tape
secured to grit; a
memory—beyond
a box of Gold Dust
laundry soap a cherry
in full flower and
later full of fruit;

a face, a name
without a face,
water with a name:
Mediterranean, Cazenovia, or
iced, or
to be flushed
away; a
flash of
good humor, no
more than a
wink; and the sun
dims its light
behind a morning
Times of cloud.

An East Window on Elizabeth Street

for Bob Dash

Among the silvery, the dulled sparkling mica lights of tar roofs
lie rhizomes of wet under an iris
from a bargain nursery sky: a feeble blue with skim milk
       blotched
on the falls. Junky buildings, aligned by a child
("That's very good, dear") are dental:
carious, and the color of weak gums ("Rinse and spit"
and blood stained sputum and big gritty bits
are swirled away). Across an interstice
trundle and trot trucks, cabs, cars,
station-bound fat dressy women
("I never thought I'd make it")
all foundation garments and pinched toes. I don't know how
it can look so miraculous and alive
an organic skin for the stacked cubes of air
people need, things forcing up through the thick unwilling air
obstinate and mindless as the glorious swamp flower
skunk cabbage and the tight uncurling punchboard slips
of fern fronds. Toned, like patched, wash-faded rags.
Noble and geometric, like Laurana's project for a square.
Mutable, delicate, expendable, ugly, mysterious

(seven stories of just bathroom windows)
packed: a man asleep, a woman slicing garlic thinly into oil
(what a stink, what a wonderful smell)
burgeoning with stacks, pipes, ventilators, tensile antennae—
that bristling gray bit is a part of a bridge,
that mesh hangar on a roof is to play games under.
But why should a metal ladder climb, straight
and sky aspiring, five rungs above a stairway hood
up into nothing? Out there
a bird is building a nest out of torn up letters
and the red cellophane off cigarette and gum packs.
The furthest off people are tiny as fine seed
but not at all bug like. A pinprick of blue
plainly is a child running.

Alice Faye at Ruby Foo's

1 from 9 is 8
and 4 from 5 is 1
K '59
a black green and white catalog from Germany
on my desk proclaims
that 18 this December's ago (when
almost any night they might just bomb
the Hotel Henry Hudson elevator ladies
who clucked because young men were "just boys")

    2
well, like I say
the chicken lady
no not in *Freaks* that was Olga
whosis Baclanova the real one
Alice Faye (glycerined feathers
humped in a rooster arch
above her butt and O those dancing shoes
stout but sporty)
dined one night in mink

blond pink and furry
or maybe just imagined it was she?

    3

" 'Driver,' this lady says, 'do I
have to ride with *this*?' So what do you think
it's right beside her on the seat
and all the time I think this navy
guy is hugging up his wife.
Me, I got a heart big as a ship.
But that lady. She was burned."

    4

White New York, and tin,
home of viscous egg drop soup, the red
baked banana, tasty yam and split persimmon,
out of the Annual Winter Guide of Uglifacts
a charm, like consulting Constella
in *The News* for fun and the oracle is apt:

        Alice Faye

smiling and smiling in the flaming night

or, THINK AMERICAN
   "dozing," as Cocteau said, "into her beard of orchids"

Don't be a goddess
Alice Faye, a democratic hoofer
a bosomy good sport
all good joes aspire to

O taxi cabs. O Ruby Foo.

Buildings

Buildings embankment parkway grass and river
all those cars
all those windows

each building shooting (straight up)
out of its small allotment
all those buildings fibered together
their flowing sap
traffic threading
the shark tooth city
O coral reef
O slick and edible matter
housed in seashell buildings
the most delicately leaved trees
on a high terrace waving
the most finely possible knotted net
of shadow on an incinerator shaft
sifting each evening its soot
in the violent atmosphere
in which white gulls are black
sickling a harvest of rinds
among swollen oceanic beauties
tugs nuzzle and badger
in the shatter surface salt river harbor
O morning light on dirty windows
sharpening the sepulchral church steeple
whitened by pigeons
the money insulated by limestone
and shining red granite reflects
such extraordinarily well dressed people
from among all of you
one can choose at a time only one
a woman striding the ragged grass
her fixed stare devouring the restless river
striding on the far side of the parkway
all those cars
all those millions of windows

Wonderful World

for Anne Waldman
July 23, 1969

"I," I mused, "yes, I," and turned to the fenestrations of the night
beyond one of Ada and Alex Katz's windows. Deep in Prince Street

lurked thin sullen fumes of Paris green; some great spotty Danes moved from room to room, their tails went whack whack in a kindly way and their mouths were full of ruses (roses). Flames in red glass pots, unlikely flowers, a spot of light that jumped ("Don't fret") back and forth over a strip of moulding, the kind of moulding that spells low class dwelling —I, I mused, take no interest in the distinction between amateur and pro, and despise the latter a little less each year. The spot of light, reflected off a cup of strong blue coffee, wasn't getting anywhere but it wasn't standing still. They say a lot of gangsters' mothers live around here, so the streets are safe. A vast and distant school building made chewing noises in its sleep. Our Lady of someplace stood up in a wood niche with lots and lots of dollar bills pinned around her. The night was hot, everybody went out in the street and sold each other hot sausages and puffy sugared farinaceous products fried in deep fat ("Don't put your fingers in that, dear") while the band played and the lady in the silver fox scarf with the beautiful big crack in her voice sang about the young man and how he ran out in front of the stock exchange and drank a bottle of household ammonia: "Ungrateful Heart." Big rolls of paper were delivered, tall spools of thread spun and spelled Jacquard, Jacquard. Collecting the night in her hand, rolling its filaments in a soft ball, Anne said, "I grew up around here," where, looking uptown on summer evenings, the Empire State Building rears its pearly height.

Scarlet Tanager

May 13, 1967

"—in the big maple
behind the willow—"
ajet with limp spring greens
lance-like, or the head of a pike
and there it flies
and there it sits
the tanager, the bright spot
in the sunny rather evil day
the red touch green
cries out for—the soldier
in "Storm at Castelfranco."
And the drums beat
in East 95th Street

for soldiers in a storm
no, it's only a parade.
A huge and sullen Buddha
of a man waits at the starting
with his sign DOWN WITH DOVES
kids cry cadence and a bunch
of thick short men in little hats
that announce them vets
of the War to End War
(It Floats, They Laughed, Chu Chin Chow)
look defiant at those
who go counter to them
though merely strolling home.

             A couple of men jump
             out of the sky
             wearing flags. Someone
             "described as a bystander"
             gets tarred and feathered.

Embittered object of our anxious
and unworthy fears, the scapegoat
in a getup like a grackle
that a cat drags in. Glorious day
in May when by the window
a wisteria hangs its violet lights
creased with a sunny pallor
and other birds than tanagers—
fluffy balls of fluffy dung—
flit to a skirl of bagpipes
in undefoliated yards
between backs of rows of houses
and men with faces like happy fists
march in well-remembered but unpracticed step
—who would study
to forget?—or is it habit, merely,
like LOOK BEFORE YOU TURN—
waving little flags, why then why then
it's hard not to believe the marchers
march for the fun of marching
to an inward tune like Mahler's happy

The Crystal Lithium

happy children's song

          drums   drums

A Sun Cab

goes by below
reflected across the street
in a window
four stories up
a train
sends up its
passing metal roll
through grills and gone
the more than daily Sunday

      CRIMINAL NEW JERSEY
      THIRSTING FLESHPOTS OF NEW YORK

buzz
horns hums and voices
a plane unravels from the Delft
a mohair thread
torn paper shadows,
dry cool and gritty
laid on
buff gray-white and pink
    The dog in its
sunspot sleep
cries in a few fine high whimpers
drips of rain
in dust on glass
paint drops

      FIDGET BALLS
      FOR AN UPTIGHT
      GENERATION

Shadows
fling out their feet

and step into sun
palpable and out
and motes of
who knows what
go by
up and out
of sight   Pale cornice
brokenly lighted
by light reflected
from the sunny side
a cab crosses
the sun
near the end of a street
to the river
unheard unseen
a fluent presence

THE ISLAND

Light Blue Above

Light blue above, darker below, lightly roughened by the stirring air
and with smooth tracks on it. There goes Reynald Hardie's lobster boat,
taking a colorful load of pleasure-seeking shoppers to Camden.

                    O Air
        the clear, the soot-bearer, the unseen that rips
        that kills and cures, that keeps
        all that is empty filled, the bright invisible

        into which we move like fingers into gloves
        that coats our rolling home with the sweet softness
        between grape and grape skin

        in silent laughter in a glass pushed down
        into a basin at retreating puzzled water
        constrained to rise elsewhere up
        the sides of the basin, of the glass
        up fingers and hand and wrist

        clinging to arm hair in mercurial bubbles
        that detach and rise and join itself

        the quick to heal
        that wriggles up from hot
        heat-wave pavement like teased hair

        or has a wintry bite, or in the dog days saps
        or is found at the bottom
        of a mailbox on an empty house
        or in a nest between twigs, among eggs

and we go on
with it within us
upon a dust speck
in bubble air

The Cenotaph

three idylls for Kenneth Koch

I *Moneses uniflora*

Rain falls on the trash burning in an old oil drum and does not put it
    out.
It smoulders.
It is not because of the widely spaced big drops that the fire smoulders.
Garbage in the trash makes the fire smoulder. Banana peels, the thin
    skin in egg shells, sots, etc.
A thick white stench moves off not much higher than the rim of the oil
    drum into the woods to the stones.
The woods reek.
The stench stinks.
The fire mumbles its food.
It is not a successful combustion.
The dogs do not agree. The yellow dog and the red dog sniff at the drum
    as close as they can without burning their noses.
They lift legs against it and make a faint steam.
Then change places and as before.
That ends the ceremony so they run and bite each other's ears.
The oil drum is weathered in gritty stains of ember and urine.
The dark day thickens.
The rain falls heartily.
The fire indoors spits sparks and black and burning lumps are stamped
    out on the wood floor.
Others fall on the hearth and are left to their own devices.
Spruce wood, full of knots and resin.
Spruce wood burns quickly, and spits.
Is it less desirable than birch or apple?
Yes and no.
Or, that depends.
Not if you want a quick hot fire.

Besides, it is plentiful.

It abounds.

The woods smell sweetly of Parma violets from moneses uniflora, single
flowered wintergreen

Trampled hay-scented fern and welcoming smoke.

The red dog comes in out of the rain to enact the chromo, *The Hound
on the Hearth.*

He garners plaudits.

The chuck wood stove is too hot.

The hand on the dial in the door has passed five hundred and can go
no higher.

Do not blame the quick hot spruce wood.

The under draft was left open.

The upper draft was left closed.

The fire burnt up in a rush.

Too hot an oven will ruin the meat thermometer.

Do not dash cold water on the red hot stove.

The iron will crack.

Today the sun came out.

Tonight we will not need a fire.

We eat aspic.

The incinerator oil drum is chockablock with paint rags and newspapers
soaked with turpentine.

The fire burns fiercely.

Its flames leap as high as the bending branches of the nearby birch.

The flames are seen but do not augment the sunlight.

If it is very hot it is still a local heat.

The dogs keep their distance.

The sun opens the flowers of the hawkweed.

Many are yellow and some are an orange red.

The hawkweed flowers are an idea about the color of fire.

The hawkweed are one thing and the fire is another.

If there is garbage in the fire it burns up too quickly to make a stink.

The fire is a hazard for the baby.

It is a good thing baby is fast asleep.

In the dark the biggest firefly is a cigarette.

The faint smell of burning is not faulty wiring.

It is the smell left by a hot day.

2 We see seals. Boats go by.

We see seals.

Boats go by.

The stones hurt tender feet, so we walk on hands.

It is easy: bodies are buoyant.

The water is clear.

It has thrown together some loose stones.

I lie on a water cushion and look down.

You lie on your back and look up.

The rocks have on seaweed.

We might slip on the weed and break my neck or at least sprain your
ankle.

Salted nuts.

I have a red toenail.

It is red dye from orange socks bought in Vermont.

If sweat causes the sock to dye the nail red why won't the dye wash off
of the nail?

It is incomprehensible.

I cannot understand it.

Some sunning seals swiftly slither and go plop.

Why?

A boat buzzed by.

The sea shapes the stones and dulls them.

Under and in it they shine colorfully.

It shows what it could do if it wished.

A final burnish is not its task.

Getting the most out of a stone might be to leave it alone.

There is nothing to eat except sea urchins and berries: blue and rasp.

There is nothing to drink except sea water full of trace elements.

That is not true.

There is a spring.

It is near here over there.

It is a good thing we did not bring the dog.

He might muddy the spring.

It is at the beach called The Beach Where the Indian Killed the Sheep.

A story about which I know nothing.

A title tells the tale.

Perhaps it is a tall tale.

It is certainly a dull one.

It is literary.

Did Beowulf call the sea "the penis-shrinker"?

The Crystal Lithium

A seal sticks his snout out and gives a short snort.
The sun has got its ribbons snarled.
It is as bright on the other side as it is on this.
It is not like the moon which will rise between five and six and maunder
among the spruce.
I am cold.
You are too.
We get out.
I dry off.
You sun.
I put on a sun-dried T shirt, shirt, undershorts, shorts, socks and shoes.
Sneakers.
You dress too.
The way to the bog through the bog to the road from the south to the
north by the silver stile over no fence to the garden by the apples
to the gate to the lupines by the well to the road and so home
to lunch.
I lie down to read.
You canoe.
Do you know a camera that "costs $1,000.00 before accessories is well
worth it?"
Oh you do did you.
Someone is twelve years old and says putting a puzzle ring together is
a "Herculanean task."

3 The Edge in the Morning
Walking to the edge with a cup of coffee.
Sunup.
The sky is red.
Sunrise.
That way, the water is blinding.
That way, the water is dusted with sleep.
That way, the water shines as freshly as lead curling smoothly under a
knife.
The bay has a skin.
It swells it without breaking like water brimming in a glass.
On its skin and on mine the sun is warm.
The slipping air is thin and cold and cools the cup.
The coffee is cold.
Small fat gray brown birds in the grass bounce up from shadow to shadow.
The false oats are ripened and bearded straw.

The sun strikes them.

They light up.

The quaking grass has collapsed in wire heaps.

It is not what it was.

The edges of the bay are thinnest at high tide.

It is low tide.

The seaweed has pods of air that are like coffee beans.

Out of the silence an engine approaches.

There are tide lines in the cup.

In the brilliance the boat is a dark chunk, bluntly whittled.

It steadily comes nearer.

It throbs.

It moves across the light and turns white.

It pays out two lines that fan and roll and add their action to the surface
friction between air and water.

The bay is 1) a continuum and 2) change.

In the boat the figure of a man is ingeniously in scale.

A crow laughs.

The engine throttles.

The boat turns.

The ripples are twisted in a knot that shatters and dissolves.

The small turbulence breaks and melts.

The engine cuts to a rale.

The figure of a man turns, steps and bends and draws out of the
dishonored and neglected grave cold-blooded fury entrapped in
a lobster pot.

Carapace and claws snapping and thrashing, mottled stormily.

Gaudy shells packed with sweet meat.

The lobsterman turns toward you a face of weathered stone that cracks
into a smile.

The price is up because the take is down.

He baits his trap and drops it in the sea.

The asthmatic purr chokes and resumes the stertorous breathing of
normalcy.

The boat goes off to grow blue with distance.

The coffee cup has found its way onto the jut of a crag the size of a
foot.

The little it holds is cold, bitter, gritty and tastes good.

The air has stopped sliding.

It is a breeze that is more like a wind.

It crumples the bay and stuffs it in a stone pocket.

The Crystal Lithium

The bay agitatedly tries to smooth itself out.
If it were tissue paper it would need damp and an iron.
It is a good deal more than damp.
What a lot of water.
A gull barks.
A baby barks back.
Three crows go by about their dark and iridescent business.
The sun is high enough to have its plain daily look of someone who
      takes in wash.
It dries the laundry.
Suppose I found a bone in the grass and told you it is one of Marc
      Bloch's?
It would not be true.
No it would not be true and the sea is not his grave.
Noble, great, and good:
It is his cenotaph.

After Joe was at the island

June 30, 1969

a good while after, on the upstairs east sleeping porch he used for a
studio, yellow petals—sharp yellow, shiny as lacquer—caught in the
tatters of a web, on the sill to the north, torn-out book matches with
burnt heads pointing all one way, laid in a likeness of a woodpile (always
making something); and a pastryboard drawing board with edge of the
paper color traces; shades of sky up to white, of leaves and needles—
All Sorts— and not much smudged rose warming, the way grass in flower
sends a terra-cotta to slide through the unmown bending, the given—
the surface of the board—its woodenness abstracted of brown pale skies,
of agitated mud rising in an unreflecting creek, of dry dirt and wet
shingle—the tide is full only twice a day and faded toward silver house
shingles; or, shakes.

"Used Handkerchiefs 5¢"

Clean used ones, of course. Also a dresser scarf, woven with a pattern
of pansies looking alternately to right and to left; a pillowcase full of

carpet scraps; underdrawers of cambric with an edging of tatting; black—shedding jet and bugles—crêpe, as stuffed with dust and as damp, or as dry, as the wrinkled hand of someone too old to die who dies because to wake up this morning just slipped her mind; bent giant postcards: Mount Pelée and a fruitless wonderland of ice prisms, clear water-diluted color chunks: blue; pink and green; sagging brown and metal-threaded tapestry cloth within the gothic arch of a table Motorola hiding a speaker from which once sped Flagstad's more than melodious shriek and, over-enunciated as plums wrapped in papers printed "Biscayne Farms," once trotted, like a quick creek, the news that flaming passengers were falling from the Hindenburg, a voice that left itself a small puddle of kerosene on the linoleum; then there is your face, floating up the stairs, big-eyed into the trash-and-treasures loft from which, finally, dressed for tennis as you came, you go down again with a find in hand: a slab of undyed linen its silverness yellowing like a teaspoon from egg yolk, ironed with too cool an iron so the washing crush marks make a pattern over the weave and, above the thick welt of the hem, a cross-stitched border of spruce and juniper unstylized (unless style is simply to choose) in shades of drab that sink in, or emerge from: the hand towel of today, embroidered forty some maybe years ago.

The Trash Book

for Joe Brainard

Then I do not know what
to paste next in the
Trash Book: grass, pretending
to be a smear maybe or
that stump there that knows
now it will never grow
up to be some pencils or
a yacht even. A piece of
voice saying (it sounds like)
"I thought her did." Or
the hum that hangs in only
my left ear. Or, "Beer" not
beer, all wet, the quiver
of the word one night in
1942 looking at a cardboard
girl sitting on a moon in

West Virginia. She smiled
and sipped her Miller's.

8/12/70

In early August among the spruce
fall parti-colored leaves
from random birch that hide
their crowns up toward the light—
deciduously needle-nested—
among the tumbled rocks—a
man-made scree below a house—
a dull green sumach blade
slashed with red clearer than
blood a skyblue red a first
fingertap, a gathering, a climax

Light from Canada

for Charles North

A wonderful freshness, air
that billows like bedsheets
on a clothesline and the clouds
hang in a traffic jam: summer
heads home. Evangeline,
our light is scoured and Nova
Scotian and of a clarity that
opens up the huddled masses
of the stolid spruce so you
see them in their bristling
individuality. The other
day, walking among them, I
cast my gaze upon the ground
in hope of orchids and,
pendant, dead, a sharp shadow
in the shade, a branch gouged
and left me "scarred forever

'neath the eye." Not quite. Not
the cut, but the surprise, and
how, when her dress caught fire,
Longfellow's wife spun
into his arms and in the dying
of its flaring, died. The
irreparable, which changes
nothing that went before
though it ends it. Above the wash
and bark of rumpled water, a gull
falls down the wind to dine
on fish that swim up to do same.

Gulls

Gulls
loudly insist on indefensible rights

Spruce
gather together on spindle shanks

Queen Anne's Lace
tip platters at perilous angles

Hawkweed
all sneeze at the same time

Rocks
go back to sleep

Birches
grunt as they scratch themselves

Stumps
grow old in hospitableness

Moss
free of dandruff

The Crystal Lithium

Bunchberries
trotting about

Closed Gentian Distances

A nothing day full of
wild beauty and the
timer pings. Roll up
the silver off the bay
take down the clouds
sort the spruce and
send to laundry marked,
more starch. Goodbye
golden- and silver-
rod, asters, bayberry
crisp in elegance.
Little fish stream
by, a river in water.

FALL AND WINTER

September

Swimming in the memorial
park pond smells of a dog

or just wading up and
down on trucked-in sand

oaks do their stuff
a dressy pine

and a kind of a mantid
that inspires respect

it isn't an insect with
only four legs when

its pincers snappily fold
back Danilova/Yastrzemski

that's it in September sun
two of its legs are like—you

know. Arms

Evening Wind

October hangs in grape
bunch lights among the leaves
of a giant tree whose leaves
are not unlike grape leaves:

a plane tree, or a sycamore?
The wind comes up the water
as water from a faucet
runs across a palm, the palm
of your hand, the water turned
on gently or broken into
cool molten wooly glass
by an aerator. And each
responds by his or its
own bending to it, tall tops
of hedge move all in a sideways
way, the grass (it begins
to have its matted resting
up for winter look) is freaked
by shade and quartz grit
bits of light, a pear tree
rocks at its roots and from
the eyebrow curves of branches
or under them flutters absurdly
its leaves like lashes. And I
am troubled by hatred for
the dead. Wind, you don't
blow hard enough, though
rising, in the smoky blue
of evening, mindless and in love.
Or would be if the wind
were not above such thoughts,
above thought, in fact
of course, though coursing,
cool as water, through it.

A Vermont Diary

November 1

                    Slowly
the dried up pond
fills again. The blackish

verge grows spongy. Packed
with seeds of which some
burst unseasonably into
life: kinds of grass in
tufted rays or with blades
folded in purple cornucopias—
low-growing bedstraw and
others to you nameless—
pushing out for room,
radiating, starring the muck.
A frail gray flower
flies off, an insect
that escaped the first
combing frosts. It's
not—"the fly buzzed"
finding moods, reflectives:
fall
equals melancholy, spring,
get laid: but to turn it all
one way: in repetition, change:
a continuity, the what
of which you are a part.
                The clouds are tinted
                gray and violet and shred
                the blue in other blues.
                Each weed as you walk
                becomes a rarity.

Quarter past four and evening turbulence begins, the sky clotted
with clouds, glazed and crazed like gray pottery.

It's warm for the time of year here—last night the Hallowe'en
weathercaster called it "living on borrowed time": last year at this time
there were five inches of snow ("On the ground?" "No. In the trees.")
50° in Burlington (at 11 p.m.)—51° in New York.

The hills that last year in early October I saw enflamed and raging
are now the browns and grays of lichened bark, the woods lit by bare
birch trunks and warmed by spruce and pine.

                                  The Crystal Lithium

In a drugstore in Montpelier—"A bottle of Fitch Shampoo—" "*Fix* Shampoo? Is it got something special about it?"

November 2

The road goes down a steep gradient through the close harmony of the fields (frowsy with opening milkweed pods) and there there is one larch, a pyramid of light among all that is faded or bare or shroudedly evergreen.

From the ceiling comes a soft irregular scuffling—Joe moving his feet as he works—a fly at the window makes a dry repetitive nagging sound, like someone trying to start a car; and on the couch Whippoorwill, all wrapped up in himself, grunts and pulls himself a little tighter.

The light on the lake and trees beyond is wintry (though the day is warm), clear as water disclosing bare stems in a harsh chill. The light is colorless, harsh as an old photograph.

November 3

As the sun goes west the shadow of the ridge brings the pond to a reflecting black, its surface on the exposed side where the road goes round crinkled by the wind. The brush piles, stumps where they cleared dead elms, the harsh light, give it a raw frontier look: beyond the fact of beauty and the appearance of beauty, life's unrelenting hardness: ice broken, jammed, grinding on itself.

November 4

Antiquing: Hardwicke.

me—"We ought to change 'Kill a cop tonight: Hallowe'en,' to 'Ball your local sheriff.' "
Joe—"Why? Is she cute?"

Thinking about Larry Fagin—"Then I went home and had this wonderful dream."

November 5

Kenward is right behind me taking wood ashes out of the fireplace to add to the compost. Actually, he is through doing that and is laying a fire, bringing big chunks of wood up from the cellar. Whippoorwill hops off the couch with a sneeze and gallops after him, then comes back to lie in some unexpected sunshine. Up until now—noon—it's been almost a snow-bearing sky, though still very warm for November, with clouds nothing like fog over the further hills, but now the middle of the sky is smeared and worn through and some pallid light makes weak shadows along the road.

> Fine lines, so many lines,
> lines on lines, the hills
> are all a haze of twigs—
>
> the armatures of summer,
> lichens on the trunks,
> are whitely acid green—

November 6

Not quite four o'clock and all heavily, snowily overcast, except down the valley in the south there is a clear strip of sky, the pale green of an unripe peach. A couple of hours ago, when I went for a nice long walk, the sky was a most tender blue—a French blue, like the sky was over Cherbourg one morning—seventeen years ago. A sky of rain clouds that morning was breaking up and the pilot boat that brought the immigration officers out bounced in heavy seas. I remember a woman in a transparent hooded raincoat sprinkled with raindrops.

My walk—the road goes steeply downhill between fields, then winds through the woods beside a stream which makes several waterfalls. Down and down, past a cleared place full of stumps where timber was cut last year and a hunter's car was parked today. Then the road levels off, a scrubby wet looking field opens on the left, and at the end of it is Farmer Martin's house, where Emslie Road ends in a right angle to the road that goes from Maple Corner to East Calais. The Martins' house, which is of a nice old kind (Cape Cod) but in need of a good deal more than paint, is built in what must always have been a rather odd place—so low and damp in the creek flats, and likely to flood in the spring—one

The Crystal Lithium

wonders what the inducement was to build there—not well water, in these gushing hills—that it was on a road, and the richness of the bottom land along the creek? Little use seems made of it now. There's always a lot of junk piled up beside the house—lately including a white toilet—and one window was propped open by a tin can. And what was once a chicken run has a rank harvest of sere thistles.

I took the right-hand turn, a long gradient that must take one up again as high as the house (well, two-thirds) and twice the length, a much easier ascent than going up the road down Apple Hill, but enough to work up a sweat. In thin woods facing south many more ferns still are green than up here, and in a growing up field old apple trees still hold a lot of fruit, yellow, or soft orange-red, and one a brilliant red, like rose hips. A lot of the land is posted, but one man's said hunting was permitted by request, and gave his phone number.

Rather a relief when the road levels out at Kent's Corners—the old brick tavern, shuttered for the winter, looking a good deal more four-square on the outside than it does inside. All the houses on this stretch of a mile or less are nicely kept up—especially the one at the first crossroads, where they keep guinea fowl (polka dots!) and there is a stream which in September is thick with forget-me-nots. A week ago this road was all churned up, but has now been leveled and rolled. A couple of big yellow dump trucks passed me going back and forth with loads of fill, which a huge complicated machine was pushing into place in front of the Co-Op at Maple Corner. The part of the Montpelier Road that comes down a short steep hill there is going to be paved—or at least, straightened. Another right-hand turn there, through the hamlet, past the school and Marian Anderson the postmistress's house and the dairy farm and its close-cropped, stony, uphill pastures. Two shaggy horses with heavy rumps were standing around looking solemn, and a lot of long clouds like old-fashioned trolley cars were going along overhead, some kind of osier was a vineyard beside the road and I thought, I wouldn't want anything to be different about this day—a sudden wonderful feeling of accepting things as they are, even the things you don't like—the plain Jane new houses, or a rough-looking dog that shot out, fiercely barking at me as I passed a garage—scary, even though chained. At the top of the rise, in the shade of some trees beside a road to a field, there was a little snow left from last night's flurries, which had been rather hard to believe in earlier, under the blue, and where this road turns off I saw through the leafless trees a pond, straight down below the fields, I never knew was there before.

November 7

A Gray Thought

In the sky a gray thought
ponders on three kinds of green:
Brassy tarnished leaves of lilacs
holding on half-heartedly and long
after most turned and fell to make
a scatter rug, warmly, brightly brown.
Odd, that the tattered heart-shapes
on a Persian shrub should stay
as long as the northern needles
of the larch. Near, behind the lilac
on a trunk, pale Paris green
as moonlight, growing on another time scale
a slowness becoming vast as though
all the universe were an atom
of a filterable virus in a head
that turns an eye to smile
or frown or stare into other
eyes: and not of gods, but creatures
whose size begins beyond the sense of size:
lichens, softly colored, hard in durance,
a permanence like rock on a transient tree.
And another green, a dark thick green
to face the winter, laid in layers on
the spruce and balsam or in foxtail
bursts on pine in springy shapes
that weave and pierce
the leafless and unpatterned woods.

Later.

Verge

A man cuts brush
and piles it
for a fire where
fireweed will flower
maybe, one day.
All the leaves

are down except
the few that aren't.
They shake or
a wind shakes
them but they
won't go oh
no there goes
one now. No.
It's a bird
batting by.
The small lake,
shrunk, shivers
like a horse
twitching off
flies. Flies
drunkenly stagger
between window
and storm sash.
They hatch, lay,
buzz and die.
The sky grows
gray, goes pale,
bears a whitlow
or splits and
shows a lining
light sea green.
But the lake
is black. Back
of the trees
where deer stoop
and step and
the independent skunk
securely waddles.
An unseen
something stirs
and says: No
snow yet but
it will snow.
The trees sneeze:
You bet it
will, compiling

a white and wordless
dictionary
in which brush
cut, piled and
roofed with glitter
will catch and burn
transparently
bright in white
defining "flame."
So long, north.
See you later
in other weather.

Late afternoon.

Another sky that looked snow-bearing breaks up and sunlight falls
hit or miss on the hills.

Country living. The Pyrofax (the gas which the stove burns) began
to give out the day before yesterday (you can tell it's running out when
you begin to smell it: spooky). So Kenward went to the Co-Op and called
for new tanks, which were to come that afternoon or, at the very latest,
yesterday. Still no Pyrofax.

Tomorrow we return to New York, a long drive, and the next night,
a big birthday party (mine).

A Stone Knife

December 26, 1969

Dear Kenward,
                    What a pearl
of a letter knife. It's just
the thing I needed, something
to rest my eyes on, and always
wanted, which is to say
it's that of which I
felt the lack but
didn't know of, of no
real use and yet
essential as a button

The Crystal Lithium

box, or maps, green
morning skies, islands and
canals in oatmeal, the steam
off oyster stew. Brown
agate, veined as a woods
by smoke that has to it
the watery twist of eel grass
in a quick, rust-discolored
cove. Undulating lines of
northern evening—a Munch
without the angst—a
hint of almost amber:
to the nose, a resinous
thought, to the eye, a
lacquered needle green
where no green is, a
present after-image.
Sleek as an ax, bare
and elegant as a tarn,
manly as a lingam,
November weather petrified,
it is just the thing
to do what with? To
open letters? No, it
is just the thing, an
object, dark, fierce
and beautiful in which
the surprise is that
the surprise, once
past, is always there:
which to enjoy is
not to consume. The un-
recapturable returns
in a brown world
made out of wood,
snow streaked, storm epi-
center still in stone.

The Dog Wants His Dinner

for Clark Coolidge

The sky is pitiless. I beg
your pardon? OK then
the sky is pitted. The yard
is sand and laced with roots
afloat on rock encasing fire.
You think so do you. No.
Yes. Don't know. Check one.
Forget all you ever knew.
Sorry. Not my romance. What
is? Sorry. We don't take
in trick questions. You mean?
I do: put down that.
Put that down too. Skies
of spit, seas where whales
piss and die to make a bar
of scented soap, uhm smells
good. She came in like an ex-
cited headline. The deer
they all were starving! To
death, even, perhaps. And
eating people! What to do
with these disordered herds
of words? I said I would
eat my words and do so, now
you see. He eats them, all
up. Greedily. Yesterday the
air was squeaky clean today
it's dull and lifeless as an
addict's armpit. Surely you
mean leafless. I have a flea
bite, here, pink, of course
as an eye disease: the cat
who brings me fleas dies
like a dog, sleepily, or
an unwatered plant. That
was exciting wasn't it. It's
not that I crave. Uh did
you say crave? Some words
are briefly worse than others:

113

The Crystal Lithium

get the Librium gun and point
it and the Kodak at that Kodiak.
You see? No hope. So don't
hope. Hop, skip, jump or
lie down. Feed your face.
Now feed the dog. He ate his.
He is eating the cat who
objects. Fix the fire. Put
out the light. An ice cold
hand slides in the window
to touch your uncovered head
forehead cheeks lips lobes
and all with worlds of fire
chilled by distance. O night.
Bedclothes loosen. Unseen twigs
erect themselves in air. You
asleep too, O magic root.

Running Footsteps

A thin brown stain
down the white brick wall
I guess yes
the new roof leaks
and there are holes
drilled in the asphalt
out there where manhole
covers used to blow:
escape for leaks. Sleet
down the chimney:
a rustle broken
into dots and dashes. Then
a midwinter downpour.
The streets are rivers
or the water streets
in a smalltown dream
"They live on Water Street
near the corner of Front Street

off Railroad Avenue."
The current fails.
Lights go out
in parts of town. In
the slosh there are
running footsteps: has
got to go though
an act of clouds would will
otherwise. Otherwise,
had stayed where was . . . ?
Couldn't. Why?
On and off lights
prolong into surges
the chatter of
rain on rain, the up
close rats' nesting noise
in the chimney: "It's
a good night to stay
in" so out you
go into it it's
almost like
that other night
you left holding
your breath to
descend and issue
screaming: your
tonight running
footsteps, rain
icy and loud
is a kind of
what to your
surprise is you
screaming in
fear, in rage,
instinctual
to find relief
muscular surges
running footsteps
the rain
rain-chilled
to be alive

The Crystal Lithium

The smell of snow, stinging in nostrils as the wind lifts it from a beach
Eye-shuttering, mixed with sand, or when snow lies under the street
    lamps and on all
And the air is emptied to an uplifting gassiness
That turns lungs to winter waterwings, buoying, and the bright white
    night
Freezes in sight a lapse of waves, balsamic, salty, unexpected:
Hours after swimming, sitting thinking biting at a hangnail
And the taste of the—to your eyes—invisible crystals irradiates the
    world
"The sea is salt"
"And so am I"
"Don't bite your nails"
                      and the metal flavor of a nail—are these brads?—
Taken with a slight spitting motion from between teeth and whanged
    into place
(Boards and sawdust) and the nail set is ridged with cold
Permanently as marble, always degrees cooler than the rooms of air it
    lies in
Felt as you lay your cheek upon the counter on which sits a blue-banded
    cup
A counter of condensed wintry exhalations glittering infinitesimally
A promise, late on a broiling day in late September, of the cold kiss
Of marble sheets to one who goes barefoot quickly in the snow and early
Only so far as the ash can—bang, dump—and back and slams the door:
Too cold to get up though at the edges of the blinds the sky
Shows blue as flames that break on a red sea in which black coals float:
Pebbles in a pocket embed the seam with grains of sand
Which, as they will, have found their way into a pattern between foot
    and bedfoot
"A place for everything and everything in its place" how wasteful, how
    wrong
It seems when snow in fat, hand-stuffed flakes falls slow and steady in
    the sea
"Now you see it, now you don't" the waves growl as they grind ashore
    and roll out
At your feet (in boots) a Christmas tree naked of needles
Still wound with swags of tarnishing tinsel, faintly alarming as the thought

Of damp electricity or sluggish lightning and for your health desiring
    pains
The wind awards: Chapped Lips: on which to rub Time's latest acquisition
Tinned, dowel shaped and inappropriately flavored sheep wool fat
A greasy sense-eclipsing fog "I can't see
Without my glasses" "You certainly can't see with them all steamed up
Like that. Pull over, park and wipe them off." The thunder of a summer's
    day
Rolls down the shimmering blacktop and mowed grass juice thickens
    the air
Like "Stir until it coats the spoon, remove from heat, let cool and chill"
Like this, graying up for more snow, maybe, in which a small flock
Of—sparrows?—small, anyway, dust-kitty-colored birds fly up
On a dotted diagonal and there, ah, is the answer:
Starlings, bullies of birdland, lousing up
The pecking order, respecters of no rights (what bird is) unloved (oh?)
Not so likeable as some: that's temperate enough and the temperature
Drops to rise to snowability of a softness even in its scent of roses
Made of untinted butter frosting: Happy Name Day, Blue Jay, staggering
On slow-up wings into the shrunk into itself from cold forsythia snarl
And above these thoughts there waves another tangle but one parched
    with heat
And not with cold although the heat is on because of cold settled all
About as though, swimming under water, in clearly fishy water, you
Inhaled and found one could and live and also found you altogether
Did not like it, January, laid out on a bed of ice, disgorging
February, shaped like a flounder, and March with her steel bead
    pocketbook,
And April, goofy and under-dressed and with a loud laugh, and May
Who will of course be voted Miss Best Liked (she expects it),
And June, with a toothpaste smile, fresh from her flea bath, and gross
    July,
Flexing itself, and steamy August, with thighs and eyes to match, and
    September
Diving into blue October, dour November, and deadly dull December
    which now
And then with a surprised blank look produces from its hand the ace
    of trumps
Or sets within the ice white hairline of a new moon the gibbous rest:
Global, blue, Columbian, a blue dull definite and thin as the first day

Of February when, in the steamed and freezing capital cash built
Without a plan to be its own best monument its skyline set in stacks
Like poker chips (signed "Autodidact"), at the crux of a view there
    crosses
A flatcar-trailer piled with five of the cheaper sort of yachts, tarpaulined,
Plus one youth in purple pants, a maid in her uniform and an "It's not
    real
Anything" Cossack hat and coat, a bus one-quarter full of strangers and
The other familiar fixings of lengthening short days: "He's outgrown them
Before you can turn around" and see behind you the landscape of the
    past
Where beached boats bask and terraced cliffs are hung with oranges
Among dark star-gleaming leaves, and, descending the dizzying rough
    stairs
Littered with goat turd beads—such packaging—you—he—she—
One—someone—stops to break off a bit of myrtle and recite all the
    lines
Of Goethe that come back, and those in French, "*Connais-tu* . . . ?"
    the air
Fills with chalk dust from banged erasers, behind the February dunes
Ice boats speed and among the reeds there winds a little frozen stream
Where kids in kapok ice-skate and play at Secret City as the sun
Sets before dinner, the snow on fields turns pink and under the hatched
    ice
The water slides darkly and over it a never before seen liquefaction of
    the sun
In a chemical yellow greener than sulphur a flash of petroleum by-product
Unbelievable, unwanted and as lovely as though someone you knew all
    your life
Said the one inconceivable thing and then went on washing dishes: the
    sky
Flows with impersonal passion and loosening jet trails (eyes tearing from
    the cold)
And on the beach, between foam frozen in a thick scalloped edging so
    like
Weird cheek-mottling pillowcase embroidery, on the water-darkened
    sand the waves
Keep free of frost, a gull strangles on a length of nylon fishline and the
    dog
Trots proudly off, tail held high, to bury a future dinner among cut grass
    on a dune:

The ice boats furl their sails and all pile into cars and go off to the super
     market
Its inviting foods and cleansers sold under tunes with sealed in memory-
     flavor
"Hot House Rhubarb" "White Rock Girl" "Citrus Futures" "Cheap Bitter
     Beans" and
In its parking lot vast as the kiss to which is made the most complete
     surrender
In a setting of leaves, backs of stores, a house on a rise admired for
     being
Somewhat older than some others (prettier, too?) a man in a white apron
     embraces a car
Briefly in the cold with his eyes as one might hug oneself for warmth
     for love
—What a paint job, smooth as an eggplant; what a meaty chest, smooth
     as an eggplant
—Is it too much to ask your car to understand you? the converse isn't
     and the sky
Maps out new roads so that, driving at right angles to the wind, clouds
     in ranks
Contrive in diminishing perspective a part of a picture postcard of a
     painting
Over oak scrub where a filling station has: gas, a locked toilet (to keep
     dirt in)
A busted soda pop machine, no maps and "I couldn't tell you *thet*" so
The sky empties itself to a color, there, where yesterday's puddle
Offers its hospitality to people-trash and nature-trash in tans and silvers
And black grit like that in corners of a room in this or that cheap dump
Where the ceiling light burns night and day and we stare at or into each
Other's eyes in hope the other reads there what he reads: snow, wind
Lifted; black water, slashed with white; and that which is, which is
     beyond
Happiness or love or mixed with them or more than they or less, un-
     changing change,
"Look," the ocean said (it was tumbled, like our sheets), "look in my
     eyes"

LOVING YOU

Janis Joplin's Dead:
Long Live Pearl

"Ever write any love poems?"

you call:
guarded voices. O
Commodore
Hotel, I like
free speech. "Free-
dom's just
a word." I bet
you think
I'm giving you
the old
McGee. I
ain't givin'
you nothin',
Buster: just
walk on in
and help yourself.
Set right down
and rap a while.
Take a toke.
Take two. Do
your thing. I'm puttin' on
Pearl (O Pearl) and
The In White Wrappers
(groovy group)
or *Company.* Couldn't
care
less. Not
true. Then
dig right
in and help yourself. You think
I don't mean it? Not

on your Kodachrome. Or
it's
a put on? Maybe
baby: that's
a game that two
can play
at: in fact it
takes two
and only two:
                    "holdin' "

"body
next to
mine"

Eyes

seta cangiante
eyes that change
changeable as changeable
silk, silk that
refracts
as bearer walks
in sunlight
into shade
from Piazza, say,
San Marco
into suncharged
shadowy arcade
or under trees
green, green
and between
blue, blue, blue
bluest blue
eyes of un-
weavable color
human eyes, man
size: unsilken

The Crystal Lithium

reflections:
hazel, gray-
blue, 'tea
ashes' Chinese,
ordinary eyes:
The Big Salty,
shifting restless,
under overcast:
smile, cold, half-
asleep
and deep in August
grass, elms, weeping
birches and all
green, too
green, so green
and the eyes
pick it up and
flash *il raggio verde*
the green ray
al tramonto
sunset flash
the red
reversal: i.e.
green

And in your eyes
your suddenly so
green eyes
the flash holds
steadily and
you smile or
I hope so: it
is not August
yet, *Occhi*
di seta cangiante
mi segue?

The Night

The night is filled with indecisions
To take a downer or an upper
To take a walk
To lie
Down and relax

I order you: RELAX

To face the night
Alight—or dark—the air
Conditioner
The only song:
I love you so
Right now I need you so
So tired and so upset
And yet I mustn't phone:
I didn't know
I touched a wound that never healed
A trauma: wounds will heal
And all I did
Was panic so briefly
On the phone
"Oh baby! you scared me."
No, what you said
First on the phone
Was, "Baby I'll be right there."
You were. You did. You
Came, it seemed, as fast
As light, you love me so.
I didn't know someone
Once hurt you so,
Went suicidal: head in the oven
Threat—that
Hysteria bit. Not
My trip.
I am not suicidal:
We are strong and
You know it and

Yet
I must sleep
And wait—I
   love you so
You will know
I know you do
Already know:
We love each other
So. Good night
My own, my love
My dear, my dearest dear
It's true
We do we
Love each
Other so

Like Lorraine Ellison

      Zéphyrine Drouhin
      lines out her
      Cerise Magic
      in pear tree shade:
      back-up group, The Persian
      Double Yellows (gone,
      about, over). And through the snares
      sexily come saxes: through
      solid shadow-green
      of brushing leaves, clear
      as a blues, violet sage,
      flowering saxes. I
      send you all the love
("Who's Zéphyrine?"
      in the world
("She was a somebody
      or would
(once, now
      if it were mine
(she is

                    to
(a rose"
                          give

Letter to a Friend:
Who Is Nancy Daum?

All things are real
no one a symbol:
curtains (shantung
        silk)
potted palm, a
bust: flat, with pipe—
    M. Pierre Martory
a cut-out by Alex
                Katz:
Dreaming eyes
            and pipe
Contiguous to
en terre cuite
                Marie
Antoinette
her brown and seeming
living curls
and gaze seen as
Reverie: *My Lady*
of My Edgeworth
("Prince Albert in
the can?" "Better
let him out, I . . .")
pipe dream. Some
Vitamins; more
Flying Buzzard
        ware:
a silver chain—my
silver chain
from Denmark from
you by way

of London—
(I put it on: cold
and I love
its weight:
  argento
      pesante)
a *sang de boeuf*
      spitoon
or Beauty bowl,
a compact
with a Red Sea
      scene
holding little
pills (Valium
for travel strain),
this French
      lamp
whose stem of
  glass
Lights softly
                up
entwined with
autumn trees
(around the base
      are reeds)
its glass shade
    slightly oiled
as is the dawn
above a swamp
lagoon or fen where
      hunters lurk and
      down *marc* or *cognac*
or home-made rotgut
  of their choice,
I—have lost
      my place:
No, here it is:
    Traherne,
Poems, Centuries
  and Three
      Thanksgivings,

a book beneath
    the notebook
in which I write
    Put off the light—
the French lamp
  (signed, somewhere)
and put it on:
the current
       flows.
My heart
beats. Nerves,
    muscles,
the bright invisible
red blood—*sang*
d'homme
  helps (is
that the word?)
      propel
this ball-point
      pen:
black ink is
  not black
    blood.
Two other books:
The Gay
      Insider
—good—*Run*
Little Leather
Boy awaits
assessment
on my Peter Meter.
A trove of glass
  within a
  cabinet
near my
    knees
I wish I were on
my knees
embracing
  yours
      my cheek

against the suiting of
                    whatever
suit—about now—
or soon, or late—
("I'm not prompt"
        you said, rueful
                    factual
"I" I said, "climb
walls")
O Day!
    literal
and unsymbolic
                    day:
silken: gray: sunny:
        in salt and pepper
tweed soot storm:
guide, guard,
            be freely
                    pierced
by the steel and
gold-eyed
needle passes—stitches
—of my love, my
                    lover,
                            our love,
his lover—I
                    am he—
        (is not
at any tick
each and every life
at hazard: *faites
vos jeux,
        messieurs*)
. . . Where am I?
        en route to
            a literal
Vermont. It's
                    time
                            to
—oh, do this
            do that—.
I'll call.

Perhaps we'll
    lunch? We
already
said goodbye a
long farewell
for a few weeks'
        parting!
My ocean liner,
    I am your
tug. "Life
is a bed
        of roses:
rugosas,
nor is it always
        summer."
Goodbye. Hello.
            Kiss
Hug. I
    gotta
run. Pierre
Martory,
his semblance,
smokes a St.
        Simonian
pipe and thinks
Mme. de Sévigné
-type thoughts.
He was, when
        posing,
perhaps, projecting
A Letter to a Friend.
        (signed)—
all my
—you know—
        ton
            Dopey.
PS The lamp is
    signed, Daum,
        Nancy.
Hence I surmise
    she made
or, at least,

designed it.
Who *is* Nancy Daum?

Letter Poem #2

Riding along in the beautiful day (there go two
blue enamel silos), half-reading about marvelous
Chamfort, thinking of "my own, my dearest," and
among other you thoughts—

> White clouds in blue above the birches
> You too are like my head, filled with
> And adrift in love, which is the sap
> That rises, stiffening these trees

We Are Leaves

There are leaves
there are trees
there is a tuba vine
"she"—a voice
she sings in other
words than what
disc grooves carry:
your name your face
our privacy in
hotel rooms with
cheap vodka cheap
quinine water our
nights are days
the morning comes
and goes and we
are pleased or
"who cares?" We
saw that view

of shimmering tall
offices. Today.
Today is muggy
gray—*I* don't
mind: why care?
Today you see
another view
desk and win-
dow ledge, while
mine—my view
that is—is
window ledge
and desk. Do
I miss you?
You know, yes
and I know,
no, you are
so with me
when apart, I
think I under-
stand you and
you me: I'm
happy as a rained
on leaf or
lettuce in a
crisper. You
love me and I
reciprocate.
The leaves—
it's almost
fall—look
to last for
ever—they will
come tumbling
down. I'm glad
we are not
leaves, or even
trees whose twigs
mesh. We are—
you are you,
I am I, and

we mesh. And
to ourselves
we speak our
thoughts and
touch and that
is love, isn't
it? What Doc
called, Gen-
ital contact.
And lighter
than a zeppelin
the sense of
touch brushed
lightly one
against the other
we two, together
here among leaves

Await

The scars upon the day
are harsh marks of
tranquility. I scarcely
know where you are:
awake? After lunch, a
Sunday snooze? Is
the ivy weeded yet?
Let the frost do
it its way. Smile, my
dear my dandy, when
you see this. That's
not much to ask, though
no smile on order
is quite the spontaneous
real thing. The day
grinds to a halt all
dusk and yellow rose.
What's a hundred some

miles or so? Or—let's
see—fifty hours?
Time of all things
is most variable, a
seed you plant to see
what in the world
it is a seed of: time,
hours compressed into
a kiss, a lick, or
stretched out by a
train into an endless
rubber band. All we
know is that for such
as us it is not end-
less: is time too to
be found of an atomic
structure? I
would be the last to
know, busily waiting
to see and smile
as you smile and bend
to kiss. Why soon it
will be only forty
nine hours, cubed in-
visibly like the sec-
tions of a creek.
A record spins,
these keys go clack
why soon I'll see
you and soon you'll
see me. I can enjoy
the here and now
but, wind shivering
clear day, I live
and love to anticipate
my hands on you and
yours on me, the
hours flow by and
a white gull is
black against
November evening

light, expressed,
it seems, from
late yellow grapes.

Steaming Ties

Steaming ties, cutting rue
when I'm alone it's hard
at times to know how unalone
I am, loved by you. We phone.
A heavy talk on real estate, you
own land. I don't. Once did.
Sold it for a trip
Italy, France, two years:
bye bye, Arkansas homestead.
Still and all on this radiant
September leaf light day
the leaves lit it seems or
seeming is from insides,
lovely inwardness of leaves
that dapple themselves with shade,
and all, and still I have a
place to lay my head
on you, oh, anywhere:
I'm no body bigot but
sometimes even yet or now, I
mean, I forget for a few
sad minutes how unalone I
am, steaming ties you gave
me, ties are, yes even ties,
are silk and real. Your
voice to me is silk and rustles.
We will meet, soon, not
soon enough. I remember I'm
unalone, you are with me,
salty sneezes off Atlantic
Ocean, there, where you are
here, in my heart and head

you blend in softly bright
September: you are moonrise
you are pain, you're mine
and I am yours, steaming
out silk ties, they bind

Watching You

Watching you sleep
a thing you do so well
no shove no push
on the sliding face
of sleep as on
the deep a sea bird
of a grand wingspread
trusts what it knows
and I who rumple crumple
and mash (snore) amble
and ankle about wide
awake, wanting to fold,
loving to watch sleep
embodied in you my
warm machine that draws
me back to bed
and you who turn
all toward me
to love and seduce
me back to sleep "You
said 9:30, now it's
10": you just
don't seem to care
cold coffee (sugar,
no milk) about time:
you never do, never
get roiled the way
I do "Should I nag
you or shut up? If
you say, I will"

always be
glad to return to
that warm turning
to me in that
tenderest moment
of my nights,
and more, my days.

Letter Poem #3

The night is quiet
as a kettle drum
the bull frog basses
tuning up. After
swimming, after sup-
per, a Tarzan movie,
dishes, a smoke. One
planet and I
wish. No need
of words. Just
you, or rather,
us. The stars tonight
in pale dark space
are clover flowers
in a lawn the expanding
Universe in which
we love it is
our home. So many
galaxies and you my
bright particular,
my star, my sun, my
other self, my bet-
ter half, my one

HYMN

TO LIFE

(1974)

FOR BOB

WATERBURY

Beautiful Funerals

Who lives in the biggest, whitest house in town?
The mortician, man.
Who's the man with all that greenery, the shrubs, the velvet turf,
who's the gink they all make fun of
in tones not untouched with awe?
They will indeed be calling on Frank C.
Campbell (Or someone like him: let's call him Frank)
in their Hour of Greatest Need.
He's no four-flusher,
kind of a con man (ask Jessica, Jessica knows).
Has he a fish eye?
Not necessarily.
Is he a creep?
Not on my street.
Is he a ghoul?
Oh get lost.
He's a Rotarian: why not?
A VIP in the VFW—
watch it, mac, so's my brother.
He's the man who can lay it out, rich and ready,
and some people rate it
no matter how they choose to go:
as mulch or ashes
(make mine mulch):
he is the mortician man, I don't
chew my cookies twice
though needs must, I will
call on Frank today,
and to him say, man to man,
                    Libby Holman's
                    Dead and gone

Hymn to Life

Way over Jordan water
God loves his children
She was and is
His daughter:
Forget the rest.
Libby Holman—
She was and is:
You were and are—
Totally great.
Libby Holman
Is laid to rest.
("Did she shoot him?"
For Pete's sake,
she was acquitted:
isn't that enough?
And don't start
whining, "We will
never know," you
busted
Broadway
Butterfly)
She will greet Louis Armstrong
at the gate
when he stomps in playing
" 'Cornet Chop Suey'
'Potato Head Blues'
and in deeper and
more deliberate fashion
'West End Blues' and
'Tight Like That' " (thank
you, Mr. John C. Wilson).
Lay it on, Frank,
lined in quilted satin
in husky hues
of blues: fittings
of bronze *doré*, for
a touch theatrical
steamer trunk type
decals on the hand-
rubbed ebony
THE LITTLE SHOW,

MOANIN' LOW, an
air from THE HOUSE
OF BERNARDA ALBA:
"But these are
grave matters."
"Sez who."
When a soul departs
on its wingèd flight
hit the vox humana
and let it rip: they
"burst out singing"
'Bye Bye Blackbird'
right at the graveside
for Florence Mills.
Vachel Lindsay, lead
Miss Holman by the hand
kindly re-introduce
her in that promised land
(they surely met) to
Messers O'Hara,
the poet Frank, and
John, the delicate author
of *Imagine Kissing Pete.*
Put silver slippers
on golden feet, call
on the choir of the
great torch singers:
Marion Harris, will
she be there? You
know it. As they
walk in meadows of
lifting mist or stop
for a quickie in a
honky-tonk saloon
all the reality
the wonderful fakery
of props and flats,
the shifting machinery
of a musical's scenery,
slap on a baby
spot and make it *blue.*

Miss Holman, shortly,
is about to sing.

Frank O'Hara chats
apart with Carole Lombard
and James Dean while
John O'Hara makes
whoopee at a dignified
gait with Scott Fitz-
gerald and Nathaniel
West. And where is
Papa? Honking where
the wild goose goes:
Zelda shimmies
in that world apart
where life to her
is a sazerac. Francis
Poulenc pounds
out *Les Funérailles.*
Libby Holman is
laid to rest.
Forget the rest.
"Miss Holman . . ."
(Povla Frisch is polite
as she is able to
Mary Garden) "presently
will sing." John
Latouche hands out
his smile extending.
The house lights darken:
immortal stuff shuffles
back from the *entr'acte.*
A trumpet in a derby hat,
a soft slide, the sax-
ophones. The house
goes black. Stage left,
the eternal flame. *L'Arc
de Triomphe, la ville
lumière.* In the night
rises a moon-blue spot:
someone is leaning

on the great stone trophy.
She is wearing what they
wore, oh, back then,
a Kiki outfit, with
tam and pumps. She
leans against a fake
it is all so real,
this artifice, not
a leaf is heard:
the mood, deep indigo.
Libby Holman prepares
to sing in a husky
untrained baritone.
Change the scene. It's
an after concert. She is,
as they say, perched
on a table edge, one
foot adangle. She wears—
let it be sable, con-
versing with Montgomery
Clift. At the keys,
Lorenz Hart (her son
is there), and
then she sings it,
her latest number,
'Dignity
in Dark Glasses.'

Roxy

a Sunday blues

You are ever
    in my thoughts
Linda Jean—
O Bob Far Out—
I used to know
your sister, Linda
Jean—"I love

you Wayne"
  indeed I do
Linda Jean
"I want you Wayne"
"I love you too"
Linda Jean, I want
to be/in your
arms/so bad tonight,
in handcuffs, Wayne
see you tonight
I love you Wayne
my Linda Jean

see you tonight
—Bob far out—
And all the flowers
don't do a thing
—I'm oh so tired
and they are too
poor Linda Jean
she needs her Wayne
Wayne needs you
too, or to be plain
he wants to screw
—O Bob far out—
and so do you.
You know, birds and
bees, and me and you
and Wayne and Lind
  Linda Jean
—Bob, you're far
away: good vibes:
it's all OK—
it's Sunday blue
the sky I mean
and nothing's right
it isn't Lind-
a Jean it's Lynn
who Wayne loves
too: and so do
you: you far out

Bob: & far away:
the sky is blue
and nothing's wrong
that is if you
like to live
locked up inside
the nut house
gate, it's great
outside the sky
today is blue
outside on grass
with friends who'll
bite your toe nail
off: that's blue
friendliness
inside outside
the nut house
gate: it's clear
it's wrong to
lock inside all the
best, the strong
the great, like
Lynn, like Wayne—
like me, like you
O Bob far out—
it's clear it's wrong
and I feel great
the sky she's
blue with
blond streaks
in it too no-
thing is wrong
I—we—can make it
right
now in
Sunday blues
so rock it
sock it Gary
knock it out
for me always
singing

wearing that hat
whispering
like a—
it is—a
song of love
to unbraiding
hair "that's
the way to be"
she smiles
and nods
she understands
—O Bob!
far out and
never from
my mind—it's
true: I
never wanted
to be
a nurse:
it may be blue
I feel great
bet you do
too Roxy:
or rock it
Gary
Green-
ly as you
can
or will you
please
do as you please
"I get so bored
on Sunday" with
this here
it is
a blues
and call it
Sunday Blue
or better
yet—I got
a great idea: the

sun is fast,
dangerous
Venus
in the night,
call it
this song—
rock it
Roxy—
Roxy Rock
or Sunday Blue
it's purple
I'm blue
you
are all
o wow
so really nice
so great
inside, outside
the nut house gate

Our Father

This morning view
is very plain: thou art
in Heaven: modern
brick, plate glass, unhallowèd,
as yet, by time,
yet Thy Name
blesses all: silver tanks
of propane gas, the sky,
Thy will,
is lucent blue, French
gray and cream,
is done: the night
on earth
no longer needs
the one white street globe light
as the light, it is

in heaven.
Give us this day
—and a Friday
13th, August '71,
at that:
our daily bread
and breakfast
(Product 19,
an egg, perchance: the hen-fruit,
food and symbol)
and forgive us our
trespasses
too numerous
to name—as we
forgive our debtors: "pay
me when you can:
I don't take
interest"
how green
the grass! so many
flowering weeds
Your free
will has freely
let us name: dandy-
lion (*pisse-en-lit*)
and, clover
(O Trinity)
it is
a temptation
to list them all,
all I know, that is:
the temptation
to show off—to
make a show
of knowing more,
than, in fact, I
know, is very real:
as real as a twelve
pane window sash
one pane slivered
by a crack, a flash,

a mountain line
that stays
to praise
Thee,
Your Name and Your
    Creation
let me surrender
ever—
poets do: it
is their way
and deliver me
from evil
and the Three
Illusions
of the Will—
for the power
that flows electrically
in me is thine
O glorious central,
O plant,
O dynamo!
and the glory
of this cool a.m.
now
all
silver, blue
and white.

Mike

for Tree Stockwell

Carly Simon
on the juke
it's
you said
"my song"
all about
marriages
don't turn out

so hot
but:
let's:
"That's the
way
to be."
Now Pearl—
dead too:
Janis
Joplin sings
on.
Look:
Mike is dead.
I can't
talk to
him. "Too much
strychnine
in the"
cap
or tab.
He paid
the tab
all right,
playing
with
death—
why?
Why not,
messer about
with pills
and
artificial
paradises?
Look out
the win-
dow
cluck:
it's real,
it's there,
it's life.
Look

at
your hand.
It's real
and so
is death.
Mike,
so long!
"He," Art
said, "is
in God's
hands."
I hope
so, think
so, know
that, a
Catholic
you—or
rather, he—
believed.
God is
good (or
He's
a nothing).
Mike was
great:
what
a
privilege!
Clued in-
to all
that en-
ergy!
Mike,
crazy
sky diver
fly high
meet Pearl—la
Joplin—
Cheap Thrills
I'll play
Carly

Simon: OK
Mike?
Great—hey
Tree,
right—
guy.

In the round

bed the inter-
loping grass
is beaded
at the wrist
the petunias
show
a crumpled horn,
morn-
ing after
rain and light-
ning the
dirt
chewed
and chewy
wet, a
mocha sauce.
"How frail
are flowers
and frailer
still are
we!" What
a dumb idea,
Dora, you
pass, stone
deaf and happy
jabbering
(a screen
door
bangs;

the little dog
is Jessica
or Josephine:
it
all depends)
a greeting
in what
may
be words
—can't tell—
deaf as a
post, happy
as a queen,
fat and in
abounding
health
on a morn-
ing of
(they weren't)
massacred
flowers
by medicinal
rain
in this
world of an
infinity—they
are finite—
of flowers:
infinite
flowers,
and only
seeming
so. "Good
morning—"
what's-
your-name.

ELSEWHERE

Poem

This beauty that I see
—the sun going down
scours the entangled
and lightly henna
withies and the wind
whips them as it
would ship a cloud—
is passing so swiftly
into night. A moon,
full and flat, and stars
a freight train passing
passing it is the sea
and not a train. This
beauty that collects
dry leaves in pools
and pockets and goes
freezingly, just able
still to swiftly flow
it goes, it goes.

To Frank O'Hara

for Don Allen

And now the splendor of your work is here
so complete, even
"a note on the type"
yes, total, even the colophon

and now people you never met will meet
and talk about your work.

So witty, so sad,
so you: even your lines have

a broken nose. And in the crash
of certain chewed-up words
I see you again dive
into breakers! How you scared

us, no, dazzled us swimming
in an electric storm
which is what you were
more lives than a cat

dancing, you had a feline
grace, poised on the balls
of your feet ready
to dive and

all of it, your poems,
compressed into twenty years.
How you charmed, fumed,
blew smoke from your nostrils

like a race horse that
just won the race
steaming, eager to run
only you used words.

Stay up all night? Who wants to sleep?
It is not your voice I hear
it is your words I see
foam flecks and city girders

as once from a crosstown bus
I saw you waiting a cab in light rain
(drizzle) as once you
gave me a driving lesson and the radio

played *The Merry Widow*. It broke us up.
As once under the pie plate tree
(paulownia)
it broke you up to read Sophie Tucker

—with the *Times* in a hammock—
had a gold tea service. "It's way out
on the nut," she said, "for service,
but it was my dream."

Unlike Joubert

Lying on the bed in the afternoon
but not "in a pink dressing gown"
in red pajamas and a yellow bathrobe
—flannel pajamas and a terry cloth bathrobe—
and for a moment, a flicked off bit
of a moment, succeeding where Joubert
failed: to think nothing; but on
second thought, failing, as it was not
by intention, nor is it certain that
there was even the shaved off edge
of a flick between the thought and
the next thought, that there had been
no thought between them. All that is
clear on this shadowless day under
a sky like a shadow is that the first
thought was gray, a harshly bright
blue-gray, a piece of too highly colored
slate, while the second was gray
as some roses are, or hair you see
was once red, a gray with the charm
and warmth to it of an intimate and
not overly cozy room, one with woodwork
by Pajou, or like worn upholstery, or
your first biplane. As different as
day from night, and as alike,
just as their connective—the nothing which
may not have been—was also a gray,
creamier, lighter, and shifty-eyed
as the sky or a big flat button
cut out of a seashell, the polished
off husk of an oyster, perhaps:

subtle days in winter when thought
sinks down in the presence of an absence.

Sometimes

I remember the synagogue at Amsterdam
    a tenderly overcast day
          ripe leaves
fell and floated
         cobbles and
    toned nuances of pink brick
            aglow
tenderly, tenderly
        what time and weather abraded
epochs of refinement
      reflected in mute lights
cross cast by shined brass chandeliers
        a kind of Quaker hush
so quiet
       and wonder how such terrible silence
came into the world

Eyes at the Window

The eyes at the window are Norma Shearer's
at the train window. Kaspar Hauser
waits at the station. He has something
he urgently wishes to say
to Alexander Hamilton's whore.
The veiled lady is Burr's daughter
under the grapes in Alexandria, Virginia.
Robert Schuyler, the great defaulter,
at a place on the plains meets
the man who robbed a Rothschild.
They set up shop in Minnesota.

The bones though are those of Ambrose Bierce.
The trap door is lowered before the door.
A tap on the door.
Amy Robsart comes to the door.
The bones though are Ambrose Bierce's.

The Veiled Lady has a story to tell: haven't you, too, old tree, new
house? Or coincidence in a name, the glamor and cash of crime without
the blood and reparation. Or to be greatness' sordid secret, object or
wish—to be purely a thought! And who never felt himself the inarticulate
stranger? A wildman without a wood. Or dreamt a Minnesota or midnight
under the warm grapes and the sound of an ambling horse comes over
the wall. And if Amy had looked before she stepped "things might have
turned out very differently from what in fact they did" says Norman F.
Cantor of Brandeis University. Nor is Bierce's death stranger than
another.

The pair of buttocks balancing
up the stairs are Norma Shearer's. The eyes
on them are Conrad Veidt's.
"The fate of an empire held
in a woman's hand!" drums thunder.
What a lot of malarkey. But Kaspar Hauser:
was he a fraud? Nor was the Veiled Lady
so to herself. It is easy
to respect such privacy and prefer
not knowing. Thieves are tedious
and about Amy it is all conjecture. Still,
this morning they came together:
they have come together this still morning
at a railway station where yuccas
grow wild in cinders and the station wall
is of oyster shells embedded in stucco
on an almost destroyed island
upon which March prepares to lay a hand.
Eyes at the window, womanly
mysteries, jabbering stranger,
consanguineous disreputability,
Bohemian Bierce lighting out like Huck,
and Amy Robsart, a thought in space, hung
there briefly. The thought
though is Walter Scott's.

Two

men in Arab robes
and hush puppy shoes
outside a pet shop
pass two others I
take or mistake for
addicts and there goes
one handsome in
the chinless wonder way
and of a dark descent
who stops and looks at
a street sign, turns,
hesitates and goes off
like the actor one often
feels: "Frowns,
looks at watch, goes
off" and in the sky
cloud words melt
and all run together.

May, 1972

Soft May mists are here again.
There, the war goes on.
Beside the privet the creamy
white tulips are extra
fine this year. There,
foliage curls blackened back:
it will, it must
return. But when?
A cardinal enchants me
with its song.
All war is wrong. The grass
here is green and buttoned
down with dandelions. A car
goes by. What peace. It—
the war—goes on. Fleeing

Hymn to Life

people. The parrot tulips
look like twisted guts.
Blood on green.
Here, a silent scream.
Can we, in simple justice,
desert our sought allies?
Draw out: I don't know.
I know the war is wrong.
We have it in us
to triumph over hate and
death, or so
the suburban spring suggests.
Here, the drive is wet
with mist. There,
the war goes on. Children
are more valuable than
flowers: what a choice
to make! The war
must end. It goes on.

June

A drum is played.
From here a rose
wears yellow studs.
A tree intrudes
upon a hedge. The
snowball bush,
lilacs, the pink
weigela. And
bridal wreath,
spirea. A piano
is played. On
the mantel, yellow
tree peonies.
The swing moves
in a light breeze.
Cymbals are played.

Silver silken sky
your name is space.

I think

I will write you a letter,
June day. Dear June Fifth,
you're all in green, so
many kinds and all one
green, tree shadows on
grass blades and grass
blade shadows. The air
fills up with motor
mower sound. The cat
walks up the drive
a dead baby rabbit
in her maw. The sun
is hot, the breeze
is cool. And suddenly
in all the green
the lilacs bloom,
massive and exquisite
in color and shape
and scent. The roses
are more full of
buds than ever. No
flowers. But soon.
June day, you have
your own perfection:
so green to say
goodbye to. Green,
stick around
a while.

For Bob Dash

on his birthday

The first three roses
opened up today, the outer petals
carmine, the inner, rosy pink.
The Old China Monthly Rose.
I send you their fragrance.
To you there where the tulips
are over, the clematis in bud
(I hope), where four plum trees
center four vegetable plots,
the rows so straight, and at
angles to each other—a Dutch
conceit? A pinwheel effect,
steadied. The lilacs here
stand in lilac glory, cornucopias
from Persia. And a white one too:
to you I send their staunchness
in beauty, to you there where
the paint on canvas flows
in sunset foldings, in branches,
rooftrees and powerlines that
catch the light. Dark strands.
The artichoke you gave me
sends up two strong and prickly
leaves. It will contrast nicely
with the soft-cut tree peony
leaves beside it, rising to tower
with its thistle blossom. To you
I send this contrast that is
harmony in all you make and do.

Song

I'm about to go shopping.
It rained in the night.
The cat is asleep on a

clothes hamper. The roses
are mouldy. Humidity.
The sun goes in and comes out.
I have a letter to answer.
A postcard won't do. This
time, God willing, I'll
remember the Ivory Snow.

Shimmer

The pear tree that last year
was heavy laden this year
bears little fruit. Was
it that wet spring we had?
All the pear tree leaves
go shimmer, all at once. The
August sun blasts down
into the coolness from the
ocean. The New York Times
is on strike. My daily
fare! I'll starve! Not
quite. On my sill, balls
of twine wrapped up in
cellophane glitter. The
brown, the white, and one
I think you'd call écru.
The sunlight falls partly
in a cup: it has a blue
transfer of two boys, a
dog and a duck and says,
'Come Away Pompey.' I
like that cup, half
full of sunlight. Today
you could take up the
tattered shadows off
the grass. Roll them
and stow them. And collect
the shimmerings in a

Hymn to Life

cup, like the coffee
here at my right hand.

A Held Breath

Dense dark day, two sun chairs
sit on the lawn in the rain.
Which stops. A mist comes to
roost in leafy intervals of
trees over-burdened in mid-
September. It still seems far
from turning time. August,
where did you go? The water
globes that are mist hang with
a look of permanence. Down the
street houses go soft in it,
color smears on water color
paper. A frowzy day, cool
and clammy. The typing paper
is limp as the skin on the
face of someone old you fondly
kiss. Summer leaves, in un-
seen ripenings, readying
to fill the air with falling.

Sunday

Pears hang on the tree by stems.
Three people cross the yard
and two of them are strangers
though not to each other, a
man and his wife. That much I
know about them. More than about
the white jet trail which inter-
sects and mixes into cloud. Slices

of light and chipped hunks and
bits of it lie all around among
dark bisecting lines, slabs and
'a face in the clouds' pieces.
The big yellow maple is now
skimped of leaves, precisely
like a cab driver who says,
'I can't change that.' And
the rain pours onto the oily
streets. Here, it's Sunday.
Put a record on, real cheery:
it goes right on, being
sunny Sunday: a feeling for
a day you never quite out-
grow. 'Not Sunday! Not again!'
Oh Monday, hurry up. But
no. I can't change that. At
least it's—in the unpeopled
yard—a sunny Sunday, un-
recorded, passing jet trail,
and oceanic sky. Goodbye,
dumped down leaves. Hi, Sunday.
The day smiles and goes
on braking down the incline.

Bleeding Gums

some poems for Michael Brownstein

Have another helping of blue snow.
Starch, what have you got to say for yourself?
Please don't play with the egg-timer.
Tomorrow is another day. But then, so was yesterday.
You have garlic on your breath. And a toy steamer.
Poised at the keys.
Let me see your tongue. Just as I thought. It's coated.
In twelve years these shoes won't owe you a cent.
Drink up.
She gave him the brush-off.
Just imagine.

Maraschino cherry, where you been all my life?
Go peddle your papers.
Here comes the night, a slow motion tidal wave.
Where do you go in your sleep? Take me with you.
In a sliced orange you might expect to find the golden section.
That phonograph. It's an amenity.
Happiness wells up, and a vee of geese pass overhead.
Happiness! Isn't that all that Matters?

The sky eats up the trees

The newspaper comes. It
has a bellyful of bad news.
The sun is not where it was.
Nor is the moon. Once so
flat, now so round. A man
carries papers out of the
house. Which makes a small
change. I read at night.
I take the train and go
to the city. Then I come
back. Mastic Shirley,
Patchogue, Quogue. And for
all the times I've
stopped, hundreds, at their
stations, that's all
I know. One has
a lumberyard. The sun
puts on its smile.
The day had a bulge
around three p.m. After,
it slips, cold and quiet,
into night. I read
in bed. And in the a.m.
put a record on to
shave to. Uptown in a
shop a man has blue
eyes that enchant. He

is friendly and inter-
esting to me, though he is
not an interesting man.
Bad news is a funny kind
of breakfast. An addict
I can scarcely eat my
daily crumble without
its bulk. I read at
night and shave when
I get up. That's true.
Life will change and
I am part of it and
will change too. So
will you, and you, and
you, the secret—what's
a secret?—center of
my life, your name and
voice engraved like
record grooves upon
my life, spinning its
tune between the lines
I read at night, a
graffito on the walls
of flowered paper I
see, looking up from
pages of Lady Mary
Wortley Montague or
a yellow back novel.
A quiet praise, yes
that's it, between the
lines I read at night.

Gray, intermittently blue, eyed hero

for Bill Berkson

Woolly-cheeked wink flasher
—a bop on your bunions, splintery toothpick:
and all for what? Because you're fog?
Rhetorical fog, leaning on a window

167   *Hymn to Life*

asking, "Can you bear to go on living?
With me for your friend?" "Sure,"
in Camel dung fug. Speak kindly to the fog,
it won't hurt you. Deep in its
penetrable blank unclarity you see
the little frizzy-headed maid
in *Umberto D,* knocked up, grinding coffee
and from ducts in rain rivulets seep
two slow tears. Fog, loquaciously
all over the lot, let's empanel
and discuss: Cinema sentiment wounds:
are they worth it? But the fog
the fog is busy too busy to
reply, absorbed in sweater moulds
and pill disintegration
(aspirin—big deal), sinus packing.
Gonna pack my sinuses make
my get-away. Albergo Turistico
Milano: reserve me a single
with shower and fog view
love to the Manzzonis. The fog
it could not care less lies down doggily
vast as an inter-galactic pooch:
"We think its grandmother was a setter"—
an amorphous asexual heredity
on the absence of whose sexual parts I
gaze with unLinnean apathy: "The genitalia
of plants we regard
with delight; of animals
with abomination; of ourselves
with strange thoughts" (my own
remind me of a ruby-crowned kinglet,
but let it pass
into the fog). Fog,
you stand, sit and lie
accused of an overwhelming list-making thoroughness
great as the great beneficent Swede's, who
"collected records of men who
had deceived their wives and had
in turn been deceived by them." Fog
you are like the tedium you recall: "Walking

168

across Central Park it was beautiful
this morning." "I know I know"
she glassily grimaced, "just like
a Chinese painting." Thanks, fog:
it's handy, getting to know someone
so instantly you don't want to
know them any better or further. "Fog,
you may go now. It's time for all
good little angels to go upstairs
and fly" blueward through blue.

Greenwich Avenue

In the evening of a brightly
unsunny day to watch back-lighted
buildings through the slits
between vertical strips of blinds
and how red brick, brick painted
red, a flaky white, gray or
those of no color at all take
the light though it seems only
above and behind them so what
shows below has a slight evening
"the day—sob—dies" sadness and
the sun marches on. It isn't like that
on these buildings, the colors which
seem to melt, to bloom and go and
return do so in all reality. Go
out and on a cross street briefly
a last sidelong shine catches
the faces of brick and enshadows
the grout: which the eye sees only
as a wash of another diluted color
over the color it thinks it knows
is there. Most things, like the sky,
are always changing, always the same.
Clouds rift and a beam falls
into a cell where a future saint

sits scratching. Or a wintry
sun shows as a shallow pan of red
above the Potomac, below Mount Vernon,
and the doctor from Philadelphia
nods and speaks of a further bleeding.

Labor Day

Not what I think
or see (I can't:
sun in my eyes)
or remember, or
will be—what
do I know of that?—
or never knew
or know for sure,
just this day
its clarity:
bliss: an un-
ending kiss:
what a gyp,
that there is
unendingness
but we, or
I, only get
to sense it.
It's not like
that, this
day. A family
of seven
walk down our
street, a tot
on his father's
shoulders. Three
policemen chat.
The fancy grocer's
is open. Liquor
store shut: I

foresaw that.
Drums in my room:
"We can make
each other happy."
Radiant clarity,
why, today, do
I think of death?

Just before fall

in the quiet spaces between equinoctial gales
silence sparkles
or in a spruce woods
shows as trunks striped light and dark
seen between each other
all the same, each different:
a woods stripped of its lower branches
that lie loosely stacked by the path through it
mossed, lichened, decaying.

The sun sits in the sky like a painting of it.
The asters bend to a breeze
it is beneath the dignity of woodier plants to notice.
Goldenrod stands in spires
or another kind, that points in Indian sign language:
"This way."

Early in the afternoon the moon slides up the sky
as the sun goes west
its light sits weightlessly
on chokecherry and elderberry brush.
They look held down
and drawn up by it
as a speedboat flees from the furrow
that seems to propel it
through illusions of green
made by black trees reflected on shattering water
shaping itself.

Hymn to Life

Marvelous universal energy,
expressed in a stellar stillness!
The Milky Way unfurled
last night above the house
and the Pleiades
to the eye faintly cried,
"The best way to see stars
is to look a little to one side"
a universe in its net of space
running down, winding up, going on

Buttered Greens

Sunshine
makes shade
acid blue
leaf work
of elms
they fell first
blown under
a big plane
tree lying
on tuftedness
the pattern
of its later
shedding. In
fields rise
as of them-
selves, houses.
Don't 'tsk
tsk' men and
habitations
are nature
too in waves
of concourse
disposable
cities give
a sense

of certainty.
"But! All
alike! How
Levittown!"
Why not
alike as
leaves which
have not
free will:
have you?
You have
you use it
unknowingly
as a house
leaf plastered
after a storm
its white
stained in
leaf marks
elm, plane
tree, a
man's will
turns in
upon it-
self if,
or rather
is it to
use or to
relax it?
Letting what
comes, go
and go in
dark, in
green and
acid blue
that fumes
as he frets
about lit-
tering houses
inside all
is not con-

tent, yet
the chance
of it is
there, free
leaves fall
and the will
stirs and
turns out
from it-
self, housed
in disposable
rib cages
(the heart
thumps) in
disposable
houses, wood
ribbed and
glazed to
flash back
buttered
green, what
it means:
leavings and
the permanence
of return
"I'll be
back by
night" wind
raking leaves
from trees
until: and
then: to-
morrow. It
is strange
and easy,
the will
exercised
within
its wind-
cleared and
cleaned

range, the
"that" not
understood
too well
the will
will heal
what hurt
though that
was what
was meant:
to do
and undo
what's
done be-
tween the
flash and
fall of
turning,
as the year
returns in
its ad-
vance to
take again
what it
last took
and what
it takes
brings back:
all done
not by
us or for
us but
with us
and within
the body
of a house
the frame
of wood or
bone it is
much the
same

Sparks

A light rain stands
in little pools
and through a green excess
bits of a white house make
for a moment a too big rose
of Sharon. Wet air lifts
wallpaper, seals
envelopes. Soon
skaters will spin in a small space
between skyscrapers, or are seen
from a train by bonfire light:
red lumberjacks in an orange glow
like sparks that die into dark
but, unlike sparks, fly back.

Deep Winter

A starling drops
from branch to
branch, it's cold
but not that cold:
the feel of cold-
ness is movement
on the skin so
walking in it
robs the air of
stillness: walking
on the half-thawed
yard you charge
the air with motion
you are a kind of
breeze a light
wind stirring still-
ness like shaking
out a rug the dust

hangs and swims
and shows a pattern
for a while, unstill.
Squirrels are every-
where, they fight
and follow "chase
the leader." Where
are their larders?
They seem still
to hunt for food
in winter-waiting
weather. The only
blue is shutters
or a car. The car
sits still behind
a house: that's Sun-
day for you. The
church bells swing
sound invisible
so palpable, it's
strange. Shops
are shut. That's
Sunday for you.
Purchases can wait
for Monday. Each
day so different
yet still alike
in waiting weather.

In Wiry Winter

The shadow of a bird
upon the yard upon
a house; it's gone.
Through a pane a
beam like a warm hand
laid upon an arm.
A thin shell, trans-

parent, blue: the
atmosphere in which
to swim. Brr. A
cold plunge. The bird
is back. All the same,
to swim, plunging
upward, arms as wings,
into calm cold. Warm
within the act,
treading air, a
shadow on the yard.
Or floating, gliding,
a shadow on the roofs
and drives, in action
warm, the shadow cold
but brief. To swim
in air. No. Not in
this wiry wintry air.
A beam comes in the
glass, a hand to
warm an arm. A hand
upon the glass
finds it a kind
of ice. The shadow
of a bird less cold.
Window, miraculous
contrivance; sun-
hot wires in
meshed cold.
The bird goes
quick as a wish
to swim up
and cast, like
it, a shadow
on the years.

So Good

Sing to me
weather about
one bird
peck, pecking
on bleached
winter grass.
March is here
like a granny
a child doesn't
like to kiss:
the farm smell,
a chill sweet-
ness. He'll
get over it.
March will pass
other birds
will sing in
other weather
time twists my
bent back.
A common cold.
And for no
reason my eyes
and the sky
fill with
tears. Two
kinds of
weather and
if you never
cry, well,
then you don't.
Snow that
turns to rain,
pain, physical
and emotive, too
these pass. They
once weren't
here: they'll go

Hymn to Life

as Granny went
embanked in flowers
so long ago, so
cold a cheek to
ask a child
to kiss. "Those
birds," she
would have said,
"are starlings.
They came from
England." Or
"This is a
monarch butter-
fly." Or, "That
is flypaper. Flies
spread germs."
Or. No. It
was all too long
ago and any
tears are for
the sullen day
suddenly so like
the inner life
that gutters,
burns and smokes.
Light the lights.
The day is dark
and where do
the starlings
sleep at night?
Goodnight Granny,
so truly good.

October

Books litter the bed,
leaves the lawn. It
lightly rains. Fall has

come: unpatterned, in
the shedding leaves.

The maples ripen. Apples
come home crisp in bags.
This pear tastes good.
It rains lightly on the
random leaf patterns.

The nimbus is spread
above our island. Rain
lightly patters on un-
shed leaves. The books
of fall litter the bed.

LOVING YOU

Was It

Was it a quarrel that barred
the spring with shadow and
brought to troubled sleep
rude awakenings? Not
exactly. The depression of
one puts pressure on both.
Distance, silence, separation.
Pop tune blues: "I miss
you so." "Bye bye baby
bye bye." An angry wish
to shake it off and be oneself
again. Goodbye: I'm glad
I didn't say it. We're
reconciled. As though this
light June wind had blown
it all away. A rose I
saw just now flat open
shook its delicate yellow
anthers in that wind. (It
whistles.) So delicate,
so tender, so strong. It
was like that when we
kissed and smiled. Nothing
lasts forever, but this way
is so much better than
any other when I
missed you so. Eyes
of changing color, to
see you smile again!
Like a pop song, "Sun,
smile down on me."

Poem

Your enchantment
enchains me, stretched
out there, planked
like a steak or
a shad in season.
And there, where
you flower there.
You're cool to my
touch, soon growing
warm, smooth but not
sleek. I love you—
too much? Not quite
possible. The thought
of harm from you is
far from me as those
Vermont hills, en-
flamed, in October,
as I by you, in their
seasonal rush. To
go up in leaves! I
wish I could, as I
sink down beside you.

Daylight

And when I thought,
"Our love might end"
the sun
went right on shining

Hymn to Life

You're

on vacation. Well
earned, twice and
more over, like a
double rose. I'll
miss you. I'm glad
you're there: you
need and want it.
Nor am I jealous
that you're not
alone. The tent
is pitched to
face away so the
wind won't fill
and belly it. There,
it's more a sand
bar than an island.
That wind: the
dune grass is
combed by it and
the surf is al-
most always up.
The same ocean
that we have here
but warmer there.
You dive into
a glassy wave
and come up
spouting, treading
water. I'll
bet you like
pissing in the
sea. People who
don't seem odd
to me. There,
think of me
and our beach
here. Dry off.
Supper time. What-

ever's on the grill
smells good: steak,
or chops. Wild horses
run there on the
dunes. The sky is
tinted green, and
rose, and blue. And
a tan, like
glowing sand. The
evening star comes
out. The moon
will rise. The foot-
steps on it from
here don't show. In
moon terms, you're
not so far away. We
see the same sky
and night. The nights
there are your
own. I'll have mine
later. In the fall,
toward which doggily
I point. Be tan,
stretch out, forget
your job, and that
which troubled you
last week. Strange
vacation days, speed-
ing by for you, so
slow for me. Time
is not our own, and
yet it is. Use it
up freely and grow
with it, relaxed.
You like to work.
You won't mind
coming back. Time,
pass more quickly
for me, more slowly,
slower, for him.

A photograph

shows you in a London
room: books, a painting,
your smile, a silky
tie, a suit. And more.
It looks so like you
and I see it every day
(here, on my desk)
which I don't you. Last
Friday night was grand.
We went out, we came
back, we went wild. You
slept. Me too. The pup
woke you and you dressed
and walked him. When
you left, I was sleeping.
When I woke there was
just time to make the
train to a country dinner
and talk about ecstasy.
Which I think comes in
two sorts: that which you
know "Now I'm ecstatic"
like my strange scream
last Friday night. And
another kind, that you
know only in retrospect:
"Why, that joy I felt
and didn't think about
when his feet were in
my lap, or when I looked
down and saw his slanty
eyes shut, that too was
ecstasy. Nor is there
necessarily a downer from
it." Do I believe in
the perfectibility of
man? Strangely enough,
(I've known un-

happiness enough) I
do. I mean it,
I really do believe
future generations can
live without the in-
tervals of anxious
fear we know between our
bouts and strolls of
ecstasy. The struck ball
finds the pocket. You
smile some years back
in London, I have
known ecstasy and calm:
haven't you, too? Let's
try to understand, my
handsome friend who
wears his nose awry.

Up

It's a Sunday kind
of Sunday, the first
one of September. The
sun was lowering in
total blue when you
called up. You drove
twelve hours in the
rain. No, towards the
end it let up. You're
back. It was great—
your vacation, that
is. How good of you
to phone. It set me
up. I'm full of
beans. I sit in shade
and see the sun draw
white lines on the
house next door. We

will meet next week.
And I see, clear as
light, your body
naked on our bed
and the white line
at the bottom of
your belly the sun
drew where you
wore your trunks.
I can't wait. Til
Thursday, love.

Saturday Night

A little drunk,
a little high,
about to go off
to a dancing
bar, I think of
you, on a yacht
or schooner or
whatever it is:
on Long Island
Sound. I guess.
Someone made din-
ner in the galley.
A bunch of you
are eating it.
You're having fun
I hope. I hope
so so much. It's
not that I
think of you all
the time. But
I think of you
a lot. The air
is still. Per-
haps tomorrow

you'll scud
before a breeze.
You're physical
and need that
breeze. Breeze,
blow for one
I love, stretch
his muscles as
he needs and wants.

Sunday

The mint bed is in
bloom: lavender haze
day. The grass is
more than green and
throws up sharp and
cutting lights to
slice through the
plane tree leaves. And
on the cloudless blue
I scribble your name.

August Night

This week we
didn't meet. I
hate that. The
bed is rumpled.
I go out onto
the lawn. The
stars are hid
in heavy haze.
The only moon
my lit room.

I put my hand
into the beam
that falls upon
a garden chair.
You've touched
that hand, and
it's touched
you. I've little
to complain of.
In fact, I'm
not complaining.
I find it
on these hot
nights, hard to
fall asleep. If
you were here!
You almost were.
Then something
came up. Back
to bed. I'm reading
about Byron and
his last love,
la Guiccioli. I
identify with
her, afraid of
losing him. When
you're down, I
get scared. What
if boredom should
set in? On your
side, not on mine.
I put my hand
on your side of
the bed. I see
you there as I
saw you sleep
there last week.
We're not like
Byron and his
Teresa, we don't
play games. (Byron,

by the way, was
great! So, in
her way, was
she.) At least,
the games we
play are sex
games, not the
kind that come
from ennui. God
damn this hot
and restless
night. I was
asleep and then
a dream that
you were angry
with me woke
me. I can't
quite shake it
off. I know it
isn't true. You're
not. It's hot:
I thought we'd
meet: we can't:
I felt let down.
I get the downs
sometimes too. And
how. I trust you.
You're as straight
as anyone I've
ever known. I hate
it when you're
blue. You plunge
so deep into it. I
feel then I'm
in the dark and
can't quite touch
you. Perhaps
I needn't, shouldn't
try. I respect
your inner life.
You have Irish

Hymn to Life

moods (and eyes).
I do too. I—
what is it that
I want to say? To
say this isn't
a complaint. It's
how I feel on
a hot night in
August, 1972,
missing you.

A blue towel

went with us to the beach.
You drove the Green Bomb,
your panel truck. Sand
dunes and signs: "No Parking
Between Signs." "Prohibited
On This Beach . . . Hard Ball . . .
Intoxication . . . Bonfires . . ."
Mist, and filterable sun.
Oh breakers, and leaping
spume! We spread the towel
where we could lie and watch
the fierce and molten wonder
of the water. You wore blue
trunks, and took off a
striped Roman shirt and kicked
off Gucci loafers (and you
think I'm hard on clothes).
We lay and watched and
smoked. I studied sand
and the sand-like freckles
on your back and, smaller
than small, one blackhead
(later removed). And thought
beach thoughts: after sex,
man is sad, some Roman said.

Did he mean, because the
pleasure's over? It's the
day after last night and I
am anything but sad. Quiet
content, a little tired: we
do go on so. Then we walked,
you in surf, I on scoured
sand, firm, and running to
escape the waves that almost
got my sneakers. Then we
walked back. Your trunks
were partly wet, as though
you'd pissed your pants. "I
think," you said, "I'll go
in after all." Then there
you were, bobbing in breakers,
leaping high to ride their
great and breaking crested
curl. It scared me (a
lousy swimmer) just a
little. "That's the way,"
you said when you came
out, "I like it. It's
almost warm enough." I saw
your chest and side be-
side me, pearled with
water drops. The mist
moved off. We sat and sunned
—it was late, no tan today—
and watched the repetitions
of the sea, each one
different from the last,
and saw how a log was
almost hurled ashore then
taken back, slipping north
along the shore. The flies
were something else. "These
insects are too much: let's
go back." The blue towel
and your trunks I hung out
on the line. You took a

Hymn to Life

shower. I made drinks. Quiet
ecstasy and sweet content,
why are not all days like
you? Happy with someone,
and that someone you, to-
gether on a blue towel
on sand beside the sea.

EVENINGS IN VERMONT

The Bluet

And is it stamina
that unseasonably freaks
forth a bluet, a
Quaker lady, by
the lake? So small,
a drop of sky that
splashed and held,
four-petalled, creamy
in its throat. The woods
around were brown,
the air crisp as a
Carr's table water
biscuit and smelt of
cider. There were frost
apples on the trees in
the field below the house.
The pond was still then
broke into a ripple.
The hills, the leaves that
have not yet fallen
are deep and oriental
rug colors. Brown leaves
in the woods set off
gray trunks of trees.
But that bluet was
the focus of it all: last
spring, next spring, what
does it matter? Unexpected
as a tear when someone
reads a poem you wrote
for him: "It's this line
here." That bluet breaks

Hymn to Life

me up, tiny spring flower
late, late in dour October.

"From the next . . ."

From the next room
the friendly clatter of
an electric typewriter.
Flies buzz in the window
pane. It is their dying
season. The house
is painted gray. The fields
befuzz themselves with
milkweed silk. By the
pond, a beaver gnaws
a tree. Those teeth, so
keen. The road winds
down the hill to here
then winds down further.
The woods are brown.
The sky is gray. What
incredible silence on
this hill surrounds
the friendly clatter,
the buzz of dying.

Standing and Watching

Standing and watching
through the drizzle
how the mist and further
edge of pond merge
into one grayness, a color
called drained-of-blueness.

Standing and watching
how the maple leaves
fall, lightly pelted by
drizzle, and turn
in air, to lie scattered,
drained, not quite of color there.

The Green Door

"We could try it,"
Ralph says to Harold.
The men are working
on the ell, a new
wing for an old house.

Out the window, the land
drops rapidly away
in wooded undulations and
fields and one larch
there turns to its own gold.

Out another window, one
bare tree laces its limbs
next to a maple which
still has half its leaves
on. Maple gold, not larch.

A plane goes over.
Ralph and Harold hammer
somewhere beyond a
green baize door. Even
the door has its story.

Many moist days, nor
is the end in sight.
I haven't seen the beaver.
The pond, the air, is still:
only the plane, only the hammer.

Hymn to Life

Sunset

The sun just
went behind the
ridge and turned
it mauve, marked
green by firs,
streaked white
by birch. Down
the valley a
line of far-
off mountains
are deeper,
bluer than the
sky. It's al-
most dinner
time, time for
a drink as
night rises
up the gulch
against the way
the water
drops from
ledge to ledge.

The Day

The day is gray
as stone: the stones
embedded in the
dirt road are chips
of it. How dark it
gets here in the
north when a cold
front moves in. The
wind starts up. It
keens around the

house in long
sharp sighs at
windows. More
leaves come down
and are borne
sidewise. In the
woods a flock
of small white
moths fluttered,
flying, like the
leaves. The wind
in trees, a
heavy surge, drowns
out the water-
fall: from here,
a twisted thread.
Winter knocks at
the door. Don't
let it in. But
those shivering,
hovering late moths,
the size of big
snowflakes: what
were they doing
there, so late
in the year? Had
they laid their
eggs, and fluttered
in the then still
woods, aware of
the coming wind,
the storm, their
end? But they
were beautiful,
there in the woods,
frantic with life.

Hymn to Life

Evening

The black marble mantelpiece
reflects a green lamp and a white.
Above it, two red candles
and a dish of fruit, painted on velvet.
What bush is that, beside the door
that faces east, that will not loose its leaves?
Snowberry, I guess. And what kind of maple
fights the evening wind to keep some of its leaves?
A few fly by. An electric heater
hums and drowns out the evening wind.
Red filaments. The sullen day
wears off in a dull blue-gray
it almost hurts to see: so like
a mood that comes upon you
unawares, uninvited, unwanted,
like missing someone, and a long goodbye.

The Walk

Out of shape,
my legs ache
going down
this steep
hill. I hear
the water
rushing down
beside me
through the
trees. Has
the creek
a name? It
somewhere joins
the brown Winooski.
The ferns
the frost

has killed and
curled: another
kind it hasn't.
One dandelion
a frayed
sun in sun-
light that
lights up the
empurpled
blackberry
leaves. Remember
when you picked
them? A dog
and a friendly
voice that calls,
"He's friendly."
One horse in
a field that
stands stock
still, soaking
up the sun.
And twelve
cows, each doing
something dif-
ferent: munching,
lying down.
The way a
white house
takes late light
and turns it
back. A tumbled
shed, once red,
with missing
windows and
gear stowed
inside. A
long and
steady climb
I've made before:
now my legs
ache, I only

want to reach
the top to where
the road ambles
down through
woods between
tumbled field-
stone walls. This
land once all
was clear. The
sun is on
the trees on
the far side
of the pond
on which they
in image lie.
The cabin, then
the house. Clear
air, warm
Indian summer
sun, the mosses
that I saw, and
delicate white
lichens, the
trees that make
it and the
trees that don't.
Soon blue snow
will shroud it
all: why take
a long walk
with aching legs?
For fun? Why
not? I can-
not tell you
all I saw,
but won't for-
get the deer
slot stamped
in the muddy
road. I love
their white
scuts when they

bound away,
deer at horseplay.

Evenings in Vermont

After two rainy days, a sunny one
of cloud curds breaking up in blue.
Now the sky is peach ice cream.
I nearly froze my hands off on my walk.
The temperature has dropped.
Turn up the thermostat. And that
dog that leapt out at me! How
I hate him, how he scares me.
"You're a good dog," I said in
feigned placating tones. He snuffed
my heels. The sky suddenly is
streaked with fire at only 4:45
in the afternoon. Or evening. Day-
light saving time is over. I liked
stopping to take a leak on dead leaves
in the woods beside the road.
That one maple by the house now
is almost bare. The pond
turns greenish-black. Downstairs
someone (you) shuts a door. Evenings
in Vermont, the fire dies in the sky,
the pond goes altogether black,
and indoors all is coziness. I study
the pattern in a red rug, arabesques
and squares, and one red streak
lies in the west, over the ridge.

Awoke

Awoke to rain
and mist, down

there in Gospel
Hollow: a cloud
that frayed and
flowed uphill
as the drizzling
day wore on. We're
not that high
up and yet to-
day we were
above a cloud.
I like that,
high on Apple
Hill beside
the pond where
you watch the
beaver and how
he uses his
tail to turn.
"And then," you
said, "he vanished."

Afterward

Then it snowed. I
saw it when I let
the dog out into
the dark yard, fat
damp flakes, ag-
glomerations of
many flakes. A
white awakening,
a drive to North-
field, picking up
mended quilts from
the quilt lady. We
used the four-
wheel drive on
the mud slick hill.

The branches bent
under their first
winter weight: it
wasn't pretty, a
thawing snow seldom
is, but it wasn't
ugly, too. In the
morning we left, all
the weeds hoar-
frosted on the hill:
a glittering gray
sheen on brown. In
the valley, the snow
was already gone. Now,
New York, in a tempest
of rain, stalled cabs
and cars, neon re-
flected on asphalt:
I like that, too.
Dreaming of a white
Vermont, scratched
by alders and firs.

THE FAURÉ BALLADE

The Fauré Ballade

*An anthology of quotes, misquotes,
and (no doubt) misremembered remarks
for D. D. Ryan*

Pyramids, Arches, Obelisks, were but the irregularity of vainglory, and wilde enormities of ancient magnanimity.

—Sir Thomas Browne

—You must excuse me for all the mistakes and errors of language of this letter. I am not instructed in the English tongue: But if you apprehend what I say to you, I shall be sufficiently fortunate. When the heart speaks, it is unnecessary to speak correctly.

—Eugène Delacroix
(To Elizabeth Salter, 1817 or –18,
110 rue de l'Université)

Brougham's review is not in good taste; he should have put on an air of serious concern, not raillery and ridicule; things are too serious for that. But it is very able. It is long yet vigorous like the penis of a jackass.

—Reverend Sidney Smith

The pearls dropped loudly to the floor.

—Frank O'Hara

"What am I supposed to be THE POEM DOCTOR?"

—Ron Padgett

"Sometimes I wish the raggle-taggle gypsies would come and take me away."   —John Ashbery

I intend the title of this book.   —Adrian Stokes

Only—but this is rare—
When a belovèd hand is laid in ours.

—Matthew Arnold

But now the customary beautiful Easter Eve Idyll had fairly begun and
people kept arriving from all parts with flowers to dress the graves.
Children were coming from the town and from neighboring villages with
baskets of flowers and knives to cut holes in the turf. The roads were
lively with people coming and going and the churchyard a busy scene
with women and children and a few men moving about among the tomb-
stones and kneeling down beside the green mounds flowering the graves.
An evil woman from Hay was dressing a grave. (Jane Phillips).

—The Rev. Francis Kilvert,
Saturday, Easter Eve, 16 April, 1870

What a hot day it is! for
Jane and me above the scorch

—Frank O'Hara

Thus, if the Firmament gave forth the sound of *f*, the Sun gave *f* an
octave higher up and the Moon gave *f* an octave higher still. Saturn,
Venus and the Earth gave *g* in these three octaves, and Jupiter, Mercury
and the Antichthon gave *c* in these three octaves also, while Mars gave
d in the lowest octave by itself. And if that is what these orbs are 'quiring
to the young-eyed cherubins,' I do not much regret 'this muddy vesture
of decay' that hinders me from hearing it.   —Cecil Torr

"Pity the bride who buys her bridal gown at Jonas."

—Jane Freilicher

Nothing in that drawer   —Ron Padgett

"My dear, you have a smile LIKE THE SUN."   —Frank O'Hara

The intelligence is part of the comedy of life.   —Wallace Stevens

Ta tête se détourne: le nouvel amour! Ta tête se retourne,—le nouvel
amour!   —Arthur Rimbaud

They saw her standing in that simple field
—Kenneth Koch

The Opera was "Il Fanatico." Naldi the father with his full low notes, Mrs. Billington his pupil daughter. She sang her solfeggi, all the exercises, and "Uno trillo sopra là"—nothing ever was so beautiful, even the memory of those sounds, so clear, so sweet, so harmonious, that voice that ran about like silver water over pearls!   —Elizabeth Grant
of Rothiermurchus

1) We had sold our house in Paris, but for very little as it stood in a shabby quarter—the Rue du Bac. 2) In the important moments of life, any thought which has not occurred in the first twenty-four hours is either pointless, or idle repetition. 3) The wedding took place at Le Bouilh on the 1st of April 1807. The only flowers in season were small red and white double daisies, so Mme de Maurville, Charlotte and I had to use them for the center-piece at dinner. We contrived a charming effect: the flowers formed the names of Henri and Elisa against a background of moss.   —Madame de la Tour du Pin

. . . on the southern side, the foot of the tower opened on a terrace, which was called the garden though nothing grew on it but ivy, and a few amphibious weeds. The southwestern tower, which was ruinous and full of owls, might, with equal propriety, have been called the aviary. This terrace or garden, or terrace garden, or terrace-garden, or garden-terrace (the reader may name it *ad libitum*), took in an oblique view of the open sea, and fronted a long tract of open sea-coast, and a fine monotony of fens and windmills.   —Thomas Love Peacock

P. S. Comme je serais heureux si je pouvais arriver à me débarrasser de cet accent américain qui fait mon désespoir.   —Robert Martin

This haughty and solitary image, by which Delacroix, rejecting the affectations of romanticism, himself decided what should be his face after death, occurs in the opening lines of his will.   —René Huyghe

Now I think of it, the severest wound life inflicts is this inevitable solitude to which our hearts are condemned. A wife who is one's equal is the greatest of all blessings. I would rather she were my superior in every way than the reverse.   —Eugène Delacroix

Raoul Dufy's sudden death in March, 1953, was like a rip in the rainbow.
—Wallace Stevens

. . . (7 Floreal, year VI) Eugène Delacroix was born in the house at
Charenton-Saint-Maurice, at the gates of Paris, which still . . .
—René Huyghe

Where there are no bushes there can be no nuts, and the way of those
you live with is that you must follow.   —*Waverly*

I am a parcel of vain strivings
—Henry David Thoreau

Dry leafless trees no autumn wind laid bare
—Jones Very

Sex to sex, and even to odd;—
—Ralph Waldo Emerson

1) Mere passive observation, even supposing such a thing were possible,
has never contributed anything productive to science. 2) We are never
quite so receptive as we should like to believe. 3) Of all the poisons
capable of vitiating a piece of evidence, the most virulent is deception.
4) It would be puerile to enumerate the infinite variety of reasons which
can lead to lying. 5) . . . what is most profound in history may also be
the most certain. 6) Anyone who took part in the Battle of Waterloo
knew that Napoleon was beaten. 7) Unfortunately the habit of passing
judgements leads to a loss of taste for explanations. 8) . . . those secret
needs of the heart which harsh daily routine has forced them to repress?
There are contradictions which closely resemble evasions. 9) . . . the
knowledge of fragments, studied by turns, each for its own sake, will
never produce the knowledge of the whole; it will not even produce that
of the fragments themselves. 10) . . . the great obstacle. Nothing is
more difficult for us than self-expression.   —Marc Bloch

All things are tragic
when a mother watches!
—Frank O'Hara

I even remember a story of a woman who prepared for the visit of what
we now so unromantically call a boy-friend by bestrewing her room and

Hymn to Life

her *chaise longue* with quantities of exotic flowers and then dying of the heavy scent just before his arrival! —Constance Spry

How Mac-Shimei will joy when their chief shall display
The yew-crested bonnet o'er tresses of grey!

—*Waverly*

POTTED HEAD
(Or Scots Brawn)
(Old Family Recipe)

Ox head, ox foot, salt, pepper, cayenne, mustard, bay leaf, mace, cloves or allspice or nutmeg, water.
Soak half an ox head and a foot for a few hours. Break them . . .

—F. Marian McNeille

. . . mysterious as breathing in sleep.   —Edwin Denby

Broke down her fence something terrible and the pigs was all over the street.   —Ron Padgett

Paganini incomparable; when he came forward and struck the first chord, my neighbor in the Opera pit (an Italian) exclaimed in a low voice, "O Dio!"   —William Allingham

The bacon too carries on its modest love affair.

—Tony Towle

Dufy's La Fée Electricité is most definitely a union of drudge and dazzling angel.   —Wallace Stevens

"What are these young people coming to?" Degas said with a smile.

—Daniel Halévy

If breakfast is enjoyed in bed, it may be served on a dazzling white tray with an exquisite cover, and white china with a deep pink border; or the tray may have a green cover and sprigged peasant china; or a delft blue and white china. For the "entre nous" breakfast there is an "entre

nous" service of violet and lavender with the coffee pot, creamer, and
sugar bowl all in one and lavender place doilies and napkins.

—Hazel M. Adler

Des ciels gris de cristal. Un bizarre dessin des ponts
—Arthur Rimbaud

moment of infinitely salty air!
—Frank O'Hara

I don't know how a poet becomes a poet. And I don't think anyone else
does either. It is something deep and mysterious inside a person that
cannot be explained. It is something that no one understands. It is
something that no one will ever understand. I asked Ron Padgett once
how it came about that he was a poet and he said, "I don't know. It is
something deep and mysterious inside of me that cannot be explained."
—Joe Brainard

and moon-like, too, the gentle Norma Shearer
—Frank O'Hara

The desire for continuous legislation is modern.   —F. W. Maitland

The subject of *Agon,* as the poet Frank O'Hara said, is pride.
—Edwin Denby

It was a few minutes after noon, Benton had been driving for hours but
he looked fresh and relaxed as he looked over at Jack and smiled,
saying, "We're just about there, Jack. In a very few minutes you'll have
your first look at New York's famous and fabulous skyline."
—Jack Love

Put out your hand,
isn't there
an ashtray, suddenly, there?
—Frank O'Hara

The window is my eye
And Frank O'Hara is the building
I'm thinking about him like mad today
—Ron Padgett

Hymn to Life

The lithographs leave us feeling that the dissipations of life inevitably arrange themselves in a final scene, a scene that fills us with optimism and satisfaction as the characters leave the stage with all the lights burning. Is not that, after all, the chief effect of this pageant?

—Wallace Stevens

Then he froze, his heart leaping quickly into his throat as he glimpsed the not far off skyscrapers looming upward into the clear blue sky and bright sunshine. His dream come true . . . NEW YORK CITY! "It—it's just great!" he exclaimed excitedly.

"Bagdad on the Hudson, someone called it. Your new home, Jack."
"And I already like what I see of it!"
"But you haven't seen anything yet!"   —Jack Love

In Centerville there lived two husky Young Fellows named Bill and Schuyler—commonly abbreviated to Schuy. They did not find any nourishing Excitement in a Grain Elevator, so they Enlisted to free Cuba.

—George Ade

I will imagine two dishes, the one of gold, the other of wood. The golden dish filled with diamonds, rubies

An evil woman from Hay was dressing a grave. (Jane Phillips).

and emeralds.—and chains, rings, and brooches of gold, while the other contains shell-fish, stones, and earths.   —William Constable

Is it not the principal thing that the individuality of Dufy should be the co-ordinating force and high issue of all these details? And is not this high issue one of those choices of the intelligence of an artist who, by making this choice, goes forward with the train of his characters, of whom he is, really one, committed to the same purpose?

—Wallace Stevens

But now the customary beautiful Easter Idyll had fairly begun
        Cannot please! Cannot charm or win
        what a poet!   —Frank O'Hara

And twenty minutes later they were again in the Mercedes which Benton was parking on Eighth Street—Greenwich Village's Main Street, he

explained to Jack, whose eyes were already bulging at the slim sleek
suits and accessories that had caught his fancy in the window of an
expensive-looking shop just opposite the car.
Benton opened the door on his side of the car, and Jack bounded after
him.
"Let's go in here and get you outfitted in some style," he said simply.
"And I don't expect you to hesitate—buy anything that catches your
eye." Lots did . . .   —Jack Love

. . . I was never afraid of Hell, nor ever grew pale at the description of
that place;   —Sir Thomas Browne

These great blues of Dufy are a kind of assertion of strength.
They create
        That's funny! there's blood on my chest
                                  —Frank O'Hara

a human self-confidence, as if one had known from the beginning the
eventual denouement of knowledge, so long postponed and so incredible.
                                  —Wallace Stevens

        It was all you, your graceful white smiles
        like a French word, the one for nursery, the one
                for brine.   —Frank O'Hara

Everything that he lost, and everything that has opened up to him since,
came from the same revolutionary process.
                      —*Times Literary Supplement*

           I rose and doused

        my hair with jasmine cologne put
        a flower under my arm and hung
        my genitals with pearls   —Frank O'Hara

Written in his program by Frank O'Hara during a performance of *Mignon*:
        où suis-je
        je respire l'air nouveau
        l'azur est plus profond

                                                      Hymn to Life

Hymn to Life

The wind rests its cheek upon the ground and feels the cool damp
And lifts its head with twigs and small dead blades of grass
Pressed into it as you might at the beach rise up and brush away
The sand. The day is cool and says, "I'm just staying overnight."
The world is filled with music, and in between the music, silence
And varying the silence all sorts of sounds, natural and man made:
There goes a plane, some cars, geese that honk and, not here, but
Not so far away, a scream so rending that to hear it is to be
Never again the same. "Why, this is hell." Out of the death breeding
Soil, here, rise emblems of innocence, snowdrops that struggle
Easily into life and hang their white enamel heads toward the dirt
And in the yellow grass are small wild crocuses from hills goats
Have cropped to barrenness. The corms come by mail, are planted,
Then do their thing: to live! To live! So natural and so hard
Hard as it seems it must be for green spears to pierce the all but
Frozen mold and insist that they too, like mouse-eared chickweed,
Will live. The spears lengthen, the bud appears and spreads, its
Seed capsule fattens and falls, the green turns yellowish and withers
Stretched upon the ground. In Washington, magnolias were in bud. In
Charlottesville early bulbs were up, brightening the muck.   Tomorrow
Will begin another spring. No one gets many, one at a time, like a long
Awaited letter that one day comes. But it may not say what you hoped
Or distraction robs it of what it once would have meant. Spring comes
And the winter weather, here, may hold. It is arbitrary, like the plan
Of Washington, D.C. Avenues and circles in asphalt web and no
One gets younger: which is not, for the young, true, discovering new
Freedoms at twenty, a relief not to be a teen-ager anymore. One of us
Had piles, another water on the knee, a third a hernia—a strangulated
Hernia is one of life's less pleasant bits of news—and only
One, at twenty, moved easily through all the galleries to pill
Free sleep. Oh, it's not all that bad. The sun shines on my hand
And the myriad lines that criss-cross tell the story of nearly fifty

Years. Sorry, it's too long to relate. Once, when I was young, I
Awoke at first light and sitting in a rocking chair watched the sun
Come up beyond the houses across the street. Another time I stood
At the cables of a liner and watched the wake turning and
Turning upon itself. Another time I woke up and in a bottle
On a chest of drawers the thoughtful doctor had left my tonsils. I
Didn't keep them. The turning of the globe is not so real to us
As the seasons turning and the days that rise out of early gray
—The world is all cut-outs then—and slip or step steadily down
The slopes of our lives where the emotions and needs sprout. "I
Need you," tree, that dominates this yard, thick-waisted, tall
And crook branched. Its bark scales off like that which we forget:
Pain, an introduction at a party, what precisely happened umpteen
Years or days or hours ago. And that same blue jay returns, or perhaps
It is another. All jays are one to me. But not the sun which seems at
Each rising new, as though in the night it enacted death and rebirth,
As flowers seem to. The roses this June will be different roses
Even though you cut an armful and come in saying, "Here are the roses,"
As though the same blooms had come back, white freaked with red
And heavily scented. Or a cut branch of pear blooms before its time,
"Forced." Time brings us into bloom and we wait, busy, but wait
For the unforced flow of words and intercourse and sleep and dreams
In which the past seems to portend a future which is just more
Daily life. The cat has a ripped ear. He fights, he fights all
The tom cats all the time. There are blood gouts on a velvet seat.
Easily sponged off: but these red drops on a book of Stifter's, will
I remember and say at some future time, "Oh, yes, that was the day
Hodge had a torn ear and bled on the card table?" Poor
Hodge, battered like an old car. Silence flows into my mind. It
Is spring. It is also still really winter. Not a day when you say,
"What a beautiful spring day." A day like twilight or evening when
You think, "I meant to watch the sun set." And then comes on
To rain. "You've got to take," says the man at the store, "the rough
With the smooth." A window to the south is rough with raindrops
That, caught in the screen, spell out untranslatable glyphs. A story
Not told: so much not understood, a sight, an insight, and you pass on,
Another day for each day is subjective and there is a totality of days
As there are as many to live it. The day lives us and in exchange
We it: after snowball time, a month, March, of fits and starts, winds,
Rain, spring hints and wintry arrears. The weather pays its check,
Like quarreling in a D.C. hotel, "I won't quarrel about it, but I made

Hymn to Life

No local calls." Strange city, broad and desolating, monuments
Rearing up and offices like monuments and crowds lined up to see
The White House inside. "We went to see the White House. It was
    lovely."
Not so strange though as the cemetery with guttering flame and
Admirals and generals with bigger gravestones than the lesser fry
Below Lee's house, false marble pillars and inside all so
Everyday, in every room a shawl tossed untidily upon a chair or bed
Created no illusion of lived-in-ness. But the periwinkles do, in beds
That flatten and are starred blue-violet, a retiring flower loved,
It would seem, of the dead, so often found where they congregate. A
Quote from Aeschylus: I forget. All, all is forgotten gradually and
One wonders if these ideas that seem handed down are truly what they
    were?
An idea may mutate like a plant, and what was once held basic truth
Become an idle thought, like, "Shall we plant some periwinkles there
By that bush? They're so to be depended on." The wind shakes the
    screen
And all the raindrops on it streak and run in stems. It's colder.
The crocuses close up. The snowdrops are brushed with mud. The sky
Colors itself rosily behind gray-black and the rain falls through
The basketball hoop on a garage, streaking its backboard with further
Trails of rust, a lovely color to set with periwinkle violet-blue.
And the trees shiver and shudder in the light rain blasts from off
The ocean. The street wet reflects the breakup of the clouds
On its face, driving over sky with a hissing sound. The car
Slides slightly and in the west appear streaks of different green:
A lid lifted briefly on the spring. Then the moon burns through
Racing clouds, its aureole that of rings of oil on water in a harbor
Bubbling up from an exhaust. Clear the sky, beside a rim of moon.
Three stars and only three and one planet. So under lilacs unleaved
Lie a clump of snowdrops and one purple crocus. Purple, a polka-dotted
Color little girls are fond of: "See my new dress!" and she twirls
On one foot. Then, crossed, bursts into tears. Smiles and rain, like
These passing days in which buds swell, unseen as yet, waiting
For the elms to color their further out most twigs, only the willow
Gleams yellow. Life is hard. Some are strong, some weak, most
Untested. These useless truths blow about the yard the day after
Rain the soft sunlight making softer shadows on the faded lawn.
The world looks so old in the spring, laid out under the sky. One
Gull coasts by, unexpected as a kiss on the nape of the neck. These

Days need birds and so they come, a flock of ducks, and a bunch of
Small fluffy unnamed balls that hide in hedges and make a racket.
"The gift of life," as though, existing in expectancy and then
Someone came up and said, "Here," or, "Happy Birthday." It is more
Mysterious than that, pierced by blue or running in the rain
Or simply lying down to read. Writing a postponed letter which may
Bring no pleasure: arduous truths to tell. And if you thought March was
    bad
Consider April, early April, wet snow falling into blue squills
That underneath a beech make an illusory lake, a haze of blue
With depth to it. That is like pain, ordinary household pain,
Like piles, or bumping against a hernia. All the signs are set for A OK
A day to visit the National Gallery—Velázquez, Degas—but, and
What a but, with water on the knee "You'll need a wheelchair, Mummy."
Coasting among the masterpieces, of what use are they? *Angel with a*
Hurdy-Gurdy or this young man in dun clothes who holds his hat so that
The red lining shows and glows. And in the sitting room people sit
And rest their feet and talk of where they've been, motels and Monticello,
Dinner in the Fiji Room. Someone forgets a camera. Each day forgetting:
What is there so striking to remember? The rain stops. April shines
A little, stormily, the ocean off there makes its freight car noise
Or rattles with catarrh and asks to have its nose wiped. Gray descends.
An illuminous penetration of unbright light that seeps and coats
The ragged lawn and spells out bare spots and winter fallen branches.
Yardwork. And now the yardwork is over (it is never over), today's
Stint anyway. Odd jobs, that stretch ahead, wide and mindless as
Pennsylvania Avenue or the bridge to Arlington, crossed and recrossed
And there the Lincoln Memorial crumbles. It looks so solid: it won't
Last. The impermanence of permanence, is that all there is? To look
And see the plane tree, its crooked branches brush the ground, rear
In its age, older than any of us, destined, if all goes well with it,
To outlast us all. Does one then resent the plane tree, host
To cardinals? I hear them call. Plaintively, in the mating season.
Why should a white city dog my thoughts? Vast, arid, a home to many,
So strange in its unamiability. Stony city laid out on an heroic plan,
Why are you there? Various answers present themselves, likely
As squills. It doesn't really matter, for instance, to miss the spring.
For this is spring, this mud and swelling fruit tree buds, furred
On the apple trees. And yet it still might snow: it's been known
Falling like cherry blossom petals around the Reflecting Pool, a sight
To see. And there are sights to hear, music from a phonograph, pop

Or classical, please choose one or both. It doesn't matter. What matters
Is how the light becomes entrapped in a dusty screen, masking out
The view into the depths of the garage where the cars are stalled like
    oxen.
Day, suddenly sunny and warming up for more, I would like to stroke
    you
As one strokes a cat and feels the ridgy skull beneath the fur and tickles
It behind its ears. The cat twists its head and moves it toward your
    fingers
Like the lifting thighs of someone fucked, moving up to meet the stroke.
The sun strokes all now in this zone, reaching in through windows to
    jell
Glue in jars (that takes time)—may I send you a warmed bottle of
    Pliobond?
It is on this desk and—here's the laugh—I don't know who put it there.
"This is something he will like, or use." Meantime, those branches go
Ungathered up. I hate fussing with nature and would like the world to
    be
All weeds. I see it from the train, citybound, how the yuccas and chicory
Thrive. So much messing about, why not leave the world alone? Then
There would be no books, which is not to be borne. Willa Cather alone
    is worth
The price of admission to the horrors of civilization. Let's make a list.
The greatest paintings. Preferred orchestral conductors. Nostalgia
    singers.
The best, the very best, roses. After learning all their names—Rose
de Rescht, Cornelia, Pax—it is important to forget them. All these
Lists are so much dirty laundry. Sort it out fast and send to laundry
Or hurl into washing machine, add soap and let'er spin. The truth is
That all these household tasks and daily work—up the street two men
Install an air conditioner—are beautiful. Flowers and machines that
    people
Love: the boy who opts for trade school while white collar kids
Call him a 'greaser.' I wish I could take an engine apart and reassemble
    it.
I also wish I sincerely wanted to. I don't. "Love is everything that it's
Cracked up to be." There's a song for you. Another is in the silence
Of a windless day. Hear it? Motors, yes, and the scrabbling of the surf
But, too, the silence in which out of the muck arise violet leaves
(Leaves of violets, that is). The days slide by and we feel we must
Stamp an impression on them. It is quite other. They stamp us, both

Time and season so that looking back there are wide unpeopled avenues
Blue-gray with cars on them, parked either side, and a small bridge that
Crosses Rock Creek has four bison at its corners, out of scale
Yet so mysterious to childhood, friendly, ominous, pattable because
Of bronze. The rain comes back, this spring, like a thirsty dog
Who goes back and back to his dish. "Fill it up, please," wag wag.
Gray depression and purple shadows, the daffodils feigning sunlight
That came yesterday. One day rain, one day sun, the weather is stuck
Like a record. Through it all the forsythia begins to bloom, brown
And yellow and warm as lit gas jets, clinging like bees to
The arching canes where starlings take cover from foraging cats. Not
To know: what have these years of living and being lived taught us?
Not to quarrel? Scarcely. You want to shoot pool, I want to go home:
And just before the snap of temper one had sensed so
Strongly the pleasure of watching a game well played: the cue ball
Carom and the struck ball pocketed. Skill. And still the untutored
Rain comes down. Open the laundry door. Press your face into the
Wet April chill: a life mask. Attune yourself to what is happening
Now, the little wet things, like washing up the lunch dishes. Bubbles
Rise, rinse and it is done. Let the dishes air dry, the way
You let your hair after a shampoo. All evaporates, water, time, the
Happy moment and—harder to believe—the unhappy. Time on a bus,
That passes, and the night with its burthen and gift of dreams. That
Other life we live and need, filled with joys and terrors, threaded
By dailiness: where the wished for sometimes happens, or, just
Before waking tremulous hands undo buttons. Another day, the sun
Comes out from behind unbuttoned cloud underclothes—gray with
            use—
And bud scales litter the sidewalks. A new shop is being built,
An old one refurbished. What was a white interior will now be brown
Behind men's clothes, there are these changes in taste. Fashion
It anew. Change in everything yet none so great as the changes in
Oneself, which, short of sickness, go unobserved. Why watch
Yourself? You know you're here, and where tomorrow you will probably
Be. In the delicatessen a woman made a fumbling gesture then
Slowly folded toward the floor. "Get a doctor," someone said. "She's
Having a fit." Not knowing how to help I left, taking with me
The look of appeal in faded blue eyes. Between these sharp attacks
Of harsh reality I would like to interpose: interpose is not the
Word. One wants them not to happen, that's all, but, like slammed
On brakes—the cab skids, you are thrown forward, ouch—they

Hymn to Life

Come. Times when religion would help: "Be merciful" "Intercede"
"That which I should have done . . ." Fear and superstition and some-
Thing more. But without the conviction of a truth, best leave
It alone. Life, it seems, explains nothing about itself. In the
Garden now daffodils stand full unfolded and to see them is enough.
They seem no more passing than when they weren't there: perhaps
The promise when first the blades pierced the wintry soil
Was better? You see, you invent choices where none exist. Perhaps
It is not a choice but a preference? No, take it all, it's free,
Help yourself. The sap rises. The trees leaf out and bloom. You
Suddenly sense: you don't know what. An exhilaration that revives
Old views and surges of energy or the pure pleasure of
Simply looking. A car goes over a rise and there are birches snow
Twisted into cabalistic shapes: The Devil's Notch; or Smuggler's
Gap. At the time you could not have imagined the time when you
Would forget the name, as apparent and there as your own. Rivers
Reflecting silver skies, how many boys have swum in you? A rope
Tied to a tree caught between my thighs and I was yanked headfirst
And fell into the muddy creek. What a long time it seemed, rising
To the surface, how lucky it didn't catch me in the groin. That
Won't happen twice, I imagine. That summer sun was the same
As this April one: is repetition boring? Or only inactivity? Quite
A few things are boring, like the broad avenues of Washington
D.C. that seem to go from nowhere and back again. Civil servants
Wait at the crossing to cross to lunch at the Waffle House. In
This twilight Degas a woman sits and holds a fan, it's
The just rightness that counts. And how have you come to know just
Rightness when you see it and what is the deep stirring that it
Brings? Art is as mysterious as nature, as life, of which it is
A flower. Under the hedges now the weedy strips grow bright
With dandelions, just as good a flower as any other. Unfortunately,
You can't pick them: they wilt. But these burgeoning days are
Not like any others. Promise is a part of it, promise of warmth
And vegetative growth. "Wheel me out into the sun, Sonny,
These old bones that creak need it." And the gardener does not
Come back: over the winter he had a heart attack, has to take it
Easy. You see death shadowed out in another's life. The threat
Is always there, even in balmy April sunshine. So what
If it is hard to believe in? Stopping in the city while the light
Is red, to think that all who stop with you too must stop, and
Yet it is not less individual a fate for all that. "When I

was born, death kissed me. I kissed it back." Meantime, there
Is bridge, and solitaire, and phone calls and a door slams, someone
Goes out into the April sun to take a spin as far as the
Grocer's, to shop, and then come back. In the fullness of time,
Let me hand you an empty cup, coffee stained. Or a small glass
Of spirits: "Here's your ounce of whisky for today." Next door
The boys dribble a basketball and practice shots. Two boys
Run by: high spirits. The postman comes. No mail of interest.
Another day, there is. A postcard of the Washington Monument,
A friend waving from a small window at the needle top. "Hoo
Hoo" he calls. Another day, and still the sun shines down, warming
Tulips into bloom, a redder red than blood. The dandelions
Cringe before them. In the evening there will be time enough
To drive from here to there, study the vegetable patch, admire
The rosy violets. Life in action, life in repose, life in
Contemplation, which is hard to tell from day dreaming, on a day
When the sky woolgathers clouds and sets their semblance on a
Glassy ocean. Only its edge goes lisp. On no two days the same.
Is it the ocean's mindlessness that troubles? At times it seems
Calculatedly malevolent, tearing the dunes asunder, tumbling
Summer houses into itself, a terror to see. They say there are
Those who have never felt terror. A slight creeping of the scalp,
Merely. How fine. Finer than sand, that, on a day like this,
Trickles through my fingers, ensconced in a dune cleft, sun
Warmed and breeze cooled. This peace is full of sounds and
Movement. A couple passes, jogging. A dog passes, barking
And running. My nose runs, a little. Just a drip. Left over
From winter. How long ago it seems! All spring and summer stretch
Ahead, a roadway lined by roses and thunder. "It will be here
Before you know it." These twigs will then have leafed and
Shower down a harvest of yellow-brown. So far away, so
Near at hand. The sand runs through my fingers. The yellow
Daffodils have white corollas (sepals?). The crocuses are gone,
I didn't see them go. They were here, now they're not. Instead
The forsythia ensnarls its flames, cool fire, pendent above the smoke
Of its brown branches. Beaches are near. It rains again: the screen
And window glass are pebbled by it. It soaks through a rain coat that
Has had its water repellency dry cleaned out of it. Most modern
Inventions don't work so well, or not for long. A breakdown occurs,
Or something simple, like the dishwasher detergent eating off
The pattern on china, even the etched florets on wine glasses.

Hymn to Life

Strong stuff. From the train, a stand of larch is greener than
Greenest grass. A funny tree, of many moods, gold in autumn, naked
In winter: an evergreen (it looks) that isn't. What kind of a tree
Is that? I love to see it resurrect itself, the enfolded buttons
Of needles studding the branches, then opening into little bursts.
And that Washington flower, the pink magnolia tree, blooms now
In little yards, its trunk a smoky gray. And soon the hybrid azaleas,
So much too much, will follow, and the tender lilac. Persia, we
Have much to thank you for, besides the word lapis lazuli. And someone
You know well is suffering, sees it all but not the way before
Him, hating his job and not knowing what to change it for. Have
You any advice to give? Have you learned nothing in all these
Years? "Take it as it comes." Sit still and listen: each so alone.
Someone driving decides not to take that curve, to pile it up
In smithereens, the anxious and unsatisfying years: goodbye, life.
Others keep on living so as not to wound their friends: the suicide
Fantasy, to awaken rested and fresh, to plunge into a deep and
Dreamless sleep, to be mindless and at one with all that grows,
Dies and revives each April, here, crying, "Stir your stumps!"
In the mental hospital a patient is ready to be discharged. "I'm
So glad to be going home!" Where the same old problems wait;
Still, to feel more equal to them, that's something. "Time heals
All wounds": now what's that supposed to mean? Wounds can
Kill, like that horse chestnut tree with the rotting place will surely
Die unless the tree doctor comes. Cut out the rot, fill with tree
Cement, score and leave to heal. The rain comes down in buckets:
I've never seen that, though you often speak of it. The rain
Comes down and brings depression, too much and too often. And there
Is the fog off the cold Atlantic. No one is at his best with
A sinus headache. It will pass. Stopped passages unblock: why
Let the lovely spring, its muck and scarlet emperors, get you
Down. Unhibernate. Let the rain soak your hair, run down your
Face, hang in drops from facial protuberances. Face into
It, then towel dry. Then another day brings back the sun and
Violets in the grass. The pear tree thickens all its boughs and
Twigs into silver-white, a dimmed brilliance, and already at
Its base a circle of petals on the unmowed grass. Far away
In Washington, at the Reflecting Pool, the Japanese cherries
Bust out into their dog mouth pink. Visitors gasp. The sun
Drips, coats and smears, all that spring yellow under unending
Blue. Only the oaks hold back their leaf buds, reticent.

Reticence is not a bad quality, though it may lead to misunderstandings.
I misunderstood silence for disapproval, see now it was
Sympathy. Thank you, May, for these warm stirrings. Life
Goes on, it seems, though in all sorts of places—nursing
Homes—it is drawing to a close. Abstractions and generalities:
Grass and blue depths into which the evening star seems set.
As windows are set in walls in whited Washington. City, begone
From my thoughts: childhood was not all that gay. Nor all that gray,
For the matter of that. May leans in my window, offering hornets.
To them too I give leave to go about their business, which is not
Nesting in my books. The fresh mown lawn is a rug underneath
Which is swept the dirt, the living dirt out of which our nurture
Comes, to which we go, not knowing if we hasten or we tarry. May
Opens wide her bluest eyes and speaks in bird tongues and a
Chain saw. The blighted elms come down. Already maple saplings,
Where other elms once grew and whelmed, count as young trees. In
A dishpan the soap powder dissolves under a turned on faucet and
Makes foam, just like the waves that crash ashore at the foot
Of the street. A restless surface. Chewing, and spitting sand and
Small white pebbles, clam shells with a sheen or chalky white.
A horseshoe crab: primeval. And all this without thought, this
Churning energy. Energy! The sun sucks up the dew; the day is
Clear; a bird shits on my window ledge. Rain will wash it off
Or a storm will chip it loose. Life, I do not understand. The
Days tick by, each so unique, each so alike: what is that chatter
In the grass? May is not a flowering month so much as shades
Of green, yellow-green, blue-green, or emerald or dusted like
The lilac leaves. The lilac trusses stand in bud. A cardinal
Passes like a flying tulip, alights and nails the green day
Down. One flame in a fire of sea-soaked, copper-fed wood:
A red that leaps from green and holds it there. Reluctantly
The plane tree, always late, as though from age, opens up and
Hangs its seed balls out. The apples flower. The pear is past.
Winter is suddenly so far away, behind, ahead. From the train
A stand of coarse grass in fuzzy flower. Is it for miracles
We live? I like it when the morning sun lights up my room
Like a yellow jelly bean, an inner glow. May mutters, "Why
Ask questions?" or, "What are the questions you wish to ask?"

Hymn to Life

THE

MORNING

OF THE

POEM

(1 9 8 0)

FOR DARRAGH PARK

NEW POEMS

This Dark Apartment

Coming from the deli
a block away today I
saw the UN building
shine and in all the
months and years I've
lived in this apartment
I took so you and I
would have a place to
meet I never noticed
that it was in my view.

I remember very well
the morning I walked in
and found you in bed
with X. He dressed
and left. You dressed
too. I said, "Stay
five minutes." You
did. You said, "That's
the way it is." It
was not much of a surprise.

Then X got on speed
and ripped off an
antique chest and an
air conditioner, etc.
After he was gone and
you had changed the
Segal lock, I asked
you on the phone, "Can't
you be content with
your wife and me?" "I'm

not built that way,"
you said. No surprise.

Now, without saying
why, you've let me go.
You don't return my
calls, who used to call
me almost every evening
when I lived in the coun-
try. "Hasn't he told you
why?" "No, and I doubt he
ever will." Goodbye. It's
mysterious and frustrating.

How I wish you would come
back! I could tell
you how, when I lived
on East 49th, first
with Frank and then with John,
we had a lovely view of
the UN building and the
Beekman Towers. They were
not my lovers, though.
You were. You said so.

June 30, 1974

for Jane and Joe Hazan

Let me tell you
that this weekend Sunday
morning in the country
fills my soul
with tranquil joy:
the dunes beyond
the pond beyond
the humps of bayberry—
my favorite
shrub (today,
at least)—are

silent as a mountain
range: such a
subtle profile
against a sky that
goes from dawn
to blue. The roses
stir, the grapevine
at one end of the deck
shakes and turns
its youngest leaves
so they show pale
and flower-like.
A redwing blackbird
pecks at the grass;
another perches on a bush.
Another way, a millionaire's
white château turns
its flank to catch
the risen sun. No
other houses, except
this charming one,
alive with paintings,
plants and quiet.
I haven't said
a word. I like
to be alone
with friends. To get up
to this morning view
and eat poached eggs
and extra toast with
Tiptree Gooseberry Preserve
(green)—and coffee,
milk, no sugar. Jane
said she heard
the freeze-dried kind
is healthier when
we went shopping
yesterday and she
and John bought
crude blue Persian plates.
How can coffee be

The Morning of the Poem

healthful? I mused
as sunny wind
streamed in the car
window driving home.
Home! How lucky to
have one, how arduous
to make this scene
of beauty for
your family and
friends. Friends!
How we must have
sounded, gossiping at
the dinner table
last night. Why, *that*
dinner table is
this breakfast table:
"The boy in trousers
is not the same boy
in no trousers," who
said? Discontinuity
in all we see and are:
the same, yet change,
change, change. "Inez,
it's good to see you."
Here comes the cat, sedate,
that killed and brought
a goldfinch yesterday.
I'd like to go out
for a swim but
it's a little cool
for that. Enough to
sit here drinking coffee,
writing, watching the clear
day ripen (such
a rainy June we had)
while Jane and Joe
sleep in their room
and John in his. I
think I'll make more toast.

Korean mums

beside me in this garden
are huge and daisy-like
(why not? are not
oxeye daisies a chrysanthemum?),
shrubby and thick-stalked,
the leaves pointing up
the stems from which
the flowers burst in
sunbursts. I love
this garden in all its moods,
even under its winter coat
of salt hay, or now,
in October, more than
half gone over: here
a rose, there a clump
of aconite. This morning
one of the dogs killed
a barn owl. Bob saw
it happen, tried to
intervene. The airedale
snapped its neck and left
it lying. Now the bird
lies buried by an apple
tree. Last evening
from the table we saw
the owl, huge in the dusk,
circling the field
on owl-silent wings.
The first one ever seen
here: now it's gone,
a dream you just remember.

The dogs are barking. In
the studio music plays
and Bob and Darragh paint.
I sit scribbling in a little
notebook at a garden table,
too hot in a heavy shirt

The Morning of the Poem

in the mid-October sun
into which the Korean mums
all face. There is a
dull book with me,
an apple core, cigarettes,
an ashtray. Behind me
the rue I gave Bob
flourishes. Light on leaves,
so much to see, and
all I really see is that
owl, its bulk troubling
the twilight. I'll
soon forget it: what
is there I have not forgot?
Or one day will forget:
this garden, the breeze
in stillness, even
the words, Korean mums.

Growing Dark

The grass shakes.
Smoke streaks, no,
cloud strokes.
The dogs are fed.
Their licenses
clank on pottery.
The phone rings.
And is answered.
The pond path
is washed-out grass
between green
winter cover.
Last night in
bed I read.
You came to
my room and
said, "Isn't

the world
terrible?" "My
dear . . ." I
said. It could be
and has been
worse. So
beautiful and
things keep getting
in between. When
I was young I
hurt others. Now,
others have hurt
me. In the night
I thought I heard
a dog bark.
Racking sobs.
Poor guy. Yet,
I got my sleep.

Dec. 28, 1974

The plants against the light
which shines in (it's four o'clock)
right on my chair: I'm in my chair:
are silhouettes, barely green,
growing black as my eyes move right,
right to where the sun is.
I am blinded by a fiery circle:
I can't see what I write. A man
comes down iron stairs (I
don't look up) and picks up brushes
which, against a sonata of Scriabin's,
rattle like wind in a bamboo clump.
A wooden sound, and purposeful footsteps
softened by a drop-cloth-covered floor.
To be encubed in flaming splendor,
one foot on a Chinese rug, while
the mad emotive music

tears at my heart. Rip it open:
I want to cleanse it in an icy wind.
And what kind of tripe is that?
Still, last night I did wish—
no, that's my business and I
don't wish it now. "Your poems,"
a clunkhead said, "have grown
more open." I don't want to be open,
merely to say, to see and say, things
as they are. That at my elbow
there is a wicker table. *Hortus
Second* says a book. The fields
beyond the feeding sparrows are
brown, palely brown yet with an inward glow
like that of someone of a frank good nature
whom you trust. I want to hear the music
hanging in the air and drink my
Coca-Cola. The sun is off me now,
the sky begins to color up, the air
in here is filled with wildly flying notes.
Yes, the sun moves off to the right
and prepares to sink, setting,
beyond the dunes, an ocean on fire.

Good morning

morning, or heartache. In
the night it rained
it misted. The walks
are dark with it, the grass
is thick with it. In
resignation I
doff my walking shorts,
put on elephant hide,
or Levi's. Bitter coffee.

Rae turns to me and
speaks her rage

but gently as a gentle
woman would. The night
nurse means well, is
something else jabbering
loudly in the hall
at night. An over-
ripe banana. I have yet to learn
to speak my rage.

Where I go books
pile up. Constable's
letters, Balzac,
Afternoon Men. It's
cool enough to
shut the window. So
I do. Silver day
how shall I polish you?

Song

The light lies layered in the leaves.
Trees, and trees, more trees.
A cloud boy brings the evening paper:
The Evening Sun. It sets.
Not sharply or at once
a stately progress down the sky
(it's gilt and pink and faintly green)
above, beyond, behind the evening leaves
of trees. Traffic sounds and
bells resound in silver clangs
the hour, a tune, my friend
Pierrot. The violet hour:
the grass is violent green.
A weeping beech is gray,
a copper beech is copper red.
Tennis nets hang
unused in unused stillness.
A car starts up and

whispers into what will soon be night.
A tennis ball is served.
A horsefly vanishes.
A smoking cigarette.
A day (so many and so few)
dies down a hardened sky
and leaves are lap-held notebook leaves
discriminated barely
in light no longer layered.

A Name Day

for Anne Dunn

You know da Vinci's painting of
The Virgin sitting in her mother's lap,
Bending and reaching toward the child:
Mary, Jesus, and St. Anne: beautiful
Names: Anne, from a Latin name from
The Hebrew name Hannah. The sun shines
Here and out the window I see green, green
Cut into myriad shapes, a bare-foot-
Caressing carpet of fresh-mown grass (a
Gift from Persia, courtesy of D. Kermani),
Green chopped into various leaves: walnut, maple,
Privet, Solomon's-seal, needles of spruce:
Green with evening sunlight on it,
Green going deep into penetrable shade:
What is that one red leaf? It's too
Soon, it's only late July. I'm frightened,
Anne, my mother, who is eighty-six, just
A few minutes ago had some kind of slight
Attack. I held her and said, "Put your weight
On me, put your weight on me." She said,
"I can't stand it." She won't let me
Call a doctor: my brother and his wife
Are out of town: they know better than I
How to handle her. I think—I hope—I
Pray, that it was just an arthritic spasm.

Beneficent St. Anne, look down and
Protect us. Mary, sustain us in our need.

Here it is all so beautiful and green:
There where you are it is night, big
Stars, perhaps: do candles flare as
You and yours gather to celebrate
Your name day, there in pungent Provence?
What would I like to give you?
Beads, a steel rose, a book?
No, flowers, roses, real roses
—Maréchal Niel, Gloire de
Dijon, Variegata di Bologna,
Madame Alfred Carrière, Souvenir
de la Malmaison, Georg Arends,
Prince Camille de Rohan: or,
Maybe better, homelier,
Canadian columbine, rusty red
(Or rather orange?), spurred,
Hanging down, drying, turning
Brown, turning up, a cup
Full of fine black seeds
That sparkle, wake-robin,
Trillium, a dish of rich
Soft moss stuck with little
Flowers from the woods—
Bloodroot, perhaps
Rose pogonia, sea lavender
And, best of all, bunches
And bunches and bunches of
New England asters, not blue,
Not violet, certainly not
Purple: bright-yellow-
Centered, so many crowded
Into vases and bowls that
The house seems awash
With sea and sun. (My
Mother is better: I hear
Her cooking supper: the throbbing
Of my heart slows down.) I
Wish I were there with you,

The Morning of the Poem

Gathered with friends
And family, to celebrate
Your name day, Anne. (Along
With the flowers, I send
You a New Brunswick lobster.)

Footnote

The bluet is a small flower, creamy-throated, that grows in patches in New England lawns. The bluet (French pronunciation) is the shaggy cornflower, growing wild in France. "The Bluet" is a poem I wrote. *The Bluet* is a painting of Joan Mitchell's. The thick hard blue runs and holds. All of them, broken-up pieces of sky, hard sky, soft sky. Today I'll take Joan's giant vision, running and holding, staring you down with beauty. Though I need reject none. Bluet. "Bloo-ay."

Afterward

is much as before. Night
slams gently down. I cannot
open this container: and
do and the pills all lie
"star-scattered on" the
rug, which by mischance is
the color of the pills. Do
you ever swear out loud
when you're alone? I do
and did, like that painting,
The Gleaners. The yellow
lamp spreads a friendly glow
on my new Olivetti and
on me. I'm drinking
Diet Pepsi. The ulnar
nerve in my right arm got
pinched I don't know how

and my little finger is
numb: a drag when typing.
The past ten months
were something else:
pneumonia, diabetes, a
fire in bed (*extase, cauchemar,*
sommeil dans un nid de flammes),
months getting skin
grafts for third-degree
burns (for laughs, try
sleeping in an airplane
splint) and getting
poisoned by the side
effects of a potent
tranquilizer: it took
two more months to
learn to walk again
and when I came out
feeling great wham
a nervous breakdown: four
weeks in another hospital.
St. Vincent's, the Neurological
Institute, Tower Nine at
Roosevelt: "You've had too
many hospitals," my doctor
said, "I'm going to get you
out of here as fast as I
can," and so he did. It's
funny to be free again: to
look out and see
the gorgeous October day
and know that I
can stroll right out into
it and for as long as
I wish and that's what I
do. This room needs flowers.

I sit down to type

So long postponed, so near at hand.
—WALLACE STEVENS

and arise whatever for?
SUGAR FREE! SUGAR FREE! TAB.
My window faces west. I mean south.
I push it up and, in
the guise of sunbeams,
God floods my room.
He's in one of his
less malevolent moods.
But God? I don't believe
in God: not for myself,
I mean. For others, it's
another story: at least
one of my friends has
a guardian angel, and
a Jesuit priest I will
call "Father Bill" is
going to heaven. Such
goodness cannot possibly
go unrewarded. But me?
I'm worm food. Someone
beautiful once asked
about religion and I said,
"I'm a crypto-Catholic."
"I'm not sure what you
mean." "Me either." In
fact, I am a Presbyterian:
but before I was
confirmed I'd read
Of Human Bondage
(if that phone rings
one more time I am
going to castrate it
with nail scissors)
and became an atheist:
imagine it: losing your
faith because of a book
by one of the most over-

rated writers of all time.
"There's this watch, see,
and where there's a watch—"
Yawn. I have a scab:
this proves there is a devil
clad in bright red
long johns. In our more
intimate moments I
call him "Sweetie Pie."
And yet I am religious: I
believe implacably in
the perfectibility of man:
to me, we are at the crux,
the most exciting moment
in the history of man:
an X ray of a brain, prisons
transposed to hospitals,
the dawning of the realization
that all men are born creative
(Kenneth Koch
could teach a golf ball
how to write pantoums),
and so on: needless to
say, this is not going
to happen in my time—
nor in yours, baby.
When I was four someone
named Mabel took me to mass:
a gray church on a gray day.
I had a vision: the first
of many. We went home and
my father said, "Did the
priest come riding in on
his ass?" "Why, Mark,"
my mother stated. Ever since
that gray vision—no
matter what I say, no
matter what I think I think—
it has been my profoundest
prayer that God will grant
me grace and I will die

a Catholic, secure in his
all-forgiving love.

The snow

that fell and iced
the walks and streets
is melted off: it's
gone. I slipped a
little as I strode.
It's early winter
yet though, more and
much is yet to come.
This gray day though
is much too warm
for snow. The window's
up a crack and I shiver
only slightly. I
think of you and then
my thought slides
on, like slipping
on a lightly iced
walk. I have no more
poems for you, chum,
only for the ice and snow.

Wystan Auden

I went to his fortieth birthday
party: was it really twenty-seven
years ago? I don't remember what
street he was living on, but he
was adapting *The Duchess of Malfi*
for the modern stage, in which
Canada Lee appeared in white face:

it was that long ago. It was in
that apartment I just missed
meeting Brecht and T. S. Eliot.

I remember Chester so often saying,
"Oh *Wystan!*" while Wystan looked
pleased at having stirred him up.

On Ischia he claimed to take
St. Restituta seriously, and
sat at Maria's café in the cobbled
square saying, "Poets should
dress like businessmen," while
he wore an incredible peach-
colored nylon shirt. And on
Fire Island his telling someone,
"You must write each book as
though it were your last." And
when he learned that in Florence
I and my friend Bill Aalto had
fished his drafts of poems
out of the wastepaper basket,
he took to burning them, saying,
"I feel like an ambassador burning
secret papers." When he got off
the liner at Naples, in black and
a homburg, he said, "I've just
read *all* of Doughty's *The Dawn
in Britain.*" And earlier, right
after the war, "My dear, I'm the
first major poet to have flown
the Atlantic." He was very kind.
Once, when I had an operation
in Rome, he wrote me quite a large
check: I forget for how much.
When I sent it back and asked
for (for a more favorable ex-
change on the black market)
cash, he sent it, along with
a cross note saying he was
a busy man. Once when a group

of us made an excursion from
Ischia—Capri, Sorrento, Positano,
Amalfi, Pompeii—he suddenly
said at cocktails on a pensione
terrace: "More of this sitting
around like beasts!" He was
industrious, writing away in
a smoky room—fug—in a
ledger or on loose sheets
poems, some of which I typed
for him (they're in *Nones*).
I don't have to burn his
letters as he asked his
friends to do: they were lost
a long time ago. So much
to remember, so little to
say: that he liked martinis
and was greedy about the wine?
I always thought he would live
to a great age. He did not.
Wystan, kind man and great poet,
goodbye.

Dining Out with Doug and Frank

for Frank Polach

Not quite yet. First,
around the corner for a visit
to the Bella Landauer Collection
of printed ephemera:
luscious lithos and why did
Fairy Soap vanish and
Crouch and Fitzgerald survive?
Fairy Soap was once a
household word! I've been living
at Broadway and West 74th
for a week and still haven't
ventured on a stroll in

Central Park, two bizarre blocks
away. (Bizarre is for the ex-
town houses, mixing Byzantine
with Gothic and Queen Anne.)
My abstention from the Park
is for Billy Nichols who went
bird-watching there and, for
his binoculars, got his
head beat in. Streaming blood,
he made it to an avenue
where no cab would pick him up
until one did and at
Roosevelt Hospital he waited
several hours before any
doctor took him in hand. A
year later he was dead. But
I'll make the park: I carry
more cash than I should and
walk the street at night
without feeling scared unless
someone scary passes.

                    II
Now it's tomorrow,
as usual. Turned out that
Doug (Douglas Crase, the poet)
had to work (he makes his bread
writing speeches): thirty pages
explaining why Eastman Kodak's
semi-slump (?) is just what
the stockholders ordered. He
looked glum, and declined
a drink. By the by did you know
that John Ashbery's grandfather
was offered an investment-in
when George Eastman founded his
great corporation? He turned it
down. Eastman Kodak will survive.
"Yes" and where would our
John be now? I can't imagine him

The Morning of the Poem

any different than he is,
a problem which does not arise,
so I went with Frank (the poet,
he makes his dough as a librarian,
botanical librarian at Rutgers
and as a worker he's a beaver:
up at 5:30, home after 7, but
over striped bass he said he
had begun to see the unwisdom
of his ways and next week will
revert to the seven-hour day
for which he's paid. Good. Time
and energy to write. Poetry
takes it out of you, or you
have to have a surge to bring
to it. Words. So useful and
pleasant) to dine at McFeely's
at West 23rd and Eleventh Avenue
by the West River, which is
the right name for the Hudson
when it bifurcates from
the East River to create
Manhattan "an isle of joy."
Take my word for it, don't
(shall I tell you about my
friend who effectively threw
himself under a train in
the Times Square station?
No. Too tender to touch. In
fact, at the moment I've blocked
out his name. No I haven't:
Peter Kemeny, gifted and tormented
fat man) listen to anyone
else.

III
Oh. At the Battery all
that water becomes the
North River, which seems
to me to make no sense

at all. I always thought
Castle Garden faced Calais.

IV

Peconic Bay scallops, the
tiny, the real ones and cooked
in butter, not breaded and
plunged in deep grease. The food
is good and reasonable (for these
days) but the point is McFeely's
itself—the owner's name or
was it always called that? It's
the bar of the old Terminal Hotel
and someone (McFeely?) has had
the wit to restore it to what
it was: all was there, under
layers of paint and abuse, neglect.
You, perhaps, could put a date
on it: I'll vote for 1881
or the 70's. The ceiling is
florid glass, like the cabbage-rose
runners in the grand old hotels
at Saratoga: when were they built?
The bar is thick and long and
sinuous, virile. Mirrors: are
the decorations on them cut
or etched? I do remember that
above the men's room door the
word Toilet is etched
on a transom. Beautiful lettering,
but nothing to what lurks
within: the three most
splendid urinals I've ever
seen. Like Roman steles. I
don't know what I was going
to say. Yes. Does the Terminal Hotel
itself still function? (Did you
know that "they" sold all the
old mirror glass out of Gage
and Tollner's? Donald Droll has
a fit every time he eats there.)

The Morning of the Poem

"Terminal," I surmise, because
the hotel faced the terminal
of the 23rd Street ferry, a
perfect sunset sail to Hoboken
and the yummies of the Clam
Broth House, which, thank God,
still survives. Not many do:
Gage and Tollner's, the Clam Broth House,
McSorley's and now McFeely's. Was
that the most beautiful of the
ferry houses or am I thinking
of Christopher Street? And there
was another uptown that crossed
to Jersey and back but docking
further downtown: it sailed
on two diagonals. And wasn't
there one at 42nd? It couldn't
matter less, they're gone, all
gone and we are left with just
the Staten Island ferry, all
right in its way but how often
do you want to pass Miss Liberty
and see that awesome spiky postcard
view? The river ferryboats were
squat and low like tugs, old
and wooden and handsome, you
were *in* the water, *in* the shipping:
Millay wrote a lovely poem about
it all. I cannot accept their
death, or any other death. Bill
Aalto, my first lover (five tumultuous
years found Bill chasing me around
the kitchen table—in Wystan Auden's
house in Forio d'Ischia—with
a carving knife. He was serious
and so was I and so I wouldn't go
when he wanted to see me when
he was dying of leukemia. Am I
sorry? Not really. The fear had
gone too deep. The last time I
saw him was in the City Center lobby

and he was jolly—if he just
stared at you and the tears began
it was time to cut and run—
and the cancer had made him lose
a lot of weight and he looked
young and handsome as the night
we picked each other up
in Pop Tunick's long-gone gay bar.
Bill never let me forget that
on the jukebox I kept playing
Lena Horne's "Mad about the Boy."
Why the nagging teasing? It's
a great performance but he
thought it was East Fifties queen
taste. Funny—or, funnily enough—
in dreams, and I dream about him
a lot, he's always the nice guy
I first knew and loved, not
the figure of terror he became.
Oh well. Bill had his hour: he
was a hero, a major in the
Abraham Lincoln Brigade. A dark
Finn who looked not unlike
a butch version of Valentino.
Watch out for Finns. They're
murder when they drink) used
to ride the ferries all the
time, doing the bars along
the waterfront: did you know
that Hoboken has—or had—
more bars to the square inch
(Death. At least twice when
someone I knew and hated
died I felt the joy of vengeance:
I mean I smiled and laughed out
loud: a hateful feeling.
It passes.) to the square inch
than any other city? "Trivia,
Goddess . . ." Through dinner
I wanted to talk more than we
did about Frank's poems. All it

The Morning of the Poem

came down to was "experiment
more," "try collages," and "write
some skinny poems" but I like
where he's heading now and
Creative Writing has never
been my trip although I understand
the fun of teaching someone
something fun to do although most people
simply have not got the gift
and where's the point? What
puzzles me is what my friends
find to say. Oh forget it. Reading,
writing, knowing other poets
will do it, if there is
anything doing. The reams
of shit I've read. It would
have been so nice after dinner
to take a ferry boat with Frank
across the Hudson (or West River,
if you prefer). To be on
the water in the dark and
the wonder of electricity—
the real beauty of Manhattan.
Oh well. When they tore down
the Singer Building,
and when I saw the Bogardus building
rusty and coming unstitched in
a battlefield of rubble I deliberately
withdrew my emotional investments
in loving old New York. Except
you can't. I really like
dining out and last night was
especially fine. A full moon
when we parted hung over
Frank and me. Why is this poem
so long? And full of death?
Frank and Doug are young and
beautiful and have nothing
to do with that. Why is this poem
so long? "Enough is as good
as a feast" and I'm a Herrick fan.

I'd like to take that plunge
into Central Park, only I'm
waiting for Darragh Park to phone.
Oh. Doug and Frank. One is light,
the other dark.
Doug is the tall one.

THE PAYNE WHITNEY POEMS

Trip

Wigging in, wigging out:
when I stop to think
the wires in my head
cross: kaboom. How
many trips
by ambulance (five,
count them five),
claustrated, pill addiction,
in and out of mental
hospitals,
the suicidalness (once
I almost made it)
but—I go on?
Tell you all of it?
I can't. When I think
of that, that at
only fifty-one I,
Jim the Jerk, am
still alive and breathing
deeply, that I think
is a miracle.

We walk

in the garden. Sun
on the river

flashing past. I
dig ivy leaves.
We walk in a
maze. Sun, shine
on. Now it is
one hour later.
Out the window no
sun. Cloud
turbulence and
the wind whistles.
Curious.

Arches

of buildings, this building,
frame a stream of windows
framed in white brick. This
building is fireproof; or else
it isn't: the furnishings first
to go: no, the patients. Patients
on Sundays walk in a small garden.
Today some go out on a group
pass. To stroll the streets and shop.
So what else is new? The sky
slowly/swiftly went blue to gray.
A gray in which some smoke stands.

Linen

Is this the moment?
No, not yet.
When is the moment?
Perhaps there is none.
Need I persist?

The Morning of the Poem

This morning I
changed bedding.
At lunch I watched
someone shake out
the cloth, fold and
stow it in a side-
board. Then, the
cigarette moment.
Now, this moment
flows out of me
down the pen and
writes.

I'm glad I have
fresh linen.

Heather and Calendulas

A violet hush: and sunbursts.
An aluminum measure
full of water. Scentlessness.
"Go to church next week?"
Fortuitous as nuts too
salty. Accordion pleats.
The phone bill is buff.
Three postcards of three
paintings. A good review.
Pale green walls and
a white ceiling. Lamps
lit in daylight. Ice.
The temperature 16. In
February. "Laugh and
the world laughs with you."
Die, and you die alone.

Back

from the Frick. The weather
cruel as Henry Clay himself.
Who put that collection together?
Duveen? I forget. It was nice
to see the masterpieces again,
covered with the strikers' blood.
What's with art anyway, that
we give it such precedence?
I love the paintings, that's for sure.
What I really loved today
was New York, its streets and
men selling flowers and hot dogs
in them. Mysterious town houses,
the gritty wind. I used to live
around here but it's changed some.
Why? That was only thirty years ago.

Blizzard

Tearing and tearing
ripped-up bits of paper,
no, it's not paper
it's snow. Blown side-
ways in the wind,
coming in my window
wetting stacked books.
"Mr Park called. He
can't come visiting
today." Of course not,
in this driving icy
weather. How I wish
I were out in it! A
figure like an ex-
clamation point seen
through driving snow.

The Morning of the Poem

February 13, 1975

Tomorrow is St. Valentine's:
tomorrow I'll think about
that. Always nervous, even
after a good sleep I'd like
to climb back into. The sun
shines on yesterday's new-
fallen snow and yestereven
it turned the world to pink
and rose and steel-blue
buildings. Helene is restless:
leaving soon. And what then
will I do with myself? Some-
one is watching morning
TV. I'm not reduced to that
yet. I wish one could press
snowflakes in a book like flowers.

Sleep

The friends who come to see you
and the friends who don't.
The weather in the window.
A pierced ear.
The mounting tension and the spasm.
A paper-lace doily on a small plate.
Tangerines.
A day in February: heart-
shaped cookies on St. Valentine's.
Like Christopher, a discarded saint.
A tough woman with black hair.
"I got to set my wig straight."
A gold and silver day begins to wane.
A crescent moon.
Ice on the window.
Give my love to, oh, anybody.

Pastime

I pick up a loaded pen and twiddle it.
After the blizzard
cold days of shrinking snow.
At visiting hours the cars
below my window form up
in a traffic jam. A fast-
moving man is in charge,
herding the big machines
like cattle. Weirdly, it all
keeps moving somehow. I read
a dumb detective story. I
clip my nails: they are as hard
as iron or glass. The clippers
keep sliding off them. Today
I'm shaky. A shave, a bath.
Chat. The morning paper.
Sitting. Staring. Thinking blankly.
TV. A desert kind of life.

What

What's in those pills?
After lunch and I can
hardly keep my eyes
open. Oh, for someone to
talk small talk with.
Even a dog would do.

Why are they hammering
iron outside? And what
is that generator whose
fierce hum comes in
the window? What is a
poem, anyway.

The daffodils, the heather
and the freesias all
speak to me. I speak
back, like St. Francis
and the wolf of Gubbio.

THE MORNING OF THE POEM

The Morning of the Poem

for Darragh Park

July 8 or July 9, the eighth surely, certainly
    1976 that I know
Awakening in western New York blurred barely
    morning sopping dawn
Globules face to my face, a beautiful face, not
    mine: Baudelaire's skull:
Force, fate, will, and, you being you: a
    painter, you drink
Your Ovaltine and climb to the city roof, "to
    find a view," and
I being whoever I am get out of bed holding
    my cock and go to piss
Then to the kitchen to make coffee and toast
    with jam and see out
The window two blue jays ripping something white
    while from my mother's
Room the radio purls: it plays all night she leaves
    it on to hear
The midnight news then sleeps and dozes
    until day which now it is,
Wakening today in green more gray, why did
    your lithe blondness
In Remsen handsomeness mix in my mind with
    Baudelaire's skull? which
Stands for strength and fierceness, the dedication
    of the artist?
How easily I could be in love with you,
    who do not like to be touched,
And yet I do not want to be in love with you,
    nor you with me,
"Strange business" the chinky Chinaman said and
    from the kitchen window

The jays are fatter than any jays I ever saw
        before and hanging
In a parlor floor in far-off Chelsea I'm
        glad there is a
Watercolor of me in blue shorts, sitting
        beside a black *Britannica*
And a green-glass-shaded student lamp and
        a glass of deep red wine
Ruby wine the throat of a hummingbird
        hanging on speeding
Wings in fierce blue delphinium depths I think
About those two blue jays, like me, too
        chubby, and Baudelaire's skull,
That sees in the tattered morning the passing of
The lost and indigent, the lost, the way
        the day when I arose
Seemed lost and trash-picking for a meatless morsel,
        a stinking
Bone, such as in this green unlovely village
        one need never
Seek or fear and you descend to your studio
        leaving on your roof
The exhalation of Baudelaire's image of
        terror which is
Not terror but the artist's (your) determination
        to be strong
To see things as they are too fierce and yet
        not too much: in
Western New York, why Baudelaire? In Chelsea,
        why not? Smile,
July day. Why did Baudelaire wander in? Don't
        I love Heine more? Or
Walt Whitman, Walt? No, they come to my death-
        bed and one by one take my hand
And say, "So long, old man," and who was it
        who in the Café Montana told,
In all seriousness, that the triumph of Mrs S.,
        future Duchess of W., was that
"They say she's a circus in bed." I like to
        dwell on that, the caged lions
And the whips, ball-balancing seals, "And now,

without a net . . ." the odious
Clowns: boring Ensor and pseudo-symbolism of
        something meaning something
That doesn't mean a thing at all: the simplicity
        of true drama, a trained and
Modulated voice, a hand that rises of itself.
        "La commedia non par finita;
Ma pure è finita" pleasant to be
        Goldoni and meet Mr Tiepolo in
The square, or Longhi, Guardi, or am I mixing
        up my dates: somebody was older
Than somebody and Goldoni went off to France
        on another gray morning in
Which the firs crowd too thickly on these village
        lawns: Chestnut Hill Road,
But the blight came and there are no chestnuts;
        the blight came, and there
Are no elms; only spruce and maples, maple saplings
        springing up in hedges,
A skinny weed, and this weed, this wild yellow
        flower lower and larger than
A buttercup, not lacquer yellow, more the yellow
        of a marsh marigold, meaty
Like it, though not so large, not nearly so
        large, sprinkled in the weedy
Wild-flower lawn, for God's sake, what is your
        name? "Will you have the watermelon
And the iced coffee, dear?" "Comrades, leave me
        read my *Times.*" She sets
The dishes out just so, as though to please me
        and to please her, a right
Way to do things and that is how she does them. The watermelon
        is fresh
And good and behind this grunt of words I see
        you, Baudelaire's mask your sign,
Legs apart, addressed to your easel, squeezing
        out the tubes of oils
Whose names you know: what is that green you
        use so much of, that seems to
Devour itself? Nor can I quite forget what someone
        said: "I got her number:

The Morning of the Poem

'Why did you tell him homosexuality is a neurosis?' "
        I said, "She said
She didn't say it, but she did." Hard to
        achieve with so much information
Available, so little to be believed. Last July
        was an inferno, tempests of
Rain, then seared grass, this July overcast
        with hottish afternoons: I
Begrudge that far-off island in Penobscot Bay,
        mossy walks and Twin Flower
Corner, icy swims in early morning off pebble
        beaches, the smell of juniper
Where my dead best friend will always walk
        beside me, stride ahead of me.
"When I walk with you, all I see is the heels
        of your sneakers": were
You buried in your sneakers? Of course not,
        though in a tender joke you were:
A nosegay tossed on the coffin: but this is not
        your poem, your poem I may
Never write, too much, though it is there and
        needs only to be written down
And one day will and if it isn't it doesn't matter:
        the truth, the absolute
Of feeling, of knowing what you know, that is
        the poem, like
The house for sale buried in a luxuriance of
        overgrown foundation planting
Across the street upon this hill (taxus,
        cotoneaster), the doctor has more
Patients in Buffalo: he moved there: I'd rather
        stay here and starve, well,
Sort of starve: yesterday I tripped on a scatter
        rug and slam fell full length,
The wind knocked out of me: "Shall I call a
        doctor?" "Please don't talk"
"Are you hurt? Can I help you?" "Shut the fuck
        up" I thought I'd smashed
My kneecap—you know, like when you really
        wham your funny bone, only
More so—but I got up and felt its nothing-

broken-tenderness and
Hobbled down this everlasting hill to distant
        Bell's and bought
Edible necessities: small icy cans of concentrated
        juice, lemon, lime, orange,
Vast puffy bags of bread, Smucker's raspberry jam,
        oatmeal, but not the good,
The Irish kind (travel note: in New York City you
        almost cannot buy a bowl
Of oatmeal: I know, I've tried: why bother: it
        would only taste like paste)
And hobbled home, studying the for-sale house
        hidden in scaly leaves
The way the brownstone facing of your house is
        coming off in giant flakes: there's
A word for that sickness of the stone but I
        can't remember it (you'll find
It in that fascinating book *Brick and Brownstone*:
        illustrative photograph)
And in July you take a picture in progress out,
        your street in snow,
Air conditioners capped with snow and in the
        distance the problem,
An office building straight from Babylon: a
        friend said of you, "With people,
He's awfully good," meaning, I surmise, "kind,
        considerate," "Oh," I said,
"When he has to, he can put his foot down," "I'm
        very glad," our friend
Said, "to hear *that*." Not that he or I meant
        you have a taint
Of toughness, just, well, time passes and
        sometimes you must say "No"
Or, "Don't tread on me" but don't change, I
        like you as you are, laughing
So loud in Sagaponack the summer neighbors
        sent the maid to poke through
Privet and say "There's too much noise": we were
        stunned: complaints about
Laughing? We go on, but, of course, it's not
        quite the same under

The Morning of the Poem

An almost autumn sky, a swimming pool awash
        with cinnamon and gentian
(The sky's the swimming pool, that is) why is
        each day dawning so alike? Overcast,
Or gray: choose one: and then there was the just-
        before-morning electric storm
Night before last: two killed by bolt in a
        Batavia park: my room lighting up
Bright enough to read by. "Fear no more the heat
        of the sun, nor the all-
Dreaded thunder-stone," funny, lightning doesn't
        scare me any more, it thrills,
So long as I'm indoors, in bed by preference,
        with pillows under which to tuck
My head against the louder claps. I'm very brave.
        Then a shovelful of earth
Is thrown into the open grave and rattles on
        the coffin. Oh goodbye, goodbye.
I want to go away into that blue or dark or
        certain or uncertain land: why
Can't we know that it is there and there we'll
        meet and grow in friendship
As we have here? You know that Austrian operetta,
        don't you, *The Land of Smiles?*
That is not what I mean. I'm often happiest
        walking crosstown on a bright
And icy day when up above mare's-tails sparkle and
        I stop to inspect the junk
In junk-shop windows and pass on feasting my eyes
        on what to me is beefy
Handsomeness, sexiness, I don't want it really,
        just to recollect or think,
My, that's nice, warm flesh on a cold, cold
        day: today, July, country edge,
There's almost a chill, and the knee I fell on
        throbs more than
Yesterday. What a drag. Michael Lally is a fine
        poet and looks straight
Into your eyes. I know someone else who looks
        deep into your eyes and under
The curly hair the lies are manufactured. Mostly,

it delights me, like
A farce, the need to dramatize, to make out, "Oh
          I was beautiful, oh the most
Famous men all fell for me and slipped it up
          my cooze. I've seen
'em all!" I believe you, dear. More kinds of
          conifers than spruce grow
On this hill. I wish I knew their names, I have
          a friend, a botanist,
Who could tell them to me, one by one. Frank lives
          in London Terrace and this
Is the London Terrace story. There's something
          called the Poison Line:
When someone, children mostly, goes, say, munching
          in the woods and gets sick
The doctors set the phone wires flashing to
          hospitals, horticultural
Gardens, informed New York. It was 3 a.m., my
          friend was asleep in
London Terrace. The phone. Off in Virginia a young
          man had quarreled
With his family so he went out in the yard and
          gathered castor beans.
They have a hard shell and if you swallow them
          like that they pass
Harmlessly through. He crushed them first.
          Eight is a lethal dose. He
Picked ten. A young man in Virginia. "What happened?"
          "I said, induce
Vomiting. I'm sure it was too late." "Did he die?"
          "I don't know: I
Tried to check back but I couldn't make contact."
          And all that castor
Oil they used to pour down me when I was a kid!
          Pity the young Virginian.
And still it's chill and overcast and in the afternoon
          we went next door
To tea: a house I'd lived next door to for
          forty years and never been inside
Of, not once, before. Mrs Blank, the dead, the former
          owner, wasn't much for

Entertaining high-school boys. She died mad, her
      little hands clenched in
Monkey fists and wouldn't eat her food. Her husband,
      the arborist, he's
Gone too, and handsome Larry, crushed by a car
      against the back wall of a garage:
Die, die, die, and only pray the pain won't be more
      than you can bear. But
What you must bear, you will. I've known a
      murderer (or two): or were
They only bragging? Not everyone is quite so nice
      as my gentle Grandma Ella
Sleeping away off there in Albert Lea, Minnesota,
      where even the lake
Is named Lake Albert Lea: who was he? A surveyor,
      it seems to me: you can
See the lake in this snapshot of my mother, kneeling
      on the lawn, using
Her turned-over hat to hold a big bunch of sweet
      William: stop stirring
The rice and come with me to Maine and we'll settle
      once for all which
Is woundwort and which Jill-over-the-ground: but
      you're painting, or sketching
In big charcoal strokes what will become a painting:
      I'm posing, seated
By the tall window and the Ming tree, and look
      out across the Chelsea street
And up to where a handsome muscular man in just
      a towel leans out into
The snow (it isn't always July, you know) to see
      what's going on: my heart
Goes pitta-pat, but you, you won't even down
      your brush and take a peek:
I call that dedication: painting, stirring rice,
      scooting off
To see the great Arletty as Garance: busy, busy:
      happy, happy? Sometimes
I think so, surely hope so: perhaps what I mean
      is happier, happier,

Plunged in work, sorting out your head: "*Bonjour,*
       madame, I am little
Marcel Proust" "I take the subway, then the cross-
       town bus, the small Rembrandt
On the wall," that's rather grand, you know, however
       small, and to the collection
Now is added one by you and that too is pleasing
       and not ungrand: July
Days pass, the brushes slide and pull the paint:
       out your window
Do the roses bloom? I hope so: how I love roses!
       Bunches of roses on
The dining table, Georg Arends, big and silver-
       pink with sharply
Bent-back petals so the petals make a point.
Or Variegata di Bologna, streaked and freaked
       in raspberries and cream,
A few gathered into an amethyst wineglass:
       nothing like it and I
Love them, not over yet early in July, this cold
       July, the grass for once
Is not overmown, burnt off: the mower is set too
       close, it frustrates
Me. Typing in my undershorts, I'm cold; abroad,
       England, France,
Denmark, Germany (oh yes, and Italy), they've had
       a four-week heat wave and
A drought. The pastures for the cows are all
       burnt off, only the grapes
In France are happy, what a bonanza there will
       be, wine, rich and grapy,
No treat, alas, for those who don't imbibe: rich
       as those Poiret robes
And dresses I went to see in the cellar of the
       Fashion Institute:
A brown that isn't purple, gamboge, celadon lined
       with jade, fat fur cuffs,
Turbans stuck with black aigrettes, luxury and
       wit: tell me, you who know,
What is that bird big as a duck that's not a
       duck on the grass with a black

                                               The Morning of the Poem

Bib and dark tan stripes, is it a kind of dove
        or pigeon? What would I gain
By knowing? Like West 20th Street, West 22nd
        Street, a white high rise at
Number 360 where the International Supermarket
        nestles? And the Seminary
Enclosing a court of grass and trees, dark-
        green-smelling cut-out shapes on
The evening we took our stroll there. Nearby,
        the sadomasochistic bars
With men in nails and boots and leather and
        the heavier sort of denim,
Clanking keys, the risky docks: you'd be
        well advised to keep
Away from: a lot of it of course is
        just for show (children playing
Dress-ups) but some of it is more, how you say,
        for real: I saw a man's
Back where someone had played tick-tack-toe
        with a knife. His wife has
Left him. "Have some speed: makes you feel
        real sexy," get away from me you
Poet with no talent, only a gift to destroy:
        when our best poet was invited
To review one of your little offerings I said,
        "Won't it be like
Reviewing your reflection in an oil slick?"
        So many lousy poets
        So few good ones
        What's the problem?
        No innate love of
        Words, no sense of
        How the thing said
        Is in the words, how
        The words are themselves
        The thing said: love,
        Mistake, promise, auto
        Crack-up, color, petal,
        The color in the petal
        Is merely light
        And that's refraction:

A word, that's the poem.
A blackish-red nasturtium.
Roses shed on
A kitchen floor, a
Cool and scented bed
To loll and roll on.
I wish I had a rose
Or butterfly tattoo:
But where? Here on
My arm or my inner
Thigh, small, where
Only the happy few
Might see it? I'll
Never forget that
Moving man, naked to
The waist a prize-
Fight buckle on his
Belt (Panama) and
Flying high on each
Pectoral a bluebird
On tan sky skin. I
Wanted to eat him up:
No such luck. East
28th Street, 1950.
How the roses pass.
I wish I were posing on West 22nd Street, seated
  by a window and the plants,
While your brush makes whorls in your painty
  palette and I watch
The street and kids skim on skateboards: it's
  summer, it's July,
Or else it's winter, December, January, February
  and the kids are gloved and
Bundled up and it's snowball-fighting time: "Gonna
  rub your face in it!" and
Does and one breaks loose and runs crying home.
  In the highest window of
A house across the street a German shepherd rests
  his paws on the sill and
Hangs his head out, gazing down, gazing down,
  gazing down and taking in the scene:

            The Morning of the Poem

These flaming Christmas plants bring to mind
    Joel Poinsett: must read up on
Him: and in September (it isn't winter, it's
    summer, it's July) I'll see your
New crop of work: I'll like that: are you staying
    off the sauce? Remember what
The doctor said: I am: remembering and staying
    off: mostly it's not
So hard (indeed): did you know a side effect of
    Antabuse can be to make
You impotent? Not that I need much help in that
    department these days: funny,
I remember walking under the palms on liberty in
    1943 with a soldier
I had just picked up and in my sailor suit some-
    thing stony as the
Washington Monument I wanted to hide from the
    officer coming toward me: I
Guess I was afraid he'd see it, get the picture
    of what was about to and in fact
Did happen, and send me back to base. Key West!
    the beautiful white houses
With the louvered upstairs, downstairs porches,
    the heavy oaks densely hung
With Spanish moss, the tall blue-blacks with
    hauteur and disdain, beyond
The chain fence, in their eyes and carriage:
    "Stay out of Jungle Town" "You
Bet I will": the barracuda and the angelfish,
    stars like the Koh-i-noor
And a full moon reflecting back the star-encrusted
    sea, a face-
Enveloping moon I want to see again casting
    black velvet shadows of
The palms and broad banana leaves. But that son
    of a bitch, that soldier:
He was trade. I was much too young in those days
    for that jazz and walked
Away and left him to bring himself off any way
    he chose, by fist, I suppose.
Sitting typing in my undershorts on this chilly

soggy morning while the rain
Comes and goes: I'd like to live in T-shirt
      and undershorts,
Bare feet, my Danish silver chain, a gift from
      the one who mattered most,
Gone as last year's roses (Souvenir de la
      Malmaison): that I'll never again
Fall asleep with my head on his chest or shoulder
      that kind of bugs me and
Pictures linger clearly: outside the Hotel Chelsea
      he stood across
The street, in tweed, a snappy dresser, feet
      apart, head turned
In an Irish profile, holding an English attaché
      case, looking for
A cab to Madison Avenue, late, as usual, looking
      right out of a bandbox,
As usual. I won't make a catalogue of all the
      times we were together I
Remember: just one more: slim and muscular you
      come out of the shower,
Wrap a towel around your waist and lean on the
      washbasin with one
Hand, then squirting Noxzema shaving foam to
      smear on your
Sharp-boned face and shave. Wilkinson Injector.
      Green eyes in the
Medicine-chest mirror. You said, "I'm sorry:
      everything just got too
Fucked up. Thank you for the book." That's
      what I get. Was it worth it?
On the whole, I think it was. Toot-toot-
      tootsie, goodbye.
The low and seamless cloud is over us, the
      all there is to it
Morning sky: again: day after day but today
      is breakthrough day, the sun
Burns through then goes away then returns
      more brightly, a breezy coolness
At the window and at my back stirs the
      Peperomia, the grass here and across

The Morning of the Poem

The street (HOUSE FOR SALE) almost glares: a
　　　lawn mower makes its heavy hum
Advancing and retreating in a dance, a reel,
　　　sweet Jesus, it's my nephew
Mike mowing his granny's lawn. "Mike, come in
　　　and have a Coke" "I
Will, Uncle Jim, soon as I'm done," he wears an
　　　Ace bandage on an elbow where
He cracked it canoeing at scout camp last week.
　　　He likes to
Ski, he likes to wrestle, he has a ten-speed
　　　bike, he likes to shoot small
Game in the fields and wood behind their house
　　　on the other side of town
Where you get the best views of the sunsets,
　　　violet laced with orange and
White fritters: kimono colors: oh, I saw those
　　　jays again at dawn
Tearing at something white and the something white
　　　was a white petunia, the jays
Are real workers at their job and the petunia row
　　　is shredded almost
All away: tall and sentinel above what's left
　　　of them a dense row of lilies
Long in bud, soon to bloom with their foxy
　　　adolescent girl smell: repellent
Yet sexy and crotch-calling: Baudelaire, I'd like
　　　to share a pipe with
You (we could both wear gloves, for fear of
　　　the itch) and I would be a nineteenth-
Century dandy dude smelling strongly of vanilla
　　　bean: did you know that
Vanilla is an orchid? And so are you, my cutie,
　　　reeking of poppers
In the parlor car, Southampton bound: you must have
　　　had quite a night of it
At the sauna: tell me what you did: you did? Oh wow.
　　　"Jimmy," you said, "don't tell
Anyone you have syphilis," "Of course I'm going to
　　　tell X, I have no secrets
From him; anyway, I've already told Y and Z, they

didn't take it big and
Laughed when I said they should have blood tests."
      I told
X in a skylit room and he was, to my surprise, cross,
      unsympathetic, in fact
Disgusted: it was all out of his range, the range of
Things that happen to folks you know: "You must
      be more careful
About catching syphilis," "When you had your accident
      I didn't say be
More careful of getting hit by trains," and "If
      I'm to have any sex
At all to do so I must run a risk" (back in the
      Turkish-bath days): no
One stayed mad, I got well, and when I went to my
      doctor for my last
Injection I walked in on his wake. Within a week
      his aide had killed
Himself, his wife had burned to death in her living
      room, all on morphine
And my doctor had cared, had tried to care for
      them all, others too.
In the cool insistent sun of this changed day—
      Scotland has gone away, western
New York is, it seems, back to stay—beneath the north
      window I see out of when I
Look left, large leaves of Solomon's-seal make light
      and shadows on themselves
Moved by air, the air is like the gray-haired striding
      slim-waisted
Man who went through the automatic doors yesterday
      afternoon at the store ahead
Of me: I wanted to tap his shoulder and say, "Excuse
      me, I'm sure that we have
Met: were you in the class of '41?" Instead I grabbed
      a cart, went wheeling
up and down the aisles trying to get a front view of
      him and see how he was
Hung and what his face was like. But when I reached
      my goal he was wearing
(I surmise) Jockey shorts (I curse the inventor of

The Morning of the Poem

Jockey shorts) and his face
Was weathered like someone who plays golf a lot,
     not handsome but a kind of
Face I like: he was smelling and squeezing honeydews
     (I'll be your honeydew,
Your Persian melon) when suddenly he raised
     his head and passed
Me, as on a tray, a plain and questioning
     straightforward hostile look: I
Dropped a green bell pepper (10¢) in the cart and
     went wheeling on:
"What am I forgetting?": when I was young I didn't go
     for guys my age, I sought
Out men his age (fifty-five?) about the age I am
     now, but now men my age are not
Interested in me, they seek out beauties, blue-eyed,
     blond and tanned, or in other
Colorations, the cult of youth, I'd like to kick them
     all: there's no democracy:
"Time to retire" when I saw a broad-beamed lady
     also frown and give me a
Different kind of look: "I know your face . . . aren't
     you . . ." you're
Right, dear, you sat in front of me in senior English
     or was it chemistry
Or French or study hall? I grab a ton of milk and
     head for the express check-
Out lane, first shoving the unwanted bell pepper
     in among some
Dog food. The man had vanished. What a great love
     ours might have been, doing
It on the golf course at 2 a.m. (he was clearly
     married, all the good ones
Are). At the hardware store I bought an onion
     chopper, glass and shrill orange
Plastic, and an old-fashioned mousetrap, up-dated
     with a scented, simulated
Piece of wooden cheese. I hate mousetraps: waking
     in the night to hear
The thrashing crashing struggle on the kitchen
     floor, the hideous trapped
Scream of pain: and I'm the one who will have

to deal with it: drowning? an
Elephant gun? Besides, what's wrong with mice? A
    few mouse turds
Are soon swept up. Now rats, rats are another story.
    This day, I want to
Send it to you, the sound of stirring air, soft
    sunlight, quivering trees
That shake their needles and leaves like fingers
    improvising on a keyboard
Scriabin in his softest mood, and the wind
    rises and it all goes Delius,
The sky pale and freshly washed, the blue flaked
    off here and there and
Showing white, flat and skimpy clouds haunting
    a bright green, a soft blue day.
I'm sorry the full moon is past, still, there
    are shadows on the grass
Fit to lie in; study the leaves or blades and let
    the scurrying
Black ants traverse your arm, your hand: the dog
    next door got in the trash
Again: a black and husky chummy fellow, him I
    can't get mad at. The days
Go by, soon I will go back, back to Chelsea, my
    room that faces south
And the ailanthus tree wound with ivy, my records,
    stacks and stacks of them,
Spohr's Double Quartet, Ida Cox, and sit in your
    parlor on the squishy chairs
On West 22nd Street, the Fauré Second Piano Quartet,
    mirrors and pictures
On the walls: next weekend I hear you're going
    To Sagaponack for a double
Birthday party and half of it is you: 37 meets
    49: many happy returns to
You and You and years and years to come: today
    is a year, a morning, this
Morning was a year, I got up at six? six-thirty?
    on the grass there lay one
Streak of morning light: the days and their different
    lights: when I
Was a child in Washington they took me to the

The Morning of the Poem

theater to see Edward
Everett Horton in *Springtime for Henry* (in which
    that master of the double
Take toured for years: catch him with Helen Broderick
    and Fred and Ginger
And Eric Blore in *Top Hat*) and when the curtain
    went up on the second
Act my breath caught: it was the light: I'd seen
    that light before in Chevy
Chase: an empty living room
    with chintz:
An old theatrical effect: then someone entered:
    left, right, center? Who
Cares? It wasn't the play I liked—too young to
    know what it was
All about—it was the magic of the rising
    of the curtain and the slanting
In of dusty golden autumn light. And earlier,
    before the divorce, at Virginia
Gold's family farm in stony Virginia, I went
    paddling bare-ass in a
Brook with another little boy: when I got back
    my mother raised heck:
"I told you *not* to go in that brook" "I didn't
    go in the brook" (how
Did they always know? I thought I was such an
    accomplished liar: I
Became a pretty good one later) "Then why are
    your B.V.D.s on
Inside out?" Unanswerable questions. The big
    barn had been struck by
Lightning and burned down. The men were rebuilding
    it: Mrs Gold fed the
Chickens and let me help: the pigs were big and
    to be kept away from: they
Were mean: on the back porch was the separator,
    milk and cream, luxurious
Ice cream, the best, the very best, and on the
    front porch stood a spinet
Whose ivory keys had turned pale pink: why? There
    was only one

Book on the parlor table and it was Lindbergh's
        We: how can I know that?
I couldn't read: someone told me no doubt and
        no doubt it was Virginia
Gold, she was a schoolteacher, I'm pretty sure.
        I don't remember much about
Her except her blueberry muffins and later
        she and my mother had
A terrible quarrel on the telephone—the
        harsh and hateful voices made me
Sick—and never met again. Mr Gold drove us
        in a Model T or
Touring car to catch a train and in the Union
        Station my father, Mark, was waiting
For us: heavy, jolly, well-read man, you've
        been gone a long time—
More than thirty years—and time I suppose
        has swept all the Golds
Under the carpet too. But I forgot: one of
        the best days at the farm:
The women put their bonnets on and I went
        with them up a hot dusty road
To fields with rock outcrops (watch out for
        snakes) and gathered poke-
Weed. Fried ham and pokeweed, and, in New
        Brunswick, a side order of
Fiddlehead ferns. Europe bores me: it's too
        late: I mean I'm too late:
I've been there: no, it isn't that: I love
        architecture more than anything,
Bernini and Palladio and Laurana, a certain
        church in Venice, Mauro
Coducci, Buonarroti's windows on the Farnese
        Palace. Architecture?
What about Donatello and della Quercia,
        Canova and Verrocchio, the Pisani?
Music and dancing, acting: the Grand Canal in
        autumn after a week of rain:
The water pours from mountains and turns milky-
        green, the tourists
And the vapid rich leave and you are left with

The Morning of the Poem

infinite riches,
The Istrian stone with the silver-pink cast to
        it of Georg Arends that
After a rainstorm enflames itself: no: that's
        the bricks (Istrian
Stone and bricks contrasted) that become petals
        of roses, blossoming
Stone. Black gondolas glide by, the sure-footed
        gondoliers bending and
Leaning on their poles, wearing green velvet
        slippers. On Diaghilev's
Tomb a French count left his calling
        card: more suitable
Than withering flowers. I left only a glance
        and a thought.
But Europe—split, twisted, shivering-leaved
        olive trees,
Grapevines strung high in swags between
        poplar trees—Europe isn't
Home. The rolling farmland of New York, or better still
        Maine and its coast and
Bays and islands, New Brunswick, Nova Scotia,
        white clapboard
Houses with red geraniums inside sparkling
        windows, eating lobster, greedily,
Vermont with a New Year gift of hellish cold and
        deep, glittering, blinding
Snow: lie face down in it and die: please don't
        die, get up and go inside
Where the logs snap and crackle and smoke and
        give off their
Heart- and flesh-warming smell: the beautiful
        humorous white whippet
No longer lies, legs in the air, on the green
        velvet Victorian couch under
Mrs Appleyard's painting on velvet of an épergne
        full of fruit: can't one,
Just one, mortal person or animal be immortal,
        live
Forever? Not shriveling like Tithonus, not in
        an improbable Cloud-Cuckoo-

Land you'd like to but can't quite believe in:
        ageless, immortal, speedy
Here in Vermont, chasing rabbits, having a wonderful
        roll in the horse shit:
"Yum! Good!" "Whippoorwill! *What* have you done?"
        (His Master's Voice), the
Graceful tail curling down and in between his
        legs: can a tail curl down
Shamefacedly? His could, and he could strew
        a house with trash, leave
An uninviting mess on stairs: "Surprise! Surprise!"
        or the night I came in
And found between me and my bed the contents
        of a three-pound box
Of the choicest candy: a cheval-de-frise of
        chocolates: and,
Most beautiful of all, on a long long lawn running,
        racing as whippets
Are bred to do and leaping straight into
        Kenward's arms, who
Casually closed them: quite an act! (That moment in
Serenade when the dancer soars across the stage,
        turns, legs in extension,
Full in the male dancer's face and he
        clasps her
By the waist. They freeze. Patricia. Nicky.)
        Yes, that whippet is
The one I nominate for terrestrial immortality:
        "They say that when
The moon is dark a thin white dog goes racing up
        and down Apple Hill,
You see the white scuts of deer fly off to hide,
        the skunks
Scuttle under maidenhair, a pond reflects the night
        and—this is the scary part—
Out of the 'transpicuous gloom' a dog
        named Nightingale
Materializes. I wouldn't live there if you
        paid me." Love, love
Is immortal. Whippoorwill, I know that.
How can I know that? God knows, I may be dumb:

may be! Was the grave
Lined with moss, a handful of wildflowers tossed
    in, did marl rattle
On a pine box? Or were the ashes scattered
    where milkweed floss
Carry their seeds like little men?
            I see a man
            naked and handsome
            in the pond. I
            see a horse
            lumber up a hill.
            I see tomatoes
            set to ripen on
            a sill. I see
            a dog, two dogs:
            Whippoorwill, of
            the mysterious
            determined inner life:
            "Let me in, let
            me out, let me wind
            myself in a
            crazy quilt," and
            pretty, trembling,
            hysterical Rossignol
            leaping out of
            the back seat of
            an open car never
            to be seen again.
            Rest, lie at rest
            among these hills
            and mountains
            in autumn flowing
            in maple colors:
            crimson, yellow,
            orange, green
            with white:
            ripeness, a resurrection,
            leaves, leaves, leaves,
            when it's time,
            cover us all.

Another day, another dolor. A shopping list:
    watermelon wedge
    blueberries (2 boxes)
                (In a far recess of summer
                Monks are playing soccer)
    Bread (Arnold sandwich)
    Yogurt (plain)
    Taster's Choice
    Brim
    Milk (2 qts)
    Whipping cream
    Dispoz-A-Lite
    Lee Riders
    Something for Sunday dinner
    Blue Top-Siders (10½)
    Little apples
    Paper napkins?
    Guerlain Impériale
    Steak
    Noxzema medicated shave foam
    Alka-Seltzer
    Baume Bengué
    K-Y
There is not one store in this good-sized village
    that will deliver. Guess
I'll have to call a cab: while I ate my oatmeal
    and read the *Courier Express*
(that fireman who's been doing it with adolescent
    girls got twenty-five years:
"Sodomy in the first degree; sodomy in the second
    degree: sodomy in the third
Degree": what's that all about? and a theater group
    is putting on a show called
Bullets in the Potato Salad) it began heartily
    to rain: not in drops,
In liquid shafts driving into the lawn and earth
    drilling holes, beating up
The impatiens, petunias, lilies (whose cock-like
    buds are turning orange) and
The bluey-purple flowers like larkspur only not
    so nice (there is a bowl

                                  The Morning of the Poem

Of everlasting on my dressing table: I'd like to
            dump it out: I hate the feel
Of their papery stiff petals: why feel it then?
            Can't help myself, feel, feel).
Rain! this morning I liked it more than sun, if I were
            younger I would have
Run out naked in it, my hair full of Prell, chilled
            and loving it, cleansed,
Refreshed, at one with quince and apple trees. As it was
            it was enough to
Sit and eat and watch it, wet weavings of a summer morning,
            and try to stop
My mother from slamming every window and shutting out
            the smell,
The sweet, sweet, sweet smell of morning rain, in
            your nose, on bare skin.
"Don't shut that window: it isn't coming in." "Well,
            it *might* come in and
I'm the one who will have to clean it up." Slam. I
            open it again: "This
Rain will last about thirty seconds (it did), I'm watching
            it and if
It starts to blow in I'll close the window." "See
            you do: and you can
Mop it." I read about Brian Goodell the great
            Olympic teen-
Age swimmer and feel like smashing dishes (never
            forget the morning when
Mother yelled, "Don't you *dare* throw that light bulb
            at me!" I didn't: I
Smashed it on the wall: when you're sound asleep
            and someone yanks the
Covers off . . .). Two people obstinate as mules, who
            love each other: I wonder
Though, do I really love anybody? I think I'll can
            it with this love
Stuff for a while; when a friend made a joke
            about death I
Laughed too and said, "I'm ready to go any
            time." "Why, Jimmy!" she said:
"No, I mean it." I wish it was 1938 or '39 again

and Bernie was sleeping
With me in the tent at the back of the yard
    the time we got up
In the starry night and went downhill,
    down Olean Road, downhill again
And through the pasture where the cows coughed
    and exhaled warm breath,
Barefoot among the cow flops (Dutchman's
    razors) and stands of thistles and
Buttercups the cows won't eat (if you're not
    a farm boy, coming up against
A cow the size of a battleship is not unnerving) (now what
    was the name of that boy, the cowfucker,
Who lived down Olean Road? To each his own), sharp cropped
    dewy grass between toes to where Cazenovia
Creek made a big bend and the warm and muddy water was deep
    enough to swim in. Starlighted silent
Ripples as you stroke: the thick black shapes against the
    black are old big trees: Bernie climbs
Up into one and dives: night air is loudly shattered by a
    splash: the crash when the curtain rises
In *La Traviata* on Act One: Violetta is "having an at home":
    we don't have towels and stand on the clay
Bank to let the air dry us off, grabbing at each other's cock:
    only, it's not that kind of friendship:
Mostly because Bernie was Catholic and worried about confession
    and such: me, in those days I was randy most
All the time. The back doorbell rings: it's the laundry
    lad, he's got my slacks, "a buck twenty-five,"
He's funny-faced, skinny and muscular, red-gold hair, and, sigh,
    wears a broad plain wedding ring. I make
Myself sound like a dirty old man, a hound, always on the sniff:
    the truth is I haven't had sex in over a year
And a half: as Ethel sang: *When the only man in the world*
                 You care about
                 Talks of somebody else
                 And
                 Walks
                 Out . . . (Mr Cole Porter, and I
                     May be misquoting)
Bob, who am I kidding? In some ways you were bright and gifted,

in others, you were one dumb ox. I insist,
Though, you were gifted, much more than, somehow, you could
    let yourself know: spending it in trivial
Ways: no: hiding it under the sod, where you couldn't find
    or use it. Love letters are said to make dull
Reading: I have one from you that's as good as Byron, and on
    it you wrote in your weird hand, "I'm not
Going to read this over because if I do I'll tear it up." I
    keep that letter, but only once have I taken it
Out and read it: ouch: cologne in a shaving cut. Where
    are you? I don't want to know (yes I do)
How are you? (who cares?) did you and your wife divorce (that,
    I am curious about: splitting after twenty-three
Years?) who got the pretty farmhouse in Jersey where the yellow
    Japanese iris I gave you flourish? and why did
You keep saying no to a clump of big white chrysanthemums?
    Splendid against deep grass at the end of August, almost
Unkillable, a perfect perennial for a lazy gardener, which you
    were (so am I), again, old chum, goodbye: I
Did a better job with Donald, I winkled him out of an antique
    shop and back into life and I didn't know I'd
Done it until he told me: they break your heart and then they
    thank you: your heart! They break your
Balls and say, "You really helped me: you know, *I*
    was in *love* with you; I think": the first,
The very first, Paul, the one in high school,
    later said, after that winter of
Silent midnight walks in the deep snow, "I couldn't take it:
    it was too heavy: you put on too much
Pressure: but I kept that letter you wrote me in that empty
    freezing house: it touched me." Every time
He thought he'd got out from under I thought of a new trick:
    a dozen dark red roses for his mother (she,
She was nice), "Paul, I'm very fond of Jimmy: I've invited him
    to dinner to help celebrate my birthday," that
Must have pissed him off: I went though and enjoyed myself:
    with Paul's parents, surprisingly, I was
Never shy, bragging about my Schuyler descent and who Alexander
    Hamilton married (it wasn't me): or the dark
Summer night when Bernie—we were getting old, planning to
    go to Guatemala, we still slept in the tent—and

I crept into their darkened house and up the stairs and into Paul's
      room and woke him up: he was furious but got
Dressed and came out to the Roycroft Inn and got mildly drunk
      on gin and Squirt: I knew it would work:
Paul was nuts about Bernie. All Bernie ever said about him was, "I
      saw your heartthrob the other night
At Kleinhans Music Hall: I knew him by his piggy little eyes."
      Then one day (snap your fingers, tap your toes)
It was over: I passed him on the street and looked at him un-
      sheepishly and said, "Hi, Paul," he was startled into saying
"Hello" for the first time in a year: later, not much later but later,
      comparing notes on our first acquaintance
With queer ("gay," if you prefer) New York, he said, "One night
      I hocked my one good suit so I could go to the
One Two Three Club and hear Roger Stearns play Cole Porter: it's
      cheap if you sit at the bar": "I'm well
Aware: did you get picked up?" "I'm not telling": which meant
      he didn't: he was not good-looking enough to
Make it in that kept-boy crowd (between sets Roger Stearns sat at
      his own table with the most beautiful sailor
I ever saw—on the nights when I went there). We were sitting on
      a sofa, side by side, and Paul reached out and
Put his hand on my crotch and fiddled with my fly (the crust) and
      got the horselaugh of his life. He sure did
Have little piggy eyes. "Let's take a walk to Stinking Pond."
      "O.K.," he said: he was a realist in a
Sickening sort of way. Years afterward he called me at the Museum
      and said, "Let's get together": "I'd love to
But I'm going out of town: a Museum show I'm working on." Finis:
      Paul, with the peculiar cock, short, thick,
Twisted, lumpy, like a piece of rotted rope (give it to the
      oakum pickers), I'll remember you one way,
Sitting in front of me in I wonder which class, with beautiful
      Patricia sitting in front of you and leaning
Back while you slowly combed her hair. You were also Luther
      Smeltzer's pet: that I did not like: it made
Me jealous: Mr Smeltzer, who opened windows for me on
      flowering fields and bays where the water greenly danced,
Knifed into waves by wind: the day he disclosed William Carlos
      Williams to us, writing a short and seemingly
Senseless poem on the blackboard—I've searched the collected

                  The Morning of the Poem

poems and am never sure which it is (Wallace
Stevens, Marianne Moore, Elizabeth Bishop, I found for myself:
    even then, there's a chance that I was somewhat
Smarter than Luther Smeltzer: "Who, where, when, what and
    why": his journalism lessons were not too novel)—
And telling us about a book that based its narrative on Homer,
    "stream of consciousness," Dorothy Richardson,
After class I asked where could I get that book? "Chuckle chuckle:
    when you're in college it will be time enough."
In my quiet way I never have cared much for horse shit so I
    went into Buffalo to Otto Ulbrich's book
Shop, where John Myers, to whom the arts stand indebted, then
    worked as a clerk: "You look interesting:
Here's a copy of my new little magazine, *Upstate*." I bought
    my book and hitchhiked home. Hiding what
It was like from old book burner, my stepfather, was an easy
    trick: "I have to write a book report: it's
A story about poor people in Ireland. Dublin." "Probably
    stinks to high hell it's so filthy. Here,
Let me see that book": he leafed through it, not knowing where
    to look for Molly Bloom, and tossed it at me:
"Still can't catch: go mow the lawn": I mowed the lawn. One
    day in American history class—taught by Miss
Pratt, so old in 1940 she still wore her hair in a pompadour,
    combed up over a rat—I was deep in the clotted
Irish rhetoric (as Frank O'Hara said about Dylan Thomas, "I can't
    stand all that Welsh spit") when a member of the
Football team leaned over: "That's the book that tells it like
    it is: it is hot—how did *you* get hold of it?"
"I guess the same way you did": bright and sassy: but to be
    spoken to by a football player and on equal
Terms! and the shock that anyone would think I was reading it
    as porn! This was art, this was truth, this
Was beauty: it was also laborious and dull, but I plowed on.
    When I first knew John Ashbery he slipped me
One of his trick test questions (we were looking at a window
    full of knitted ribbon dresses): "I don't think
James Joyce is any good: do you?" Think, what did I think! I
    didn't know you were *allowed* not to like James
Joyce. The book I suppose is a masterpiece: freedom of choice
    is better. Thank you, "Little J.A. in a

286

Prospect of Flowers." Last evening Mike mowed the lawn again:
in the silken dawn each leaf and blade and
Needle bore its crystal drop, diamonds cut into pearl-shaped
perfect globes (I never have seen a round
Diamond: why not? I'd like a few to rattle in my pocket: a
change from rattling change), and the silk
Grew worn, and strained and frayed away and sister sun sipped
the droplets up, not all at once, nor one at
A time, a steady vanishing into the air, sweetening, freshening,
endewing the day. The days go by like leaves
That fall in fall, not yet, soon, so soon, I feel my death in
currents of damp air on the back of my neck,
Filtered through a window screen (a casement window screen I
open in the watches of the night, too lazy
To make it to the john, and take a moonlit piss into the taxus),
death, my death, over fifty years and that is
What I am building toward. No cremation, thanks, worm food,
soil enrichment, mulch. Another morning and
I hand you a hammered silver brooch dripping wet, fished from a
stream. Like a curse in a Greek myth, water,
Not rain in drops or streams, in sheets, water solid as that in
a swimming pool, massively falls, bending the
Thick-stemmed orange lilies to the ground, turning overmown
grass back from scorched tan to succulent green,
Curling (I've never noticed this before) maple leaves in on
themselves like cupped hands and disclosing
Coral petioles: that one red leaf burns on in rain. Here is
a story about Fairfield Porter. A long long
Time ago he went to paint in "the fairy woods" beyond the
Double Beaches on Great Spruce Head Island.
He had his portable easel and was wearing, oh, sneakers, shorts,
a shirt, and a straw hat, a farmer's hat. He
Set up shop and got to work: a view of Bear Island (owned by
Buckminster Fuller and his sister Rosie). It
Was a fine hot day so Fairfield took off his clothes to enjoy
what salty breeze there was and went on smearing
Maroger medium on his canvas. From Bear Island put out a
rowboat or a canoe (I can't remember everything), in
It a couple, a man and a woman, rowing or paddling over the
sunny bouncing water to the rocky point beyond where
He was painting. Fairfield thought of dressing, but on second

The Morning of the Poem

thought reflected, "This *is* my island." Now he
Was working the pigments into the medium. The couple beached
    in a coign of the rocks, took ashore their lunch
Hamper, and took off their clothes. They were under forty and
    handsomely built. They ate their lunch, basked
In the sun and Fairfield forgot them as he went on painting.
    After a rest, the stranger got up and left
His mate to wander into "the fairy woods" (so named by Fairfield's
    German governess when he was a child: because
Of the silvery beards of moss that hung from the spruce), picking
    and eating wild raspberries that flourish there.
He looked up and the naked men confronted each other. Nobody
    said "Hello," "Goodbye," "Fine day" or "What's
Your name?" He went back to his woman, they dressed and
    returned to Bear Island over the broken gleaming water
Where seals snort and play. Our painter, in his farmer's hat,
    naked as a snake—to quote William Faulkner—
Finished his painting, dressed and ankled home. A winter or two
    later, in brash New York at a party, Fairfield
Noticed a man across the room who kept frowning at him. The
    frown broke into a smile, the smile broke into a grin.
The man pointed at him: "I know you: *you're the man in the hat!*"
    I wish I could say they went on to become the
Best of friends: they didn't, though I suppose they chatted:
    "How's Buckie? How's Rosie?" The painting?
The painting did not turn out one of the best. I think Kenneth
    Koch has it now. Fairfield's life was full of
Incidents like that, and he always carried them off with aplomb.
    Like the time he was canoeing naked and guess
What got sunburned. I like to think of sunburn on a day like
    today, rain in sheets and thunderclaps and
Lightning bolts: in the house the lights flicker on and off:
    we may go up in a sheet of flame: would the
Rain put it out? Who knows? I wish I were paddling an Old Town
    canoe with red and peeling shoulders, bouncing
Over and cutting through curling and icy water: fluent below
    me the giant seaweed called devil's-apron,
While there in the pebbly shallows off Landing Beach John
    gathers mussels to scour and beard with a wire
Brush and an oyster knife, to steam and serve hot in soup plates,
    rich with the salts of the sea. "Do you often

Experience déjà vu, Jimmy?" Edwin asked me. "Why yes," I said
(old Truthful Thomas). He and George exchanged
A look like a nod, "That proves it," it seemed to say. A lot of
people believe that a proneness to déjà vu, that
Strange and not unwonderful feeling, I have experienced this, this
light, these trees, these birds, heard the very
Words you are saying, before, or, it all clicks into place and
I know what you are about to say: "Please
Stop picking your nose": there, you said it: they see this as
a symptom of schizophrenia. Hence
The look between wise old Edwin (the color of silvery parchment)
and knowing George (whose looks were beginning
To go: it wasn't déjà vu that told me they both were hung like
stallions: only a slight case of experience)
I was feeling upset enough God knows, the sanatorium door stood
agape: but I subscribe to a simpler explanation:
One lobe of the brain registers the event, what in simple reality
is said or happens or is seen, while the other
Lobe takes it in a split second, an infinitesimal split second
later, so, in a sense, there is a real déjà vu,
Half the brain has experienced the experience: "I have been here
before": you have: so know-it-all George and
Edwin can go screw themselves with stalks of glass wheat. Like
my dream this morning, casting a pall over
This part of the day (why did it have to stop raining?): Donald
and Roy exchanged a sharp glance, it meant,
"Jimmy is going over the hill": I left in pique and took the
funicular down the sandstone cliffs: on either
Side businessmen in hats and carrying briefcases were sucking
each other off in cave-like cubicles: on
The sunless beach, the day after a storm with screaming and
wheeling gulls and flotsam and jetsam, boards
Stuck with bent and rusty nails and wound with bladder wrack,
they—the border patrol, the cops, the fuzz—
Stopped me and asked to see my passport: in my mind I could
see it in a desk drawer in an orange room:
In this land you can't forget your passport: I turned and left
them and they let me go: I climbed the gritty
Steps which soon penetrated the cliff, the rear entrance to a
horrible apartment house in the Bronx: to
Go forward could only get worse: I turned and ran back down

to where the tunnel issued from the cliff:
Below me boys were gathering rocks on the beach with which to
    stone me. I woke up, glad to get out of my
Fresh white bed (usually, I would rather sleep than do anything):
    why should a dream like that fill me with gloom,
A kind of moral hangover: "I may want to die, but at least I
    am still alive"? Was it only yesterday I
Awoke to streaming rain from a dream, a vision, like a late painting
    of Fairfield's, one of the ones of a misshapen
Sun burning through mist over a sliding morning sea? There is
    only one sky: a pewter plate, easily bent:
There are two windows: out one grass may be damp but looks dry;
    out the one to the east, enclosed by trees, the
Broad and pointed leaves of Solomon's-seal are thickly set with
    water drops, as easy to gather as colorless wild
Berries in a cleft in a cliff, as beads on a Patou dance frock:
    green barely freaked with blue and glitter:
Japanese lanterns and serpentine, a confetti blizzard, New Year's
    Eve on a ship at sea, Isham Jones, the Coon Sanders
Band: "And now for your pleasure, ladies and gentlemen, Miss
    Irene Bordoni." Or was it Fifi D'Orsay? Last night,
Driving to the Old Orchard Inn, a flash flood. "Why would a
    bank," my brother asked, "be crazy enough to finance a
House on the flat by a creek where the cellar is bound to flood
    whenever it rains?" Why, indeed? Crossing
Cazenovia Creek the smoothly racing water was almost up to the
    bridge, silent, smooth and creased, a tossed-
Out length of coffee-colored satin. Sadistically, I hoped to
    see a drowned Holstein floating by, a ship of
Furry flesh, its udder like a motor. Drowned Holstein eyes; but
    not a Jersey.

        A better morning comes to pass
        Sunlight buttered on the grass
        Late, late, I lie awake
        Finding pleasure for its own sake
        Reading books to pass the time
        Print on paper, algae, slime
        Until before the dawn a gray
        Light breaks, will the day be gay
        Or will thunder-stones roll this way?
        The former, yes, it may turn out,

Though, no, the latter still come about.
    In jinglejangle the day may pass
    Light freshly buttered on the grass.
My mother goes off to the podiatrist: she has an ingrown toe-
    nail, it's turning black and looks infected.
My sister-in-law will drive. It hurt so much yesterday
    morning (Sunday) she almost didn't go to church:
Unheard-of. Every weekend we have the same talk:
    "Jim, wouldn't you like to come to church?"
Sometimes I'm rude and say, "Lay off!" Mostly I manage a polite
    "No thank you." "I wish you would." "If
wishes were horses then beggars could ride. In other words, I'm
    not going to church." "I wouldn't object if you
Want to go to the Catholic church." "If I wanted to go to the
    Catholic church, then I would go. As it happens
I don't." Then why do I carry a rosary with me? Partly because
    a half-mad old woman gave me one (I have two,
As it happens). "You look like a good boy," she said, "here, take
    this": a handful of beads and a dangling crucifix.
I remember the beads slipping through my fingers, decade after
    decade, as the car spun east through Newport, the luxury
Cottages, the cliffs, the sea: what happened to what I thought
    were my resolutions, praying in the Lady Chapel
At St. Patrick's, going to Mass with kindly Father Lynch,
    attending a lecture by Karl Stern, the
Catholic psychiatrist? That was a turn-off: his idea of sin
    was certainly not mine: I have never been
Sure about sin: wrong, yes, but sin and evil, it all gets too
    glib, too easy. Then meeting the head of Fordham,
Like a handsome snake with George Raft hair (only silvery) who
    gave me the fish eye: except for Father Lynch, I can
Live without Jesuits. I can live, it seems, without religion,
    though I have never wanted to. Brush in hand,
You've slipped out of my poem: I have such confidence in your
    future, in what you'll create, with paint and
Canvas, Conté crayon and heavy paper, views, faces, a pier glass
    in a long room, a fence hung with roses out a
Garden window: is the stereo playing, and if so, what? *The Ring*,
    Scriabin, moth-wing strokes of Sviatoslav Richter's
Steady fingers? Here, I have no phonograph: television. My mother
    watches (i.e., dozes off) while I sit and read.

                                                                The Morning of the Poem

The Olympics were fun, marvelous slow-motion underwater shots,
    replays, of swimmers' arms and shoulders
Flexing and pulling and the turn and push off the wall, the
    high divers leaping and spinning to straighten
And smoothly slice the water; the gymnasts, the
    fourteen-year-old girl from Rumania who could do
Anything, anything she pleased, delightful, enchanting, and how
    the crowd went wild when the Russian weight
Lifter broke the Olympic record and then came back to break all
    other existing records: "He's the strongest
Man in the world!" the announcer squealed. "Ladies and
    gentlemen, you've just seen him: the world's strongest
Man!" His voice broke in his excitement. Then horses and hurdles
    and Princess Anne: her horse was too feisty to
Handle: the royal family decorated a box: the Queen, Prince
    Philip, the Prince of Wales, his brothers: a
Close-up shot: my mother came to long enough to ask, "Does the
    Queen have any children?" And dozed off again.
I switch to *Mod Squad*: Adam Greer (played by Tige Andrews) is
    shot by almost invisible poison pellets:
He passes out on the grass: will Peggy Lipton and Clarence
    Williams III find out what the poison is in
Time to obtain an antidote? It seems likely. But what *are* you
    painting, oh you who paint on West 22nd Street?
You're not much of one for writing letters, are you? But then,
    you said you weren't so I can't complain. No
More am I. A bundle of postcards, all of them dull, sits and has
    sat on this desk for days. This afternoon I must
Mail them to you. But it looks like rain! Not again! I wish
    I could send you a bundle of orange lilies
To paint. They stand—and lean—in a row, at the top of a wall
    by the drive. Their anthers are so delicately
Hung that just walking past makes them swing, and if they brush
    your clothes they leave brown stains. Wake up
In the night, after midnight, and open the casement screen and
    study the road gliding downhill, brightly
Lighted by a misshapen half moon, almost white, scooped out of
    lemon ice. How can macadam (or is it called
Asphalt or blacktop?) return this lunar light as a river or
    creek might? On this quiet small-town street,
Whose car coasts quietly up the hill at this late hour? Returning

from a social event? A night worker going home
To bed? Haven't I seen this car at this hour before? About
now Mr Talbot used to drive home from the
Buffalo paper for which he wrote a nature column, hunting and
fishing, the ways of wildlife and what was and
Wasn't burgeoning in fields and swamps. And a little later Joe
Palmer's sedan slid by, also home from a Buffalo
Paper, a different paper, a rewrite man. Other people live in
their houses: I know a lot of dead people: I
Don't think of them much. Standing at the window, staring at the
street, staring at the tree behind which swiftly
Slips the bright twist of a demi-moon, I wish for someone to take
a nocturnal stroll with, like the moonless
Night on Great South Beach when the waves broke and sprayed us
and you put your arm around my shoulders and
I thought, "Why can't we walk on like this forever?" Sandy
sneakers. A car (called the Green Bomb), a drive, home, a
Shower, mussed sheets, bed, sleep as total black at four windows
melted into the false dawn. Sleep into sunshine,
A Crenshaw melon, and you drive away. I'm chilled at this window
here in western New York, studying and losing
What's left of the moon: tomorrow night there'll be a bigger
serving. An August morning, cool and cloudless,
Maple leaves lightly moving, conifers perfectly still, robins
skimming the grass where a fat black dog named
Cornelia just took a dump, a sky not blue but white, up the valley
from Olean a freight train passes (the distant
Sound of breakers), down the valley toward Olean the loudness and
smell of diesel trucks, children's voices: shrill:
Back-yard swimming-pool voices. One train rolling toward Buffalo
right after the other: that's rare: it's
Raining not knowing why. You put down your brush and sit down
and stare at what you've painted. You light a mild
Cigarette, or a thin cigar. Whoever knows what a painter is
thinking? Is it obscure and muggy in Chelsea, or light and
Shivery the way it is here? What shall I do with the rest of
the morning? Shower, shave, write to Barbara,
Go uptown and buy cool milk in waxy cartons? Call my nephew
and go for a walk? Try to remember what I
Forgot? What I can't remember is the name of my New York
doctor: "Murray." But Murray what? I must have it

The Morning of the Poem

Written down someplace, and if I haven't "you" can tell me.
        When you read this poem you will have to decide
Which of the "yous" are "you." I think you will have no trouble,
        as you rise from your chair and take up your
Brush again and scrub in some green, that particular green,
        whose name I can't remember. Thank God the
Sky cleared: I think it's tonight that the moon is full! Round
        and white as opaque ice, hung from a sky hook
Over a city avenue, tonight, riding slowly up a rural sky, a wheel
        of Gourmandise with the foil peeled off, smelling
Sweetly of cherries, the colorless side of a Royal Anne cherry,
        shedding light perhaps, perhaps with a ring on
The blue-serge night: does a ring around the moon portend rain?
        I bet it does, I bet it will, this dank and
Somber summer. The screen through which I peer cubes all into
        sampler stitches: the suppertime shadows laid
Out in topiary work, a dolphin, a spire, a dog, your name, flat
        and roughly clipped, dark on light, dark green
On bright moon green, the world smells of mown grass. I think
        I see a mountain it must be a cloud: there is
No mountain. Let there be a mountain: Why not? Didn't Long
        Island have a hurricane last night? Didn't
I long to be there in the four-poster bed and hear the shutters
        rattle and the windowpanes whistle and sing
And the thunder of the surf, wind in the giant plane tree? And
        to get up in a cleared-off day and go to the beach
And the dunes and see the scattered wrack, fish and weed and
        (always) some cast-up surprise: fishing
Gear, net, an ominous object of red and orange plastic, breakers
        rough, dull and full of sand and the sinus-
Clearing oceanic smell. Dunes carved into new shapes, salt
        air, combing through the cut grass, beach plum,
Unkillable rosa rugosa. Maybe a big beach cottage has had its
        foundation of sand eroded by water and wind:
Toppling, ready to tumble: why so much pleasure in wrack and
        ruin? A house falls into the sea: my heart
Gives a jump. But the paper says the eye of the hurricane and
        the moon-drawn high of the tide did not coincide:
Probably nothing much happened. What a gyp. Or better this way?
        At least I needn't feel guilty for my pleasure
In wrack and ruin. Suppertime shadows sneaking over the lawn,

a buzz saw slicing a tree into portions, cars
Coming up the hill to dinner (they all eat Jell-O), me smoking
     and you painting: no: cleaning your brushes
(Though about that you are not quite so scrupulous as some I
     know): what's for dinner? Shrimp croquettes?
Barbara Guest sent me a card, "Architectural Perspective, Italian,
     late 15th Century," that gave me a pang, that makes
Me long to take you to that loveliest land and we could visit
     Vicenza, walk up the drive to the Villa
Rotunda, the building with the noblest profile in the world,
     see the cut of the flights of steps as you
Slowly perambulate through grass scattered with pecking white
     chickens, go to the hilltop wall and look
Down at the fields below, where peacocks fan their tails. I doubt
     it will happen: still, there's our projected trip
To Washington and the National Gallery, that's to look forward to.
     Paintings are such a pleasure: can I tempt you
With Cleveland and Boston and Baltimore? California, frankly,
     is just too far. Suppertime shadows, my gastric
Juices are beginning to flow. Barbara writes, "I can see you working
     & poking your head outdoors in the evening—or
Taking a late walk—" she may be right. She was right, I poked
     my head out of doors after supper (beef in
Tomato sauce—ick) and there the tiger lilies were, in a row
     above a low wall above the drive in which grew
A few more tiger lilies, reddish orange, petals turning back,
     dark brown pollen, no scent, the strong
Thick stems beaded with round black seeds. Further on, past
     the birdbath, its basin partly filled with
Gunk (childhood memory: "Put down that book and go scrub the
     birdbath"), to the apple and quince trees
Looking so old, so unkempt: I remember planting them, they were
     just seedlings, or do I mean saplings? Now
They stand, unpruned, unbearing, smothered in swags of Concord
     grape leaves lightly, heavily moving like the
Heave of the sea, leaf over leaf, and hung among them cloudy
     green bunches of grapes. I would like to wait
And see them empurple, I would like to wait and taste that
     particular taste, so sweet when they're really ripe: did
They tell you that if you swallow them the seeds will catch in
     your appendix and give you peritonitis? I

The Morning of the Poem

Always swallow them, don't you? Letting the oozy grape meat slide
    down my throat like an oyster: grapes, oysters
And champagne: bliss is such a simple thing. A faded photograph
    shows (it says in pencil on the back), "This is
What the woods are like": white-stemmed trees, smudges (needles),
    rough soft grass. (I made limeade: sticky
Fingers: I drink and type: sticky keys.) Those woods, that
    island and the bay, I won't forget them soon,
Nor that same moon I saw last night hang in glory over this small
    hill I used to see ride, embosomed, in the fullness
Of the sky it lit etching the tall, still spruce and casting its
    light on the rippled water that led off and off
To ocean and to where you cannot see: to go out through the
    dining porch among the daisies and the crags
And moon-bathe. Have you ever swum at night in water so cold it's
    like plunging into a case of knives, your quickly
Moving limbs dripping with moonstones, liquid moonstones? I
    turned my back and this small green world went shadowless:
The nimbus is back at four in the afternoon: no moon tonight.
        Before dawn I woke and made my oatmeal, orange juice and
Coffee and thought how this poem seems mostly about what I've
    lost: the one who mattered most, my best friend, Paul
(Who mattered least), the Island, the California wildflower paper,
    the this, the that, Whippoorwill, buried friends,
And the things I only write between the lines. What can one write
    between the lines? Not one damn thing. Look over
Your shoulder, into the future: one thing I want to see is heavy
    snow falling in Chelsea, to walk in it, snow
Blowing in my face, from where I live to where you live, to stomp
    the snow off in your vestibule, to punch your bell,
To hear the buzzer buzz, to push the door and see the open inside
    door and you smiling there: "Hi-ee: how *are*
You? What will it be? The usual?" A tall cold glass of Vichy.
        Winter in New York, when the big wet flakes
Stream horizontal. (Funny, I haven't beat my meat in days—why's
    that?) I think it may rain again tonight—a
Shower, a smattering—suddenly I feel it in the breeze that
    lifts the paper on which I type. I smell
It, faintly, the fresh faint smell of coming summer rain. I
    used to climb out my first-floor bedroom
Window, naked, into it: the slippery wet bathmat grass, the

rain, both cool and warm, plastering down
My hair, rain running all over me as I danced or stood in it,
    the long persistent tongues of summer rain:
"Want a trip around the world?" "OK" And so it did, the
    licking, bathing summer rain. Another dawn as
Gray as hands that shovel pea coal into an Aga cookstove: under
    it, the walks and road shine slick as though
Greased with Vaseline: in the middle of the night, deep in
    the dark of that time of the morning when it
Seems light will never return and only a weight of black go on
    and on, what a storm we had, the lancing of the
Rain, the thunder cracks and lightning bolts happening as one: I
    thought the house was struck, or at least a
Nearby tree, my bedroom lighting up in flares like the strobe
    light in a discotheque. You bet I didn't go out
In that for any sexy rain bath: no-siree-bob. The air is cool
    but heavy, clammy, robins are garnering earth-
Worms from the lawn: I see one long worm wriggle as it's
    swallowed. Early, so early, it lightly rains again: or is
It drops showering down from leaves on other leaves? So early
    that the morning paper hasn't come yet: Eric
Larsen brings it, he's about thirteen, with yellow Scandinavian
    hair: first his older brother passes, with
Papers for houses further up the hill, then, at, oh, seven or
    so, Eric trudges across the grass to leave the
Courier Express on the brick steps: "Good morning, Eric," "Good
    morning," gruff, but with a shy smile, and I
Sit down to coffee and the news: the Republican Convention, rapes
    and muggings, arson: arson—I don't know why—
Is very big on the Niagara Frontier. A barn burner has been busy
    on these summer nights: the *Courier* keeps
Pointing out he doesn't seem to want to hurt anybody, he just
    wants to see the wood flame and roar up into
The night sky (although one herd of Holsteins were roasted in
    their stalls: perhaps our friend didn't know
That they were there?): I'm glad his meat is not small white
    clapboard houses. A day comes in a month, in a season, and
You wish it were some other month, another season. I never have
    liked August much, I wish it were September,
October, I wish it were the fall. Falling leaves, glittering
    blue skies, in the country, late goldenrod

The Morning of the Poem

And asters, in the city, a crackle to the air, a crackle, and
      at the same time a balminess. The Bluebird
Laundry truck comes and goes (I missed my chat with the freckled
      driver), there are small dandelions scattered
On the lawn: no, yellowed Euonymus leaves blown down by last
      night's storm. With all that sudden force, not
A single lily stalk was bent or broken. They stand in rows in
      metal strength and curve their petals back
And give a point to August. "All he cares about are leaves and
      flowers and weather": and who are you, which
Maple are you I mean, the one who curves its leaves like hands
      disclosing pink palms, growing in clusters on
Branches with silver bark and already bearing five, six, colored
      (a light rich red) leaves? A silver bark?
A swamp maple: isn't that the one whose leaves turn first? I
      think it is, I remember one, deeply blazing
Full in late summer, growing in swampy ground where the waterfall
      tumbled and tinkled down to feed the beaver pond.
The other evening my mother and I were watching TV in the living
      room when something fell, a metal clang on the
Back stoop. I went and put the outside lights on and looked:
      the trash-can lid had been knocked off and
Perched on the can full of trash was the biggest raccoon I've
      ever seen: he turned his head and looked me
In the eye, hopped down and walked sedately off into the shrubs.
      I put the lid back on and dragged the can into
The vestibule. "I wish you had seen him," I told my mother, "he
      was beautiful: he was so *big*!" "Maybe he
Was a dog," she said, deep in her program. I don't know why,
      but that breaks me up, like telling someone
You've seen a rat, and they say, "Maybe it was a fat mouse."
      I'd love to have picked him up and held him,
Only, frankly, I thought he might incline to bite. I would like
      to put food out for him, but how could I know
He was eating it and not the dogs that swarm around this hill?
      The dogs, they get enough to eat at home.
The mail comes, the mailman smiles and goes away in blue, slowly
      and steadily, to the next house behind a screen
Of trees and shrubs (spruce, forsythia). Letters from Kenward,
      Trevor, Anne Porter, Darragh and "Domaine de Ste.
Estève, Lambesc," in other words, Anne Dunn, who writes:

It was nice having the Hazans here but unfortunately I had to leave midway through their visit as my brother was dying and I wanted to be with him. In so far as dying of cancer is bearable his death was, his wife, two daughters and myself never left him, until the last 24 hours the grandchildren and the dogs ran in and out as usual, he was heavily doped but conscious and felt reassured by our being there. I must admit his dying was pretty harrowing, I have never sat holding someone's hand before as they "take off." After the funeral Rodrigo and I went to Lincoln to see the cathedral which was one of Philip's last wishes so we filled in for him, on the way there we went to the Peak District which was beautiful, rolling country flecked with stone walls and dreamy cows, we stayed at Bakewell and ate Bakewell tarts, also visited Chatsworth Gardens which are sensational and put the Himalayas to shame, the scale is so cunningly manipulated, extraordinary growths of giant cow parsley by rushing streams, I wish you had been there. The temperature was in the 90's which you wouldn't have liked much. I fell in love with the Lincolnshire wolds. We came back by the Boston Stump (St. Botolph's) restored by the good people of Boston, Mass, and Ely whose cathedral I really loved, much more so than Lincoln.
How English, the children and the dogs—especially the dogs—
    running in and out of the room where the man—
The son, brother, husband, father, grandfather—lay slowly dying.
    "In the midst of life we are in death, in the
Midst of death we are in life": I know how harrowing it must
    have been for you, but, though I'm not much of
A mystic, I'm sure in that long last handclasp he gave you
    something: not just love, the electric flow of his failing
Power: a gentle charge: and in exchange took with him from your
    physical grip all that you felt for him all those
Years, condensed in a red pulsation. And what a fine memorial, to
    take a pleasant pilgrimage he would have liked to
Take: Lincoln, the Lincolnshire wolds, the Peak District, Ely, the
    gardens at Chatsworth (Paxton, surely?): yes,
I wish I had been with you. Perhaps one day I will. Dear, dear
    Anne. What is "the Isle of Ely"? Is there
Really an island? And when next you come to 185 East 85th, please
    bake me a Bakewell tart: I'm sure there's a
Recipe in that Florence White cookbook I gave you (and I would
    not mind a Grassy Corner pudding). Here,

The Morning of the Poem

Stillness, and a car honks twice, lunchtime stillness: all
      morning we lived in a barbershop, the
Perpetual power mowers shaving away the relentlessly growing
      grass. Peace and quiet, a sullen, sultry sun
Slants under a leaden sky. A fat woman in a loose dress pads
      down the hill: who's she? A big white
Butterfly zigzags by, and a smaller yellow one: distantly,
      a dog barks, nearby, a young child yammers
And squawks (the neighbors have children and grandchildren
      visiting), I subside into the quiet of my
Room, annunciated by the rapid ticking of my cheap alarm clock.
      (The phone bill came: last month I spent
A hundred dollars on long-distance calls: I must be bored here,
      without my friends: I shouldn't do it, but
Calling France is so much fun: "Give me the overseas operator":
      oh to be rich, to do all you want, to visit
Chatsworth and Bathurst, in New Brunswick: oh, you know.)
      August half over, and another dawn that is no dawn, a
Mezzotint of a morning: how I used to pore over Pennell's *Etchers
      and Etching*, plate after plate, weird, smeared,
Sooty, scratched: Rembrandt, Whistler, Goya, Félicien Rops, an
      Irishman whose name I forget, a stream densely
Banked by unmown grass: water, sunlight, succulence, a curve.
      I'd like to collect etchings of the post-Whistler
Period, minor works by minor masters, evocative and fresh. My
      heavy naked calves are etched with hairs, worn
Off on the inner side where my legs rub against my jeans. On
      this miserable Sunday morning ("Jim, are you
Sure you wouldn't like to come to church?") I like to sit in this
      Hitchcock chair and idly pull my foreskin—I'm
Sitting in my undershorts—and drink iced tea and smoke and have
      a passing sexy thought for someone I won't ever
Have—the eyes, the wide slope of the shoulders, the thighs—and
      let tunes play in my head: Carly Simon singing
"Anticipation," Mado Robin singing "Fascination," golden oldies.
      I know someone who when he wakes up in the
Morning likes to just lie there and feel himself all over (maybe
      he's afraid he vanished in the night: I rather
Wish he would): I like to lie in bed at night and read and feel
      myself, shoulders, armpits, chest, belly, crotch,
And maybe tweak a hair. Once I found a kind of a swarm of moles

on my rib cage—only I don't think they were
Moles: I don't know what they were, not scabies, not a rash: little
    lumps, growths, a colony. I put rubbing alcohol on
Them and in a few days they were gone. I don't like any funny
    business, stuff like that. Herpes simplex! That's a drag:
Eye salve is good for it, I found that out from a doc in Zurich
        where I stayed in a snow-white hotel beside the green glassy
And rushing river on which swans pointed upstream toward the
        bridge on whose balustrade I was drunkenly leaning one
January night when some men came by and spoke to me in
        German: "Surely you speak English?" I said: they thought
I was a gas. We went somewhere to drink and soon I was in bed
        with a supple, gray-haired man, playing snakes, flailing
About and knocking the bedside lamp on the floor. He ran one of
        the big hotels and used to send me packets of
Marrons glacés sprinkled with candied violets: the desk clerk
        gave me funny looks when he handed me
My daily tribute. How I gobbled them up! I wonder what my
        chum's name was? Once, when we were dining, the
String quartet played "Wien, Wien," and he leaned across the table
        and took my hand and said, "This will be our team
Song": it took a while to figure out what he meant. And once he
        said, "Come": we stepped into his bathroom,
He picked a razor up and shaved my sideburns off. What crust. I
        didn't really mind though: I'd only grown them
Because what else do you do on a nine-day crossing? What I did
        mind was that it emerged he was a major bore, so
I packed my duds and took an express train to Geneva, which I
        only went to because I wanted to stay at a hotel where
Henry James had stayed: it had fallen on sorry days and my view of
        Lake Leman was one of banks of fog. I walked past
Calvin's house on moist cobbles, bought a volume of Gide's diary,
        saw George Raft in *Scarface*, and took the train
To Italy, passing the inspiration of Byron's "The Prisoner of
        Chillon." Switzerland, so long. July is gone,
A hunk of August, a few blank days got lost (I couldn't stop
        sleeping), the sun came cloudlessly back, hot yesterday,
Hotter today, hotter still tomorrow the TV set predicts: shower
        baths help: I'm well bedewed this minute, my
Hair slicked down, and icy orange juice and iced tea with lemon—
        both are on my desk—no wonder my time is spent

The Morning of the Poem

Hanging out over the toilet, splashing away like a mountain
        rill. Late in the afternoon and suddenly a cool
Breeze springs up and streams in the window: the leaves shudder:
        how sweet, when something you really enjoy
Unexpectedly arrives, like the postcard I got this morning from
        Ned Rorem, with flattering words about some
Poems, how kind, how nice, but I'm glad I'm not with him on
        Nantucket, where I got one of the worst sunburns of my life—
I wonder what it's like, being a composer? Writing goes by so fast:
        a couple of hours of concentration, then you're
Spent: but music takes so much time: the sounds come into your
        head, but then, the writing them down, the little
Notes. I can see Nantucket now, sand and whipping grass under a
        glare of sun. There are not many islands I really
Like, the ones where the rocks are slithery under the
        thick seaweed when the tide is out, where the
Heart of the island beneath tall trees is all overgrown with ferns
        and moss begemmed with fog and is silent, spongy
To walk on: on other days, a scented springy mattress to stretch
        out on. Little boats emerge from behind other
Islands: utter peace and total privacy. Still, Nantucket has its
        points, but I prefer to go north and further north:
Maine, New Brunswick, Nova Scotia. Oh, what's to make such a
        fuss about? I like all sorts of places. I can't
Believe it, I have to go piss again: it's like that night in
        Paris when I first got bombed on Pernod: I
Was making my way along the boulevard back to the hotel when
        my bladder flashed the message that I had to go and
I had to go *now*, not in two minutes: up ahead, in the same block,
        I could see a pissoir (I mean, a *vespasienne*)
But that just wasn't close enough, nor could I run. I plunged my
        left hand in my pocket, and got a good grip, like
Stopping the flow in a hose, and walked stiff-legged along: the
        pressure, the pain, was something else: "My
Brow was wet": I made it: there I was, confronting a urinal: I
        inched down my zipper and put my right hand into
The opening: hideous trauma, there was just no way I could
        transfer my swollen tool from hand to hand without a great
Gushing forth (inside my pants), like when Moses hit the rock: so
        I did it: there was piss all over Paris, not
To mention my shirt and pants, light sun tans: why couldn't it

have been the depths of winter, and me in heavy
Dark overcoat? I was so mad I stomped on my way, thinking, "Well
    if somebody wants to make something out of it . . ."
(Young and dumb, it never occurred to me that if I'd spilled a
    drink in a café, I'd have looked the same.)
But Pernod, Pernod is murder. I wish I had some now, but tea
    and orange juice will have to do:
Tomorrow: New York: in blue, in green, in white, East Aurora
    goodbye.

The Morning of the Poem

A

FEW DAYS

(1 9 8 5)

FOR TOM CAREY

The Snowdrop

The sheath pierces the turf
and the flower unfurls: drooping,
pendent, white, three-petalled,
the corolla with a frill
of green: the virgin of the spring!
In earliest spring! (Reginald
Farrer hated snowdrops: in his
Yorkshire rock garden the rain
beat them down into the mud
and they got all dirty. Why not
pick a few, wash them off and
make a nosegay in a wineglass,
Reginald?) And when the flower
fades and dies, the stem
measures its length along the sod,
the seed pod swelling like
a pale green testicle.

The Rose of Marion

for Harold Talbott

is pink and many-petalled:
it rests on the rim
of a shot glass on the desk
in my room in this
eighteenth-century house in,
of course, Marion, Cape Cod,
Massachusetts (for
further details, see Thoreau
or *The Outermost House* by
whats-his-face).

The window is filled
with leaves! So different
from my urban view
in stony-hearted New York.

I love leaves, so green,
so still, then
all ashimmer. Would
I like to live here? I
don't know: it's
far from friends
(for me) and others
I depend on. But
it's awfully nice to visit,
a whaling port
like Sag Harbor, Long Island.

Pink rose of Marion, I
wish I knew your name.
Perhaps one day I will.

Gray Day

"There is a cloud,"
Fairfield used to say,
"that stretches from
Richmond to Bangor:
its center is Southampton."
Today,
gray day,
its center is
Bridgehampton,
a nimbus over the pond
you made,
where a willow
jerks its leaves
and the oxeye daisies
stand in unserried ranks.
Helena is on a bench
by the pond, writing
a poem, I bet.
I opt
for the living room and

the squishy chairs
and Rachmaninoff
played by Richter
(who else?) and
here comes Oriane
with her ragged ruff:
"Oriane, there are hairs
all over my blazer:
would you care
to discuss it?" She
would not and stalks
haughtily out of the room,
leaving me with the music
and a window
full of leaves.

This notebook

is small and stamped,
MADE IN ITALY.
It's bound in
Florentine art paper:
a design in blue and brown
of Maltese crosses
and what looks like
bladder wrack. How it takes
me back! To our
pensione on Piazza Frescobaldi,
Ponte Santa Trinità
(replaced, in postwar '40s,
by a Bailey bridge),
the Via Tornabuoni, and
Doney's and Leland's, in
one of which
Ronald Firbank
dangled grapes—before
my time. When
I walked in Florence I

used to see it not
as the Medici's stamping ground,
but through the eyes
of one of Henry James's
heroes or heroines:
Isabel Archer, perhaps.
To walk up to
Bellosguardo, to look
and wonder and remember
what I never knew!
Little notebook, I
love you, and the friend
who gave me you.

Lilacs

for Helena Hughes

Helena brought me
hang their heads
heavy with fragrance
—what other
is like it? roses?
lilies of the valley?
freesias? (not tube-
roses: they're
too much)—and
prove that fat
can be beautiful:
not on me, on them.
Each truss of seemingly
myriad, four-petalled
flowerets of that color
(lilac) Persia dreamed up:
would they could last
forever, were of porcelain
or silk: silk lilacs?
I
think not. I love them as
they are, seeming so

permanent, yet even more transient than we!
Now I think I'll have
a sniff of lilac,
then eat a wedge
of rhubarb pie:
rhubarb and lilacs:
could life hold more?
Perhaps:
there is, for instance,
Helena.

Thursday

A summer dawn breaks over the city.
Breaks? No, it's more as though the night
—the "dark," we call it—drained
away into the sewers and left transpicuity.
You can see: buildings, dogs, people,
cement, etc. The summer city, where,
I suppose, someone is happy. Someone.

The other bright evening cabbing
down Fifth Avenue past the park I
saw all the leaves on all the trees
and counted them: not one by one, in
bunches. I forget precisely how many
there were: quite a few. Oh yes, more
than you could count. Not me, though.
I counted them, bunch by bunch.

As I said above, it's summer: not
my favorite season. I prefer the spring,
when the leaves bud and unfurl, or
autumn, when the leaves
color and fall. Or winter, when
the leaf-bearers stand naked,
flexing their biceps like bodybuilders
exhibiting their charms.

311

Then there is a fifth season,
called—but that's my secret.
Yes, my secret, and I'm going
to keep it that way. Yes, my secret.

Cornflowers

After the stormy night:
the crack of lightning and
the thunder peals (one bolt
fell in my street!)
the cornflowers (or are they
bachelor's buttons?) stand,
ragged scraps of sky, in
a shrimp-cocktail glass on
thin green stems with thin
green leaves, so blue, so blue
azure as sky-blue eyes
the cornflowers (I wish
I were wading through a
field where they bloom)
tattered tales of my life.

Velvet Roses

Katie is making
velvet roses: next
to a green pair, she
fastens a bunch of
wooden spoons. How
striking they will
look, on the bodice
of her dance frock!

And Anne is cooking,
and Lizzie is there . . .

Sleeping again,
dreaming again.

August first, 1974

was yesterday. I went out in the yard
in back today. I didn't stay: too hot
for comfort even under the apple trees
hung—smothered, in fact—by Concord
grape vines, unpruned, run rampant. But
then, my stepfather, the gardener, is
dead. The garden that he took such pride
in isn't much really anymore. I don't
mind it this way. It's dry (rain predicted)
and from this desk it used to be—say,
more than thirty years ago—you could look
right down the valley that leads to Olean.
Now, in August, the leaves of young trees
across the street hide all that view of
uncultivated fields, where sometimes
a horse would unexpectedly appear: Jim
Westland's. Jim's dead too, and Katharine,
his wife. So kind to me when I was
in my teens. A hot breath of wind stirs
a white voile curtain: or are they
organdy or net? It couldn't matter less.
Below the window a taxus hedge: Japanese
yew, so popular for foundation plantings
in suburbs and small towns. *Qualunque:*
commonplace. I like a house to rise up
naked from the ground it stands on. Oh,
honestly, I don't much care one way or the
other. And what's that small purple
flowered weed or wildflower that grows
in grass, making something like a herb

A Few Days

lawn? Typing this makes me sweat. No
more today. You see, I'm waiting.

Sleep-Gummed Eyes

for Geoff Young

With sleep-crowned eyes I
see the morning sunlight
lie, a pinky-yellow rose
petal, on the building
across the street: the radio
plays and says the day
is cloudy, overcast! How
can it be so different
between Twenty-third Street
and wherever in the Fifties
the broadcast originates? On
the building across the
street there is a stone or
concrete escutcheon: an
oeuf à la Russe or an *oeuf
en gelée,* a white egg in
pinky-topaz jelly. A funny
conceit for a downtown
loft building. I rub my
eyes and roll the gunk
between my finger-ends: it's
February first, 1982,
and they say (on the radio)
torrents of rain will
descend and the temperature
drop to well below
freezing. So be it.

Overcast, Hot

It's a hot day:
not so hot
as the days before:
it's *that* July,
the one in 1981,
the hot one. Alice
said, "I lay in bed
all night with
my face sweating."
I lay in bed
all night with
my ass sweating.
Darling Helena sends
a card from England
where it's overcast
and cool. Lucky
England! And
Prince Charles is
about to marry
Lady Di! "Will you
get up at four-thirty to
watch the wedding
on the tube?" Elinor
asks. Not
bloody likely; though
if I'm still awake,
which is bloody likely,
I guess I'll watch
it. I remember how
lovely Julianna
Slosson looked coming
down the aisle. All
in white and lace!
But that was plenty
some years ago. And
it sure is hot, muggy
July.

At Darragh's I

lie in bed and watch the night
rise slowly, implacably, out of
evening, darkening
the lance-shaped leaves of that
nut tree whose name I never
can remember: only, those leaves
are too wide to be called
lanceolate: why, they're oval!
(A childhood memory, the
cookies that were called "fruited
ovals," molasses with a
white icing, that came from the
grocer, not made at home, and
oval
oval
oval.) When a firefly dances
into my view (a black window):
another childhood memory:
in Maryland we used to catch
them and put them in jars
and watch their silent, sexy
signal. We also used to tear
their phosphor off: children
can be real fun people!

Or I sit on the porch as
a light rain slants down
onto the pond Darragh made,
the wind riffling the water
and the rain making rain rings
on it. Oriane, the lurcher,
wants in, wants out, full
of the *va et vient* of life
(speaking of French, did
you know that in Paris bi-
sexuality is known as
voile et vapeur? I
like that).

Then we all pile into
the Toyota and drive off
into the
World of Roses.

White

I came back from Cape Cod
last night (Cape Cod? So
far away, so long ago) and
found "they" had, as I
asked them to, painted my
hall and bathroom fresh
stark white! White as snow,
white as an icebox:
too white: I wish I had
asked for a light pink, or
pale blue with white trim
or lemon yellow. Or perhaps
had it papered in some
design or other. Oh well,
there's nothing really
wrong with white. And the
dum-dums shut the French
windows, which I had care-
fully left open, so the
place really stank, reeked
of paint: not nice oil
paint and turpentine, but
latex, rubber-base paint,
like old tires burning. It's
airing out. Only now, by
contrast, the big room,
the room where I live and
read and eat and write and
listen to music and watch
the tube and dish with Helena
and Tom, looks distinctly

A Few Days

shabby: it will have to be
painted too. Perhaps also
white, but with a French blue
ceiling. Now, I think I'll go
and take a dump
in my snowdrop-colored bathroom.

Dear Joe

for Joe Brainard

I can easily believe that I
am fifty-eight, but that you
are forty fills me with won-
der! I remember
how young you seemed (and were)
the first time I met you,
when Kenward invited a few
of the younger poets
(Ted, Tony) to meet me and
you came too. You didn't say
much (you said nothing) but
looked at books in that little
house in Cornelia Street, not
aware of what would come to pass
for you there: why, you came
to live there! And you came
to visit me at 49 South Main
in Southampton, wearing worn-
out shoes. I gave you a hand-
me-down pair of—sneakers?
moccasins? I
forget. My room here in the
Chelsea is bright with art
works by you (a "fake Fairfield
Porter" I especially
love), and though I don't
see you often I think about
you a lot:
for your birthday I would like

318

to send you a bunch of lilies
of the valley, which mean,
in the language of flowers,
"I love you since long."

Amy Lowell Thoughts

What are you, banded one?
H.D.

The sea opened its lips
blue with cold
and coughed up
a cabin cruiser

Covertly, in the mist,
the sun
is fingering some spruce

Draped one,
speak.
Are you a larch?

Just at the surface
toothed rocks
spit foamy mouthwash

The Five Sister birch clump
chopped down.
Thoughts
of Charlotte Mew.

Over the sea
she strolls
in fog shoes

319

The morning

breaks in splendor on
the window glass of
the French doors to
the shallow balcony
of my room with a
cast-iron balustrade
in a design of flowers,
mechanical and coarse
and painted black:
sunbursts of a coolish
morning in July. I
almost accept the fact
that I am not in
the country, where I
long to be, but in
this place of glass
and stone—and metal,
let's not forget
metal—where traffic sounds and the day
is well begun. So
be it, morning.

October 5, 1981

"A chance of a few morning sprinkles . . ."
says the weather on the air. It's
October, my favorite month, and where
is "October's bright blue weather"?
Day after day of it, gray after gray:
this isn't the October I know
and love, leaves turning, that
scintillating sky . . .

Moon

Last night there was
a lunar eclipse: the
shadow of the earth
passed over the moon.
I was too laze-a-bed
to get up and go out
and watch it. Besides,
a lunar eclipse doesn't
amount to much unless
it's over water or
over an apple orchard,
or perhaps a field,
a field of wheat or
just a field, the kind
where wildflowers
ramp. Still, I'm sorry
now I didn't go out
to see it (the lunar
eclipse) last night,
when I lay abed instead
and watched *The
Jeffersons*, a very
funny show, I think.
And now the sun shines
down in silent brightness,
on me and my possessions,
which I have named,
New York.

Virginia Woolf

I wish I had been at Rodmell
to parlay with Virginia Woolf
when she was about to take
that fatal walk: "I know you're

A Few Days

sick, but you'll be well
again: trust me: I've been there."
Would I have offered to take
her place, for me to die and
she to live? I think not. Each
has his "fiery particle"
to fan into flame for his own
sake. So, no. But still I
wish I'd been there, before she
filled her pockets with stones
and lay down in the River Ouse.
Angular Virginia Woolf, for whom
words came streaming
like clouded yellows over the downs.

Oriane

My name is Oriane,
the lurcher:
half whippet, half border collie,
bred to course
for hares and rabbits
(there are no hares,
only rabbits):
and so I do,
and chase my rubber ball
and play in waves,
and cuddle
in arms that love me.
This is my home:
its name is
          Oriane

Beaded Balustrade

The balustrade along my balcony
is wrought iron in shapes of
flowers: chrysanthemums, perhaps,
whorly blooms and leaves and
along the top a row of what look
like croquet hoops topped by a
rod, and from the hoops depend
water drops, crystal, quivering.
Why, it must be raining, in Chelsea,
NYC! How I wish I could look out
and see rain-washed grass, and is
it not forsythia time? There, where
I dream of, the elms are gone (Dutch
elm blight), but the giant plane
tree, last to leaf out, last to
shed (but that's not until almost
winter, half a year away, or
so) and the shrub roses, waiting
to do their stuff! Oh well, if
I haven't got that, at least I've
got a beaded balustrade . . .

People who see bubbles rise

for Darragh Park

may be swimming, not drowning,
or merely diving, rising.
Or watching goldfish in a tank.
Or, "That's a vodka and soda?"
"Yes, please."

I'm on a train (Bridgehampton–New York)
Darragh is with me, reading Proust
—in French, of course: India paper,
a brown leather binding, brown
as the October leaves we pass:

scrub oak, I guess. No, they
still are green. Leathery, but green.

This noon, or early afternoon, I
walked down through still-unharvested potatoes
(one chicory was in blue, blue bloom)
to Sag Pond—Sagaponack Pond, I mean.
Across it winter rye made its
incredible green haze, so soft, so clear,
and trees around a yellow house,
trees I didn't recognize, were
a deep wine red. To their right, maples
did their flamboyant thing.

The dogs, the chat, the dinners,
the insomnia and the sleep:
the lousy book about V. Sackville-West:
for me, a rather mixed-up weekend.
And yet I loved it. I always
love the garden and the house Bob made
and the way the early light comes
in the guest-room windows
through violet curtains. To lie there,
watching it, like someone diving,
who, open-eyed, sees bubbles rise.

Autumn Leaves

Mountains and mountains and mountains
rolling, rolling, rolling:
all overgrown with trees, trees, trees,
turning, turning, turning:
but in the field where we are
strolling, strolling, strolling,
the leaves on trees
are green, green, green.
"Soon," I say, "these leaves,
the ginkgo, the willow and the beech,

will all be
turning, turning, turning.
That smouldering red off there
is swamp maple."

Then we come to a fence
where one who has given
his life to poetry leans.
Next to him a sign proclaims,
ETERNAL HAPPINESS. Am I
dreaming about Frank again?
Frank among the leaves
all turning, turning, turning.

En Route to Southampton

In a corner of a parlor-car
window, a thin crescent is
the moon. Below,
the sky on the horizon
is oily bilge.
The leafless trees go by,
the ugly houses,
the parlor car
is much too hot.
The whistle blows
its warning:
such very ugly houses.
But in that corner
of the window,
the ice-white,
eternal promise
of a new moon.

Tomorrow

for Helena Hughes

is Helena's birthday:
she isn't getting any
younger, but not even
the meanest guy in town
(we all know who *he* is)
could call her old. She
likes to think I'm still
fifty-six, because that
makes her feel that much
younger. Well, I've news
for her: I'm not, not
that I'm all that old!

It must seem a long way
from Bristol, England
(daughter of Irish parents:
the girl with two passports)
trundling, a little
Catholic, in the shadow
of the walls of Clifton
College, where Thoby Stephen,
Virginia Woolf's brother,
went to school, to New York
and the Buddhist Center,
where she does right by
the lamas and . . . and . . .
I love her very much and
wish her all the happy re-
turns she may want, the
bodhisattva of tomorrow.

November

for Helena Hughes

is a nice month to be
born, don't you agree,

Helena dear? We both
were, five days apart:
five days and twenty-
eight years. When I'm
pushing daisies you'll
still be spry as a
chicken. But let's not
dwell on that. A couple
of sexy Scorpios (very
heavy sex sign, you
know), hung with topazes:
golden and glittering,
smoky topazes. November,
the month when the leaves
in the parks finally
come unstuck and tumble
down, bump, bang, the
stately paulownia, the
rugged sycamore: last
to leaf out, last to
fall! Soon, soon. But
no snow: which is all
right with you, though
not with me. A nice
month, though not much
to say about it. So,
as Tom calls you, "the
Divine Miss H.," many
happy returns on your
birthday, many and
many and many . . .

Fauré's Second Piano Quartet

On a day like this the rain comes
down in fat and random drops among
the ailanthus leaves—"the tree
of Heaven"—the leaves that on moon-

lit nights shimmer black and blade-
shaped at this third-floor window.
And there are bunches of small green
knobs, buds, crowded together. The
rapid music fills in the spaces of
the leaves. And the piano comes in,
like an extra heartbeat, dangerous
and lovely. Slower now, less like
the leaves, more like the rain which
almost isn't rain, more like thawed-
out hail. All this beauty in the
mess of this small apartment on
West Twentieth in Chelsea, New York.
Slowly the notes pour out, slowly,
more slowly still, fat rain falls.

A Belated Birthday Poem

for Robert Dash

You are walking in the grounds
on the second day of summer
taking snapshots, the seeds
of future paintings, under
a June sun already hot
on this Sunday morning.
A red-winged blackbird sits
on the finest top (the
growing point) of a ginkgo
or maidenhair tree.
You got up at seven and went
right to work: how I envy
you your creative energy!
Painting, painting: landscapes
of Sagaponack.
You make houses out of
sheds. You cook, you
garden: how you garden!
One of the best I've ever seen.
"It's a sort of English cottage garden."

"It's a seaside garden," D. V.
flatly stated. Those dummies
what do they know? The big
thrill these past few days
is the opening of the evening primroses
—*Oenothera missourensis*, perhaps?
I love them, their lacquered
yellow petals and a touch
of orangey red. You mowed
the small field (I'd heard)
and I was worried. I like it
when the wind-bent grasses
rush right up to a house.
But you were right: how
the mowed grass (you
almost might call it a lawn)
sets off the giant shrubs
of dog roses, drenched in white
so you hardly see the green
that sets them off. Last evening
the young honey locust gleamed
against a sunset of fire
and green, blue-green. I
can't describe the color
of that tree. Imagine—
no, I can't do it. The roof
of your grand *couloir*
sprang some heavy leaks
in the last cloudburst.
It's going to cost a mint
to fix it: tar and pebbles.
It will cost a mint and
where will the moola
come from? Don't worry,
it always comes, to you
at least (somehow, we get
through). I sit at the dining table
staring out at a dark pink weigela—
it's going over. For your
birthday I gave you five
of the rose Cornelia. They're

pretty shrimpy but will
grow to great shrubs, the canes
bending, studded with
many-petalled blooms: how
I wish I had the dough
to shower you with shrub
roses! But I haven't. I
sit and stare at a blue sky
lightly dashed with morning
clouds and think about
these paintings, this house,
this garden, all as beautiful
as your solitary inner life.
Your moon last night was gibbous.

Poem

I got my hair cut
    and it rains
I'm waiting for the papers
    and it rains
I'm waiting for pretty Helena
    and it rains.

Red Brick and Brown Stone

for Darragh Park

He arises. Oriane
the lurcher wants
her walk. Out into
the freeze. Oriane
pees and shits. The
shit is scooped up
in a doggy bag, ac-
cording to law ($100
fine) and is disposed

of somewhere.
The sun peers down
and sees them. Ov-
altine, a fag, WNCN:
unspeakable Telemann.
The dinner table is
mahogany and silver
gleams. A carriage
clock chimes eight,
sweetly. The front
room north-facing
studio, its two long
windows divided by
a pier glass. Canvas,
eight by six, cars
charge down Ninth
Avenue straight at
you. Parked, a yellow
cab. A bending tree.
London Terrace, an
eighteenth-century
house now a shop,
work in progress.
Brush in pigment:
scrub stroke scour.
Hours pass. Hunger
strikes: Empire Diner
silver metal art deco.
A porkburger, salad,
tea (iced). Home. Oriane
wants out. So they do
as before. Oriane goes
home. Off by cab to
Florentine palazzo
Racquet Club: naked,
the pool, plunge, how
many laps? Home. (Through-
out the day, numerous
cigarettes. I forget
which brand. Tareytons.)
A pencil drawing of

a vase of parrot tulips.
Records: Richter:
Scriabin: Tosca: "Mario!
Mario! Mario!" "I
lived for art, I
lived for love." Sup-
per: a can of baked
beans, a cup of raspberry
yoghurt. Perrier. Out?
A flick? An A.A.
meeting? Walk Oriane.
Nine p.m. Bed. A
book, V. Woolf's let-
ters. Lights out, sleep
not quite right away.
No Valium. The night
passes in black chiffon.

Tom

They told me, Heraclitus,
they told me you were dead.

A key. The door. Open
shut. "Hi, Jim." "Hi,
Tom." "How didja sleep?"
"I didn't. And you?" "A
log." Blond glory, streaked,
finger-combed, curling
in kiss curls at the nape.
A kiss, like bumping fore-
heads. A god, archaic Greek
Apollo in a blue down
jacket. Fifteen degrees
no snow. Tom hates that;
me too. "French toast?"
"Of course." With apple-
sauce. The *Times*, the
obits, a great blues singer
has been taken from us

and a businessman. OJ,
coffee with milk, lecithin
to control mouth movements,
a side effect of Thorazine.
At the stove Tom sings the
release of his rock song,
"Manhattan Movie." His voice
is rich, true, his diction
perfect. I'm so in love
I want to die and take
my happiness to heaven!
No. To be with Tom, my
assistant, three hours
a day four days a week.
(Tom likes "assistant"
I
prefer "secretary."
No sweat: "Ain't no
flies on the lamb
of God." Ahem. Phlegm.)
Tom's eyes are "twin
compendious blue oceans in
which white sails and
gulls wildly fly." We'll
never make it. Tom's
twenty-eight, I'm fifty-
six: he isn't Proust's
"young man born to love
elderly men." He loves E.
an eighteen-year-old
poet, whose mother feels
concern at Tom's two-
year pursuit (they only
lately made it). I'm
going to tell her how
lucky her son is, if he
is to have a homosexual
episode (or be one, as
I think he is, pretty
boy), to have a lover so
kind, so loving, so

witty—that thrash-about
laugh—I've said it
and I will. At Number
One Fifth Avenue I tell
E., "You should un-
reservedly make love
to Tom and be cosy and
tender." "I'm sorry, I
don't feel that way
about him." Later
he tells Tom,
"We had a man-
to-man talk." Sad.
I only care about Tom's
happiness. "He's not
very sexually oriented.
Here." The French toast
and applesauce are
delicious. We settle down
to read: he, a Ross
Macdonald, me *Phineas*
Redux. How superb is
Mme. Goesler when she
repudiates the Duke of
Omnium's bequest of priceless
pearls and diamonds and
a fortune (she already
has one) so they will
go to Lady Glencora, the
rightful heir, and no one
can ever say her three years'
tenderness to the dying
man was motivated. In
Tom's book a corpse is
found in corrupt upper-
middle-class L.A., where
he comes from. Beauty.
We might some
day shower
together, wash
each other's back.
Travelling share a bed.

Flesh on flesh,
a head pillowed
on an arm. Touch.
Running from a cab to
the deli, the energy
(graceful) of youth.
Thomas Paul Carey of
Sherman Oaks, California,
who writes and sings
his own rock songs, the
son and grandson of two
great movie actors, the
two Harry Careys. Love
is only and always beautiful.

Tom's Attempt to Seduce Big Brother Steve

"I went
 into
 his

   room!!!!!
 in
 my
 u
 n
 d
 e
 r
 w
 e
 a
 r

 and & and
 said,
         "Let's
          wrestle!"

A Few Days

Sleep

with its burden of dreams:
a smart boutique, small,
with a funny counter, where?—
the cliffs of Rome, the seas
of Venice? Italy, anyway. Scraps
of colorful vinyl properly
put on compose an intriguing
rain garment. Chic. And
a costly tweed suit! Who
needs a costly tweed suit?
I can't say I need one, but
I sure would like one. Sleep,
with its burden of dreams.
He was much as usual, my
dearest friend, but why
was he wearing a beautiful
Fortuny evening gown? "Perhaps,"
my therapist said, "he was
not only a good father
to you, but a good mother
as well." What an insight!
(An orgy on the lawn: the
neighbors are so shocked
they won't speak to me.)
Then there was the night
I dreamed I was fucking
you. "Jim," you said, "tell
me you love me." "Tom," I
said, "I love you." Then
I woke up and shed
tears: it was only a dream
and you weren't and never
would be there. That's all
over now, though I still and
always will like to dwell
on your thighs. "Tom," your
Dad said, "you've got
good legs." Why, I

believe you're vain
of them! But that's all
right: anything goes in
sleep, sleep,
with its burden of dreams . . .

The Day

Because of a coolness in the air,
because of the henna in your hair,
(it turned it orange, boy)
because of Helena's perky boobs,
because of Tom's insouciant buns
(M. is really gone on them),
I would like to celebrate today.

But how can I, in this stony gulch?
"Questo popoloso deserto che appellano . . ."
New York. How I miss the country,
how I miss that island in Maine!
Never to gather tiny sweet-scented
white violets again! Never to piss
again out the window on the juniper
while I dig the moonstruck bay!
O bay!

A Table of Green Fields

on which to shoot pool (that
boring game)
for cows to munch upon
where lambs may gambol
come spring

these thoughts haunt my dreaming
nights, and when I wake I think
of you, blond curls crushed
into your pillow, one hand grasping
your————

The year goes by, it's spring
again. I wonder why. I
sleep and wake and take
a little stroll to see
those thin trees whose name
I do not know, abloom, again . . .

Tom's Dream

Tom dreamed he was visiting
Lillian Hellman in her kitchen:
"the famed Miss H." was baking
a ham: for him . . . for her . . .
for them. She took the ham
out of the oven and broke off
a bit of bone to test its
doneness. "It's done on that
side," she said, "but not on
this." Then she put the ham back
in the oven, being careful
to put the undone side in first.
That was Tom's dream, the night
he slept over and came
down with that terrible cold
for which I gave him
Alka-Seltzer Plus Cold Remedy.

Perhaps

Perhaps there's time to write a poem.
There is always time to write a poem.
Not literally true . . . what to write about?
How about, the love I bear thee?

Love, how I would love to bare thee!
In your summer clothes I can see
you're quite a stud. Not mine to handle.
Oh well, the hell with that.

There are plenty of things to write
poems about besides unrequited love.
Name one. Food. Poodles. Old age
(fast approaching). Middle youth.

And so forth and so on. I really
love this day, so unexpectedly
springlike in mid July. If only
fall would come! When Helena and I
are going off on our jaunt to Venice,
Florence, Rome, the beauty spots.
Now I think I'll wash my hair. G'bye.

O Sleepless Night

I lie down and spread my legs and arms
out upon my firm mattress on which there is a
                    white
percale sheet and two blankets
with which I never never never never cover myself:
"Jimmy likes to sleep cold," Fairfield
told Anne, after he awoke me with a kiss
in my south-facing room with California
wildflower paper, books (more
in adjoining guest room: Lawrence's room: how's Lawrence?

A Few Days

Is he in Lansing? Still teaching French
at the U? I suspect he is.)
As I say, I lie down, spread-eagle, and
the radio plays, classic, not
rock or pop or show tunes or film scores or jazz or blues:
it merely is (you simply must forgive me:

                    you you you you you you you

)
a preference. I love all music
except Bach—I do like the sonatas
for unaccompanied cello: how
many are there? Six,
I'm pretty sure. Divine Pierre Fournier!
He draws the bow across the strings (five? six? seven?)
which are not catgut
                              &
the sound box resonates: a cello
which is not most beautiful of instruments (did
I say that I always sleep
with the two lamps on? I like light
at night
moonlight
enshrouded in parchment shades).
I wake up
once or twice
a night
and by the light
(starlight, enshrouded in a parchment shade)
of lamplight
check out the time: three a.m.:
"the Dark Night of the Soul"
about which F. Scott Fitzgerald
was mistaken: he
thought it was some sort of sudden unendurable angst
or anguish or plunge into the pit of hell:
no:
it is the moment
when a mystic like St. John of the Cross
                              kneels outdoors
                                        and
                              prays: his

very soul
rises in a beam or column or like morning mist
and intermingles
with the divine essence of the Godhead:
love, love, love,
pure and unalloyed, simon-pure, the real thing:
beyond, way far beyond
all human comprehension:
love, pure love, its essence:
gilded clouds, rainbows, no sky, no moon, no sun, no stars,
and yet
light
gentle and bright
light:
Angels, Archangels, Cherubim, Seraphim and Cupidons
choiring together
melodiously
in song that is not plainsong
to the music of plucked harps, wind harps, o-
                    carinas and the nose flute
and the oot of instruments: most beautiful of all,
the pianoforte
        played by Sviatislav Richter
            and Marguerite Long (Vuillard).
                Shit, piss and corruption:
did I or did I not
take my Placidyl, which is a sleeping pill
"take two at bedtime"
and the tiny, tiny antidepressant (I
                have suffered not one second
of depression
dans toute ma vie).

A WHITE NIGHT

a sleepless night, total insomnia, no sleep
to lie there
open-eyed
and wonder
dreaming and not dreaming
thoughts stream by
slow, slow, slow, slow, slow, slow,
                flights

A Few Days

of total recall:
all those telephone numbers and addresses including zip code
almost every word Leopardi ever wrote (I
                             have not read
Il Zibaldone, the notebooks,
                    and never will)
"Canto notturno di un pastor errante dell' Asia"
           "Sous le Pont Mirabeau
               Coule la Seine . . ."
      "The Moon has set
                and the Pleiades,
the night is passing, passing
                        &
          I lie alone"
          a few words
              more
                 which I
                   do
                     not
                        recall
Upon the striking of the hour of one
I know
decisively as the swift descent of the knife blade of a guillotine
                   that I
will not sleep this night: insomnia, a white night, a sleepless
                                    night

                 piss
Once,
on the Porters' Great Spruce Head Island I
                went
without sleep on
           Great Spruce Head Island
                    which is in
Penobscot Bay
—what was I going to say? I forget. Oh yes
I went for two weeks
without sleep: I lay in the dark
with shuttered eyes and rested:
nothing happened: I
felt A.O.K.:
At Ellen's party:
      "Really great seeing you again after

all these years"
                    and
"I'm Jim Schuyler: I'm a poet: and you are . . . ?"
"Did you see Alex—Alex Katz's show?"
I loved it, most of all Ada
in a sable hat
among a few, few, few,
slow-falling
snowflakes, one
of which had
adhered
to her coat. Also,
something immense called "Their Eyes Met"
the color
about as great as color ever gets
             last night I
                         was briefly brushed
                         by the wind of the wing of death:
waiting for a cab outside the Chelsea
to go up to upper Fifth Avenue
to dine with Barbara Guest—Mrs. Trumbull Higgins—
when, no, not when
a car was
proceeding crosstown at a
                         normal rate of speed
when
it spun round twice and
shot up on the sidewalk
brushing against my winter overcoat, which is not lined
with sheepskin
and slammed into the brick wall of the hotel
:actually, to be frank and open and sorta truthful
             (You
                 look like a clean-cut kid:
                     have a linea speed:
                         makes
                     you feel real sexy
                         pop, sip, swallow, rush)
Where am I?
In my room at historic Hotel Chelsea:
Dylan Thomas, Thomas Wolfe, Virgil Thomson, me and
                 one more whose name

                              escapes me
                              O. Henry, Brendan Behan
What was I saying? Oh yes
          (and the sheep
          half asleep
          upon the greensward
          sheep
          half asleep
          as they creep
                    creepy sheep

          we're three little lambs
                    who have lost their way: baaa, baaa, baaa
                    a crystal bead
                              and ropes of amber)
Well, folks, dat's about all
                    sleepless night
                              A White Night
                              a sleeping no a sleepless night
                              insomnia
Tom Tom Tom, I want my Tom:
Tom Tom Tom, where's my kiss?
Tom Tom Tom, where are you?
                              Tom, Tom, Tom
why do you not lie beside me
I mean to say, why
Oh, tell me why
why do you not lie beside me
entwined in one another's arms
my head upon your pliant marble shoulder
you asleep and me awake,
decked beside me
body pressed body to body?
Tom Tom Tom Tom, Thomas Paul Carey
I love you so: forever and forever and forever
                              and a day
through all eternity
and yet beyond that
                    buona notte
(when the inspiration
to write this poem

came to me
en route to see my shrink
I envisioned
twenty or so pages and this is only six: oh well, can't win 'em all)
Tom, Tom, Tom, sleeping beauty, sleep well, Tom, Tom, Tom
                    "Good night, sweet prince,
                        And flights of angels sing thee to thy rest"
                                        "Give me the Knife"

Suddenly

it's night and Tom
comes in and says,
"It's pouring buckets
out," his blond hair
diamond-dusted with
raindrop fragments.

345

THE FIREPROOF FLOORS

OF WITLEY COURT

English Songs and Dances

Witley Court

In northwest Worcestershire
in eighteen-sixty
Samuel Dawkes installed
the fireproof floors of Witley Court

Put to the test in a fire
the firemen could not extinguish
the fireproof floors
failed to distinguish
themselves and are no longer
really to be trusted

Visitor to Witley Court
enter at your peril

Below the Stairs

I
Anaemia, dyspepsia and ulcer
afflict the chambermaid

It's the damnable food you give her
"kitchen" tea
"kitchen" meat
"kitchen" butter

that force her
to indulge in
unhealthy "between meal" snacks

    II
Brown and Lilly Bungalows
Boston Garters Simpitrol

The search for health and pleasure
leads to no fairer clime

Laxton House and Hamble Bank
The Grange and Brinkley Grove

How is it you got out so early?

Oh, the missis bought a vacuum
and it do the work in no time

In a Churchyard

Where droop the little ivy shoots
the sun slants down to kiss
the heaps of mellow headstones
brown and gold with tender lichen

Where soil runs deep and loamy
sturdy, unabashed,
singly, in pairs or in great batches
everywhere the sun shall be their lover,
daffodils!
who need slight wooing
to flaunt their winsome charms

Hats

A cherry-colored picture hat
of tagal straw, its only trimming
a black-and-white windmill bow
at one side, or in front

A shady hat in silver straw
the brim rolled up
and on the crown a clump
of blue wings from an Indian jay

Frock

I love crystal fringe on a dance frock
and the ripple of light as you pass
in a plain little chemisette bodice
drawn down from your shoulder
by long heavy tassels that match
your tunic of pale rose-pink charmeuse

What Ails My Fern?

My peonies have lovely leaves
but rarely flower.
Oh, they have buds
and plenty of them. These
grow to the size of peas
and stay
that way.
Is this
bud blast?

What ails my fern?

I enclose a sample
of a white disease
on a leaf
of honesty
known also
as the money plant

My two blue spruce
look worse and worse

What ails my fern?

Two years ago a tenant
wound tape around my tree.
Sap dripped out of the branches
on babies in buggies below. So
I unwound the tape.
Can nothing be done
to revive my tree?

What ails my fern?

I hate my disordered
backyard fence
where lilac, weigela
and mock orange grow.
Please advise
how to get rid of it.

Weeping willow roots
reaching out
seeking water
fill my cesspool and well.
What do you suggest?

What ails my fern?

Wild Eggs

For her size the moor hen
lays a large egg
and many of them
and the eggs make delicate eating

By abstraction she
can be made to lay
more than her normal number
and her eggs make delicate eating

Boer War Bread Strike

Oversifted fine white flour
with little crust
and that not crisp

We cannot fight on this glue
give us the bread we are used to

Of stone-ground flour
the kissing-crust
the color of the rest
and baked right through

Bread for bread, bread
for the prisoners
each craving what
from his youth he ate
not the bread of exile
and that not crisp

Procession

Serene and purple twilight of the South
the wind-distorted olives
so dim beside the road
so very still tonight
the sea delicately touches
the shore with foam

Black clad, glimmer of white
pyramids of trembling gold
up the white road wind
in misty iris blue

a cross, a crown, a spear

the air is drenched

the nails, the hammer

fragrance of lemon and orange

the scourge, a sponge

salt perfume of the sea

Adverts

I
Ambrosia

Fry's Cocoa! The word
means food of the gods

So perfect, so peerless
nothing to throw away
more and more relied on

351   *A Few Days*

Fry's Cocoa! I repeat
there is no better food

        II
Good-bye, Cheap Lamps

What fine lamps
these Mazdas are!

We were wise to say,
Good-bye, cheap lamps

And to heavy bills
for current, too!

Yes. There's no doubt
about it. So-called

cheap lamps cost
most in the long run

In future we
will stick to
Mazda lamps
            with the wonderful no-sag filament

That's what I
call a good light

        III
Swan and Edgar   Good Linen

We sleep on linen
we dress in linen
we clothe our table
with a linen cloth

Constant service
lasting pleasure
indeed it is
a royal fabric

Swan and Edgar
        Good linen
Swan and Edgar
        Good linen

A FEW DAYS

A few days

are all we have. So count them as they pass. They pass
    too quickly
out of breath: don't dwell on the grave, which yawns for
    one and all.
Will you be buried in the yard? Sorry, it's against
    the law. You can only
lie in an authorized plot but you won't be there to
    know it so why worry
about it? Here I am at my brother's house in western
    New York: I came
here yesterday on the Empire State Express, eight hours
    of boredom on the train.
A pretty blond child sat next to me for a while. She
    had a winning smile,
but I couldn't talk to her, beyond "What happened to
    your shoes?" "I put them under the seat." And
so she had. She pressed the button that released the
    seat back and sank
back like an old woman. Outside, the purple loosestrife
    bloomed in swathes
that turned the railway ditch and fields into a
    sunset-reflecting lake.
And there was goldenrod and tattered Queen Anne's lace
    and the noble Hudson
on which just one sailboat sailed, billowing, on a
    weekday afternoon.
A tug towed some scows. Sandy red earth and cows,
    the calves like
big dogs. With Fresca and ham and cheese on a roll the
    eight hours somehow passed.
My sister-in-law met me at the Buffalo Central Station
    and drove me out to their house.

Hilde is just back from a visit home to Augsburg,
    where she was born
not too long ago. She taught herself to speak English, which
    she does extremely well.
My mother now lives with them in the house my brother built
    himself. She's old: almost eighty-nine
and her sight is failing. She has little to do but sit and
    listen to the TV rumble.
When I came in she said, "I can't see you but I know your
    voice."
"Some corner of a garden where the soul sinks down under
    its own weight . . ."
But this isn't about my family, although I wish it were. My
    niece Peggy is at
camp in the Adirondacks so I am staying in her room.
    It's essence of teenage
girl: soft lilac walls, colored photographs of rock stars,
    nosegays of artificial flowers,
signs on the door: THIS ROOM IS A DISASTER AREA, and
    GARBAGEDUMP.
"Some ashcan at the world's end . . ." But this is not
    my family's story, nor
is it Molly's: the coon hound pleading silently for table
    scraps. The temperature
last night dipped into the forties: a record for August
    14th. There is a German
down pouff on the bed and I was glad to wriggle under
    it and sleep the sleep
of the just. Today is a perfection of blue: the leaves
    go lisp in the breeze.
I wish I were a better traveler; I love new places, the
    arrival in a station
after the ennui of a trip. On the train across the aisle
    from me there was a young couple.
He read while she stroked the flank of his chest in a
    circular motion, motherly,
covetous. They kissed. What is lovelier than young love?
    Will it only lead
to barren years of a sour marriage? They were perfect
    together. I wish
them well. This coffee is cold. The eighteen-cup pot

A Few Days

like most inventions
doesn't work so well. A few days: how to celebrate them?
    It's today I want
to memorialize but how can I? What is there to it?
    Cold coffee and
a ham-salad sandwich? A skinny peach tree holds no
    peaches. Molly howls
at the children who come to the door. What did they
    want? It's the wrong
time of year for Girl Scout cookies.
My mother can't find her hair net. She nurses a cup of
    coffee substitute, since
her religion (Christian Science) forbids the use
    of stimulants. On this
desk, a vase of dried blue flowers, a vase of artificial
    roses, a bottle with
a dog for stopper, a lamp, two plush lions that hug
    affectionately, a bright
red travel clock, a Remington Rand, my Olivetti, the
    ashtray and the coffee cup.
Moonlight Serenade:
            Moon, shine in my yard,
            let the grass blades
            cast shadows on themselves.
            Harbinger of dreams,
            let me sleep in your
            eternal glow.
That was last night. Today, the color of a buttercup,
    winds on the spool
of time, an opaque snapshot. Today is better than yesterday,
    which was too cold for
August. Still, it had its majesty of tumultuous cloud wrack.
    Here and there a sunbeam
struggled through. Like the picture in my grandmother's Bible
    of Judgment Day:
Rembrandtesque beams of spotlights through cloud cities on a
    desolate landscape. I
used to feel frightened when I saw that effect in the sky. The
    August coolness:
a winter's-coming autumn feeling of it's time to pull our
    horns in and snuggle

down for winter. The radio, the anodyne of the lonely, speaks
    or rather sings:
                    I love you only
                don't want to be lonely
delectable, deleterious trash. Three in the afternoon, when
    time stands still.
Is your watch right? Rest after labor doth greatly ease. There is
    no place to put
anything. These squandered minutes, hours, days. A few days, spend
    them riotously. There
is no occasion for riot. I haven't had a drink in years, begging
    a few glasses of
wine. I dream at night about liquor: I was mad at Fairfield because
    he invited people
to dinner and all he bought for them to drink was a pint of rum.
    I poured some for Anne
in a crumbling eggshell. And what does all that mean? I'm no
    good at interpreting
dreams. Hands fumble with clothes, and just at the delirious
    moment I wake up:
Is a wet dream too much to ask for? Time for a cigarette. Why are
    pleasures bad for you?
But how good the tobacco smoke tastes. Uhm. Blow smoke rings
    if you can. Or
blow me: I could do with a little carnal relief. The yard slopes
    down to a swampy bit,
then fields rise up where cows are pastured. They do nothing
    all day but eat:
filling their faces so they'll have a cud to chew on. I'm not uncowlike
    myself: life as a
continuous snack. Another ham-salad sandwich and then goodbye.
    Will you say no to a
stack of waffles? I need a new pastime: photography turned out to
    be just too expensive. I
miss it though, stalking the motif, closing in on a flower, my
    photograph of Katherine Koch
laughing and leaning back in a porch that blazed with sunlight.
    You went off to Naropa
in Boulder, Colorado, and I have a postcard to prove it.
    I think about your
lesbian love for your roommate. You're a modern miss and I like

you as you are.
Today is tomorrow, it's that dead time again: three in the afternoon
    under scumbled clouds,
livid, that censor the sun and withhold the rain: impotent as
    an old man ("an
old man's penis: limp as a rabbit's ear"). It's cool
    for August and I
can't nail the days down. They go by like escalators, each alike,
    each with its own
message of tears and laughter. I could go pick beans only Hilde
    beat me to it.
The drive to the village: a whole generation younger than I
    seem to rule the
roost. Where Sipprell the photographer used to live and work
    is someone else's
now. He was a kind and gentle man. I knew his sons. The one I
    knew best is dead
and gone now, as he is himself. Life sends us struggling forth
    like "the green vine
angering for life" and rewards us with a plate of popovers
    labeled "your death."
Where is mine waiting? What will it be like when there's no
    more tomorrow? I
can't quite escape the feeling of death as a sleep
    from which we awaken
refreshed, in eternity. But when the chips are down I plunk
    them on nothingness;
my faith ran out years ago. It may come back, but I doubt it.
    "Rest in peace"
is all I have to say on the subject. I drink too much strong
    German coffee and
can't sleep at night. Last night I woke up laughing from
    a beautiful sensual
dream: a man who looked like a handsome woman who looked like
    a man. He told
me I should read in the sun to get a better color. But oh, the
    delicate touchings!
Venison stew, rank and gamey. Choke it down. Have a dumpling.
    Once again it's
another day, a gray day, damp as a dog's mouth, this unlikely
    August. In the vegetable

plot the squash are ripening, and tomatoes. Perhaps there are
        nematodes: cucumbers
won't grow here. They start to produce and then the plants die
        back. In the garden
(the flower garden) edelweiss thrives and so do China asters.
        Here, at home, I'm
lonelier than alone in my New York digs. There is no one to talk
        to, nothing to talk
about. "Tell me the story of your life," in great detail. Your first
        memory, the scariest thing
that ever happened: travels and food, the works. "Are you really
        interested?" "Passionately."
When you rest your head like that you suddenly look like an
        old woman, the old
woman you may one day become. Struggle into the shower to wash
        your hair, then crimp
it in rollers. You have a corrugated head. Can't you throw
        caution to the winds
and buy a little of some decent scent? Scent is one of the great
        amenities. Smelling like
a whore's dream. The dream shop and the dram shop. Dram shops
        in Amsterdam, old and cozy
enclosing the small fires of marvelous *ginevra*. It burns
        my throat and my eyes water;
so good to be free in the mid-afternoon, free to be a slightly
        drunk tourist, eyeing
the man-made wonders along the Amstel. Go to Naples to buy
        striped socks off a barrow.
Besides the dram shops there is the Pleasure Chest, with its
        edifying displays: pleasure takes
        many forms: keep it
simple is the best bet. I especially hate the picture of two
        Scotties with pink bows
on their heads. Sentimentality can go further than the door to
        the cellar and the
braid of garlic. Guess I'm ready for lunch: ready as I'll
        ever be, that is.
Lunch was good: now to move my bowels. That was good too:
        "Oh shit," she said,
"I stepped in some doggy pooh." Worse things could happen
        to you. Meeting a

A Few Days

man-eating tiger in the street, for instance. A little
    trembling worthless
thing: a mobile. It balances five angels and I lie in bed
    and throw puffs of
breath at it. It does its shimmering dance. Sunday, "the
    worst day," and we
all sit snowbound in drifts of Sunday paper. No news is
    good news but it
sure makes Jack a dull boy. "I can't get in there: my grades
    aren't good enough."
My nephew Mike came home at two in the morning from his
    hitchhiking trip in the Middle West. He
liked Springfield, Mo., the best. I can't make out why: a
    girl perhaps. He's
sixteen and smokes, which makes my brother see red. I wanted
    to ask him if he ever
smokes pot, but a sudden shyness came over me, the way
    the white sky overcame
this bluest of mornings. A sound of rolling peas:
    traffic goes by.
"Is Fred your uncle?" my mother asked out of the dimness
    of time. "No: he's
my kid brother." "Oh, I see." It's time for Hilde
    to brush and comb
her hair, a glory of white. She sits all day, a monument
    to patience, almost eighty-nine
if she's a day. We talk, but nothing comes of it. Minnesota
    winters when the sleighs
whirled over the snow-covered fences and jokes were
    made about the Scandinavians.
Exhilaration: one night we took the toboggan and went
    to Emery Park, where
there was a long, long slide, on which we sped
    into the night. "I'll
wash your face in the snow!" "Get away from me, you
    punk rock rabbit."
I just sat outside with my mother: my one good deed
    of the day.
That day passed like any other and I took the train from
    Buffalo to New York.
Buffalo, the city God forgot. Not even the Pope is going

to visit it,
and he should: it's the largest Polish city in the world.
Now I'm back
in New York on West Twenty-third Street with the buses farting
past. And the one
dog that barks its head off at two or three in the morning.
I hate to miss
the country fall. I think with longing of my years in
Southampton, leaf-turning
trips to cool Vermont. Things should get better as you
grow older, but that
is not the way. The way is inscrutable and hard to handle.
Here it is
the Labor Day weekend and all my friends are out of town:
just me and some
millions of others, to whom I have not yet been introduced.
A walk in the
streets is not the same as a walk on the beach, by
preference, a beach
emptied by winter winds. A few days, and friends will
trickle back to
town. Dinner parties, my favorite form of entertainment.
Though in these
inflationary times you're lucky to get chicken in
place of steak.
What I save on meals I spend on taxis. Lately a lot
of cabs have
signs: NO SMOKING, PLEASE, or NO SMOKING DRIVER ALLERGIC.
A quiet smoke in
a taxi is my idea of bliss. Yes, everything gets more
restricted, less free.
Yet I am free, one of the lucky ones who does not
have to show up
Monday morning at some boring desk. I remember the years
at NBC, looking
discontentedly out at grimy Sixth Avenue, waiting for
the time to pass.
It did. Pass, I mean, and I took ship for Europe. A
pleasant interlude
on the whole, despite my operation. I miss Rino, my
Roman lover, and

often wonder how he is and what he's up to. Probably
     a grandfather by
now. Good day, Signor Oscari: are you still a grocer
     by trade? Did
your uncle die and leave you his shop in the *periferia*?
     Italy seems so
far away (just a few hours by plane), and, you see,
     since I was there
I fell in love with an island in Maine, now out of
     bounds. I'd like to
find a new place, somewhere where there are friends and
     not too many
houses. This summer has passed like a dream. On the last
     day of August
I feel much better than I felt in June, heaven be praised.
     Who said, "Only
health is beautiful"? There's truth in the old saw. I
     have always been
more interested in truth than in imagination: I
     wonder if that's
true? I have one secret, which I sometimes have an almost
     overwhelming desire
to blurt out; but I won't. Actually, I have told it to
     my shrink, so it's
not an absolute secret anymore. Too bad. Are secrets a
     way of telling lies,
I wonder? Yes, they are. So, let it be. I don't drink
     anymore, still, I
just had four double cocktails: margaritas. At least I
     stopped there. I
like not drinking. Hangovers were too horrible. I MEAN THAT.
     Really mean it.
Tomorrow is another day, but no better than today if
     you only realize it.
Let's love today, the what we have now, this day, not
     today or tomorrow or
yesterday, but this passing moment, that will
     not come again.
Now tomorrow is today, the day before Labor Day,
     1979. I want to
live to see the new century come in: but perhaps it's

bad luck to

say so. To live to be seventy-six: is that so much
        to ask? My father

died in his forties, but his mother lived to be ninety,
        as my mother seems

likely to. In what rubbishy old folks' home will I
        pass my sunset years?

A house on the edge of a small town, private but
        convenient, is my

wish. I won't say no to Vermont or Maine, not that
        I want to spend

my old age shoveling snow. I spent my youth doing
        that. Our drive

was cut into the side of a hill and no sooner
        was it cleared

than the wind would drift it full again. Monotonous
        days, daydreaming

of any place but there. It rained earlier today: I
        lay on the bed

and watched the beads it formed on the foliage of
        my balcony balustrade

drop of their own weight. I remember the night the
        house in Maine

was struck by lightning. It was attracted to a
        metal flue

and coursed harmlessly down to the wood-burning
        stove that heated

the bath water for my end of the house. I could
        write a book about

the island, but I don't want to. I want to write

more novels. I've made more false starts than anyone
        since Homer was a

pup. Now it's dinner time: time to feed the inner man. I
        wish I could go

on a diet of water for a few days: to reduce the outer
        man to weigh what

he should weigh. A letter from Joe Brainard: he's
        my favorite pen pal.

Joe decides what he's going to do, then he does it.
        This summer it's

been sunbathing and reading Dickens and Henry James.

And he sends a poem:
      "Ah! the good old days!"
      "If gobbled then—digested now.
      (Clarified by time—romanticised by mind.)
       For today's repast remembered."
          and:
      "Reminds me of you—Jimmy—out in
      Southampton in the big Porter House in your
      little room of many books it takes game-
      board strategy to relocate now, as then."
          and:
    "Out trekking up South Main Street
    you are:
    a pair of thick white legs
    sporting Bermuda shorts
    (of a *most* unusual length)
    and plain blue sneakers so 'you'
    they are."
I tripped and fell the other night and struck the curb
    with my head,
face forward. I went to the emergency at St. Vincent's.
    They put stitches
in my chin: I look like "The Masque of the Red Death."
    Feel like it, too.
I wish this humid unsunny day would get its act together
    and take it on the road.
It's no day for writing poems. Or for writing, period.
    So I didn't.
Write, that is. The bruises on my face have gone, just
    a thin scab on
the chin where they put the stitches. I'm back on Antabuse:
    what a drag. I
really love drinking, but once I'm sailing I can't seem
    to stop. So, pills
are once again the answer. It must have been horrible
    to live before
the days of modern medicine—all those great artists going
    off their chump
from syphilis or coughing their lungs out with TB. But
    they still haven't
found a live-forever pill. But soon. Across the street

        sunlight falls like
a shadow on the Palladian office building. This room
        faces north, which
usually I don't like, but the French doors to the
        balcony make it light
enough. I ought to buy a plant, but plants are too much
        like pets: suppose
you want to go away (and I do), someone has to take care
        of it. So I waste my
money on cut flowers. I'm spoiled: I'm used to gathering
        flowers for the house,
not buying them. Thirty-five dollars for a dozen roses,
        Sterling Silver:
not today. Always thinking about what things cost: well,
        I have to, except
when a cab comes in my view: then I flag it down.
        I'd be scared to
figure up how much I spend a year on chauffeur-driven
        comfort. I'd like to spend
        part of this lovely
day in a darkened movie theater: only there's nothing I
        want to see. Fellini's
Orchestra Rehearsal was too much like *Alice in Orchestralia*.
        Perhaps a good
walk is more what's called for. I could tool down to
        Dave's Pot Belly
and have a butterscotch sundae: eating on the pounds I
        walked off. Or
I could go shopping: I need cologne. Taylor's Eau de Portugal
        for choice. In the
country you can take a walk without spending money. In
        the city it isn't
easy. This soft September sun makes the air fizzy like
        soda water: Perrier
in the odd-shaped bottle from France. I dreamed last
        night about autumn
trees: orange, red, yellow, and the oaks dark green. I
        wish there were
something besides ginkgos and plane trees to see short
        of Central Park.
"It does wonders for your back . . ." The radio is on:

365   *A Few Days*

                perhaps this will
be a lucky day and they'll play something besides the
        New World Symphony
or Telemann. I could call Ruth and chat, only it isn't
        noon so she
isn't up yet. It still isn't noon: it's tomorrow
        morning. The risen
sun almost comes in the north windows: I see it lie
        along the balcony,
cut into shapes by the wrought-iron balustrade, a
        design of crazy
chrysanthemums and willow leaves. This old hotel is
        well built: if
you hold your breath and make a wish you'll meet Virgil
        Thomson in the elevator
or a member of a punk rock band. I still want to go to
      a movie but
there isn't any. A month ago when I wasn't in the
        mood there were lots:
Flying Down to Rio, Million Dollar Legs, Blonde Bombshell
        or do I date myself?
A red, pink and blue slip on my desk tells me that
        I am going to
spend forty dollars to have a jacket relined. A child
        of the thirties,
that seems to me what you spend for a new suit. More
        money! I got that
cologne: sixteen twenty. Think I'll splash some on
        right now. Uhm. Feels good.
        I think I'll take a shower.
No. That would mean taking my clothes off and putting
        them on again. I
haven't got the energy for that. And the waste of hot water!
        And I should wash my hair.
But that would mean putting my shoes on and a tromp around
        the corner to the
drugstore that isn't open yet. Or I could wash it with plain
        cucumber soap and
rinse it with lime juice (I think there is a lime). I
        think I'll leave it matted
and get it cut—oh—tomorrow. For a while I let it get

really long, I
looked like Buffalo Bill's mother. Ruth says, "Oh, Jimmy,
    you look much better
with short hair." "Graciousness, part of the Japanese
    character." The radio
is still on. "It's time for one of our classical hits:
    you'll recognize this
one." But I don't. Good grief, it's "Greensleeves." I'm
    a real music lover!
I'd rather listen to rock, but if I tune WNCN out I
    can never find it
again. Last night they played the Brahms Second Piano
    Concerto, which sent
me off contentedly to bye-bye land. The sleeping pills
    I scoffed helped too.
It used to be when I checked out a medicine chest there
    would be lots of
amphetamines. No more. Doctors won't prescribe them.
    I heard a rumor
about a diet doctor in Queens who will. Must find out
    his address. But
Queens seems awfully far to give the day a gentle lift.
    I can do it with
coffee, only that much coffee gives me sour stomach. Urp.
    Belch. Guess I'll
make a cup of Taster's Choice. My sister-in-law and
    Donald Droll both use
that brand. Not bad. *The Burning Mystery of Anna in 1951*:
    I prefer the genteel wackiness
of John Ashbery's *As We Know*. A poem written in two
    columns, supposed to
be read simultaneously: John is devoted to the impossible.
    The sunlight still
sits on my balcony, invitingly. I decline the invitation:
    out there, it gives
me vertigo. People who come here say, "Oooh, you have a
    balcony," as though I
spent my days out there surveying Twenty-third Street:
    Chelsea Sewing Center,
Carla Hair Salon. Twenty-third Street hasn't got much
    going for it, unless

you love the YMCA. I once did. I remember Christmas '41.
    I was in the shower
when a hunk walked in. I got a hard-on just like that.
    He dropped his soap
to get a view of it and in no time we were in bed in
    his room. Sure was
a change from West Virginia. When I told Alex Katz I
    went to college in West
Virginia, he said in that way of his, "Nah,
    you're Harvard." Wish I
were, but I'm a lot more panhandle than I am Cambridge,
    Mass. Which reminds
me, I saw in the *Times* that my old friend Professor Billy
    Vinson died of the
heart condition he knew he had. Billy was the Navy officer
    who, when he was
getting fucked by an apelike sailor, lifted his head out of
    the pillow and
said, "I order you back to your ship." His camp name was
    Miss Williemae.
He was a virologist who detected two new viruses, which he
    named for Chester
Kallman and me: Fiordiligi and Dorabella. If anybody called
    me by my camp name
nowadays I'd sock them—I like to think. I remember how
    I felt when Chester
dedicated his book to me and wrote the poem in "camp": "Wearing
    a garden hat her mother
wore . . ." Bitch. Chester's gone now, and so are Wystan, Billy Vinson,
    Brian Howard, Bill Aalto and Brian's
friend, the red-haired boy whose name I can't remember.
    Chester was a martyr
to the dry martini. So, in his way, was Wystan. Brian
    committed suicide:
Why do people do that? For fun? Brian was the most
    bored and boring man
I ever met. He was what the French call *épatant*: he told
    an American officer
that he was a clandestine homosexual. The officer knocked
    him to the barroom floor.
Brian looked up and said, "That proves it." I could tell

a thousand Brian
stories, the way some people can reel off limericks. For
a great poet, Wystan
Auden's dirty limericks are singularly uninspired. Sorry
I can't remember any
to quote you. *The Platonic Blow* gives me hives. Funny porn
I guess is a gift,
like any other. Who wrote:
"Lil tried shunts and double-shunts
And all tricks known to common cunts . . ."?
A tired newspaperman? A gifted coal miner in West
Virginia? The morning
passes like an elephant in no stampede. The morning passes like
Salome's veil. Famous last
lines: "I am still alive!" and "Kill that woman!" Fast
curtain. The morning
passes too slowly. I want it to be seven forty-five in the evening,
when I'm invited
to dine on delectables chez John Ashbery. I wonder if the
cuisine will be
Indian? The little minx took a course in it, after all
those years in France.
Tall Doug and blond Frank will be there: I wonder about
David Kermani of the
shoe-button eyes? Lately whenever I've gone there he's
been out on some
important errand: is he avoiding me? I hope not. I like
him. What a
devil he is for work. I hope his boss, Tibor, values him
at his true worth.
The sun is off the balcony. The sun is off: a scrim of
cloud obscures the
sky. Yesterday was such a heaven day: blue, warm, breezy.
When I cabbed up to Barbara's
I found the park full of joggers: men and women whose
breasts and buttocks
went jounce, jounce. Uhm: a shave and a splash of Eau
de Portugal,
Taylor's best. I mustn't use it up too fast: think what
it cost. The only trouble
with it is that it doesn't hang on: I like a cologne that

makes people say, "You
smell good," like Guerlain's Impériale. Paco
    really hangs on:
people who say "You smell so good" look as though
    they're going to retch.
I threw caution to the winds and threw it out. I
    would like to go
in the bathroom and swizzle on some of Taylor's best,
    but the maid is in
there stinking up the house with household ammonia.
    "Is that girl who
comes and takes care of you your niece?" she asked me.
    No, Eileen Myles is
my assistant: she comes and makes my breakfast and
    lunch, runs errands
to the grocery store, the p.o., the bank, mails letters,
    and always arrives with
that morning's *Times*. I lie in bed and read the obituaries
    and smell the French
toast frying. Served with applesass. I think I'll
    let her take the laundry
out; she needs the exercise. The sun is off the balcony,
    the air is cool
as one of Barbara's kisses, which don't make me feel
    I turn her on.
Her husband won't give her money to pay the cleaning
    woman and they
have a huge co-op. It is all neat and tidy. Barbara is
    very organized
for a literary lady. She loaned me a book about Natalie
    Barney I thought
would be fascinating but the writing is much too coy,
    "Amazon" instead of
dyke or Lesbian. I always think I can read anything
    but some things turn me off:
like trying to read jellied gasoline. I could almost
    put a sweater on
the air from the French doors is so cool. But I think
    I like to live
cold, like George Montgomery and Frank O'Hara wearing
    chinos and sneakers

in the snow at Harvard. It was the thing to do. "I'd like
        to kiss Jimmy," said
a dope who came to the door. Frank made a grand gesture at
        me lying reading on
the couch and said, "Help yourself." So he did. I wonder
        what I was reading?
I should keep a reading diary of all the books and mags
        I read, but what
would be the use? I can't remember what I read. I read
        Graham Greene's *A*
Sort of Life and a week later reread it without remembering
        anything, except his
playing Russian roulette. It's a lovely book, the writing
        is so concrete. I
have a foible for books of family life, like Gwen Raverat's
        Period Piece and
Frances Marshall's *A Pacifist's War.* I went out to post
        some letters (Chemical
Bank, Denver Art Museum, Richard Savitsky, my lawyer) and
        the sun was hot. In
the shadows it was cool but when you stepped into a sun-
        spot you felt the heat.
It's a beautiful day, the gray nimbus devoured itself. No
        clouds at all.
I bought the *Post.* More mothers killing their babies be-
        cause they're mad
at their husbands. What kind of sense does that make? Maybe
        they wanted to have
abortions and their husbands wouldn't let them. How
        does that grab you?
Eileen took the double-breasted blazer Joe Hazan
        gave me to have
the sleeves shortened half an inch. It came from Hunts-
        man! I used to have a
Huntsman hacking raincoat. In Alex Katz's painting
        Incident you can see
me wearing it, flanked by Ada Katz in a hat and Rudi
        Burckhardt with a
camera. That was a long time ago. I wonder if they still
        have their Teddy Wilson
record? The Alicia de Larrocha of the hot piano.

A Few Days

A few days! I
started this poem in August and here it is September
        nineteenth. September
is almost my favorite month, barring October and May.
        November, my natal
month, is too damn wintry, I don't like it but I like
        my birthstone, the topaz.
In Venice I saw a pair of cufflinks, square topazes
        edged with paste
diamonds—sixty-five bucks, but Arthur, who was
        picking up the check,
wouldn't buy them for me. Cheap is cheap. It was funny
        having no money of
my own. Every time I went out sightseeing I would see
        a black-and-red knitted
tie I wanted passionately to own. Last weekend I spent
        at Barbara's in
Water Mill: a funny turreted house, commodious within
        (this coffee is too strong),
all the woodwork very nineteen-hundred, dark wood balusters
        and cream walls,
Barbara's pictures: Paul Georges, Robert Goodenough, Fairfield
        Porter. We went
to call on Anne Porter, who is selling the house at 49 South
        Main, where I used
to live. The library was void of books: it made me sad, the
        way it did when
my mother sold her house. That one back room in the ell was
        my room. I could
lie in the four-poster on the horsehair mattress and stare
        at Fairfield's color
lithograph of Sixth Avenue and the Waverly Theater en-
        tranced by its magic.
The cover of *Hymn to Life* is Fairfield's version of the
        view from my
south window: the wondrous pear tree in white bloom. Did
        you know that you
can force pears to bloom? Go out in the snow and cut a
        few knobbly twigs
with buds. Soak them overnight in water, put them in a vase
        and hold your breath:

a Chinese print is what you have. A haircut: Breck's
      Shampoo for Normal Hair.
I looked for the *New York Review of Books*, which has a
      review in it of my novel
by Stephen Spender. Couldn't find it. Damn. It's funny,
      having a review come
out a whole year later. Everyone on the street was wearing
      sweaters. There was a
man lying on the sidewalk, one shoe off, his shirt un-
      buttoned down to his
navel. Passersby looked at him coldly; nobody offered
      to help him. I
curbed my Good Samaritan instincts. Poor guy: once he was
      a little boy. How
do you degenerate that way? There aren't any novels about
      blindstiffs these
days: *Tramping on Life* and Jim Tully. Joe Hazan, who lives
      in a Fifth Avenue penthouse,
went on the bum when he was young. I'm thinking about D. D.
      Ryan and her "mothwing" eyebrows.
She says they grew that way, but in a bright light I
      wondered.
She never appears until her face is on. Her boys, Beau and Drew, are
      match-happy. I went
outside and there in the autumn leaves was a circle of flame.
      We managed to stamp
it out. It was right by the house: Kenward's little cottage
      reduced to ashes! Almost.
D. D.'s Vuitton cosmetic trunk that weighed a ton. When we
      stopped at the diner
in Rutland I saw a stark-naked man in the john. He dashed
      into a stall and hid
himself. "I really hate to do this," D. D. said, passing a
      car on the right
at ninety miles an hour. *"On ne voit pas le rivage de la
      mort deux fois, D. D.,"*
as Racine said. When we got to New York Kenward and I
      went to Casey's
and got hysterical with laughter.
Blossoming afternoon, what can I tell you? You tell me that
      my hair is clean and cut.

Breck's Shampoo for Normal Hair, 40¢ off. It's nice and
     gloopy. I'd like to
take a bubble bath but I haven't got the stuff. Bath oil
     is risky business:
it coats the tub with slime and taking a shower is a perilous
     stunt. Help! my Eau
de Portugal is half empty. I've been slathering it on. I
     love it. I ought to
get a Caswell-Massey sampler and see what smells best. Patchouli.
     Vetiver (ugh). September
evening, what have you to say to me? Tell me the time. Still
     two and three-quarter hours
until John's. I'm reading Osbert Sitwell's autobiography
     stitched in brocade. I
read a page, then rush back to my poem. I would once have
     thought that Sitwell
was "influencing" me. I'm too me for that. Poor trembling
     Osbert, suffering from
Parkinson's disease. I met him at a party Wystan gave for
     them. John was
dashing tears from his eyes: "What's wrong?" "I just met
     Edith Sitwell." Tender
heart. Edith looked less like her photographs. She was
     creased and had that
famous nose. September day, how shall I color you? In blue
     and white and airy tones.
September evening, you give your benediction. Ruth is
     in love with a priest
(an Episcopalian) who smokes grass. Ruth can convert from
     Judaism and wear a
hat in church. "The Overture to *Zampa* led by Leonard Bernstein
     with the New York
Philharmonic." The radio is such a pleasure. A Hand in
     a Glove: a vase
you couldn't believe. "Price includes round-trip air fare."
     Oh, the radio! I
can't live without it. Yes, I must put a sweater on. Brrr.
     September, how fickle you are,
there is the shadow of a flapping flag. The Plaza Hotel
     was flying a Japanese
flag: who was staying there? I have on a George Schneeman

T-shirt, a plaid
shirt on a coat hanger. Useless gas. Here is my Blue Cross/
   Blue Shield number: 11223677
Ho8. I don't know my social security number. It's in two
   names: James Ridenour
and James Schuyler. Ridenour was my stepfather's name,
   and when I went to
Europe in 1947 I found my name had never legally been
   changed. Sometimes someone
comes up to me and says, "Aren't you Jimmy Ridenour?" I
   plotz. It's good to
have your own name. Ask me, I'll tell you. It's pink!
   the light I mean
shining from the west on the office building. The sunset.
   That's the trouble with
a north view: you can't see the sunset. North is kinda dreary.
   Will it be dark
when I set out for John Ashbery's? It spooks me. His
   apartment is so nice:
full of French antiques and oriental rugs and collectibles.
   An angel wing begonia
and wandering Jew, peperomia. He has willowware china
   which reminds me of
the Willow tea room, where I used to eat in eighth grade.
   Salisbury steak. Chop suey.
There were motifs from the willowware painted on the walls.
   It's Wednesday morning, but
later than I got up yesterday: the sun is off the balcony.
   There's a chill in the air,
I put on a Jaeger sweater, sand color. The dinner was
   nice: cold soup, veal
collops with a brown sauce, broccoli, noodles, pineapple
   upside-down cake, whipped cream.
The latter had rum in it and I ate it rather nervously but
   it didn't activate the Antabuse.
Rather nervously describes the way I was all evening: just
   sat and drank Perrier
and smoked. Didn't say a word, even when someone spoke to
   me. I meant to say
to John, "Is there any coffee in the house?" Instead I said,
   "Is there any liquor in

A Few Days

the house?" He looked astounded. I faced it out, didn't tell
   him what I really
meant. I have a sleeping-pill hangover; my head feels like
   Venetian glass. I
only took two pills, not three, which puts me to sleep but
   makes me feel crappy.
The *Times* says there's a vogue for pumps: Eileen and I did
   the galleries and I
watched the women's feet: they were all wearing sandals,
   very chic, especially
a black chick who had on a stylish suit. I thought I could
   beat the starting gun
by taking my pills at seven: seven Sleepeze, two Nembutal,
   the scoffed pills, three
antidepressant pills, a red pill that controls the side
   effects of the antidepressants.
I went to sleep like a babe, and here I am wide awake at
   eleven. Anne Dunn is here.
She can't see me until Saturday lunch. I wanted to have
   dinner with her tonight.
Christ, I feel shitty. I took two more sleeping pills and
   what I feel like. Creamed
shit. I lay in bed for an hour; it was torture. It's the
   witching hour of night.
I feel great. This is the morning; it's wonderful. I can't
   tell you about it.
It's a grand day. I feel cold and I
   mailed letters today:
Denver Art Museum, Chemical Bank (that should bring in
   money), Savitsky, my lawyer: he pays my bills, like
the rent ($550). I went back to bed and slept some after
   all. Eleven hours
   all told. Not bad
but I still have the old sleeping-pill hangover. "He brought
   it on himself."
I know I'm going to regret it but still I do it—take that
   one extra pill at
the wrong time. I could kick myself around the block. It's
   getting light out
not sunlight, just morning gray. It looks the way it feels—
   chill. THE LAW FIRM

OF RICHARD D. SAVITSKY, a card says. I wonder if I trust him?
    There's no reason why
I shouldn't. I wonder how they broke the news to him. "There's
    this guy who keeps
having nervous breakdowns and he can't pay the hospital
    bills—state hospitals being of course out of the
question." Bellevue is proof of that: the scary patients,
    the nothing to do, the
insolent staff (that one nice girl), the egg for breakfast,
    One morning I had a bowl of cream of wheat, the black guy
sitting next to me said, "Hunh, putting sugar on
    grits," so this is
what grits are, people stealing cigarettes out of your pajama
    pocket while you sleep,
patients who will share a cigarette with you, you have to
    be an enforced abstainer
to know you'll never give up smoking, Christ I'm cold,
the up in the air TV you can't see, just a blur, the ennui,
    the doctor: "If there's anymore
smoking on this side smoking privileges will be taken away,"
    that's when you know
you'll never give up smoking. When I was in you could
    only smoke if you had money to buy the cigarettes.
I didn't have any money and had to depend on the charity of
    others. It was surprising
how many there were who were charitable. I swore I'd never
    give up smoking. I
did though. It turned me into a fiend. I took up the costly
    cigar. My first cigarette
tasted good. I talk big: I have a pain in my chest and
    worry about lung cancer.
Better make an appointment with the doc. I don't like my
    doctors, except the dentist and my shrink. "Come on
in, Jim." "What are you thinking about?" "Nothing." Not
    true: you're always thinking something.
I'm thinking about this poem. How to make it good, really
    good. I'm proud of my poems.
I wrote a poem about Ruth Kligman in which
    every line began "Ruth"—
talk about maddening. Ruth claimed to like it. When I
    told her it was a

stinker she said, "I didn't think it was one of your best."
 I've got to find that
notebook and tear it up, when I'm dead some creep will
  publish it in a thin
volume called *Uncollected Verse*. It will be a collector's
  item. I hate to think
of the contents of that volume. "Dorabella's Hat," "They
  Two Are Drifting Uptown on a
Bus." Bill Berkson asked me to send him any writings I had
  so I sent him "They Two." He didn't publish it. It's
very funny. The two are Frank and Larry. It's not a poem.
 It's a playlet. I used
to write lots of playlets. "Presenting Jane" is lost.
 It was produced. By
Herbert Machiz. It was horrible thanks to Herbert. When
  I first met Herbert
he said, "A nice-looking boy like you shouldn't have
  dirty fingernails." I blanched. I looked at my
nails: I felt creepy. "I work in a bookstore," I
  extenuated. "Is it
a second-hand bookstore?" he demanded. "No,
  it specializes in
English books." "English dirt." I recounted this to Frank,
  who broke out laughing!
"Jimmy, Herbert is a wit." Herbert dropped dead, on a
  rug? John Latouche
fell down a flight of stairs in a small gray clapboard cottage
  at Apple Hill
among the leaves at Calais (pronounced callous), Vermont.
  Wystan died in his sleep
in a hotel in ring-streeted Vienna not far from his
  country home in verdant
southern Austria: Austria utterly turns me off: the
  goldenesdachtel at Innsbruck
is the worst thing, except for the dragon of Klagenfurt,
  Egg-am-Fackersee. The train
through torrrent-torn needle-clad (I mean trees like
  spruce, pines and firs)
mountains and granite-boulders, then you're in Italy
  among the lemon
lamps and *"Permesso,"* which means "Move or I will mow you
  down with this dolly of

bricks." Then there's "*Ti da fastidio?*" which means "If
    I smoke will it give you the fastids?"
Then one day
the telephone:
it's Hilde:
"Mother passed on
in her sleep
last night. No,
you needn't
come, it's not that
kind of a ceremony.
Fred is seeing
to it all right
now. The last
three months were
pretty grim."
And so I won't be
there to see my Maney
enearthed beside
my stepfather:
once when I was
home a while ago
I said I realized
that in his way he
loved me. "He did
not," my mother said.
"Burton hated you."
The old truth-teller!
She was so proud
in her last dim
years (ninety years
are still
a few days) to be
longest-lived of
the Slaters: for-
getting her mother
was the Slater, she
a Connor:
Margaret Daisy Connor Schuyler Ridenour,
rest well,
the weary journey done.

LAST

POEMS

Mark

My father was ribald
about religion: when
he said, "Did the priest
come riding in on his ass?"

My mother said, "Oh, *Mark*."
Confusing, if you're only four
and everyone else so serious:
mother, her friend who took me

to that big empty box of
a room where all was gray,
empty, ugly: only the priest
and Mabel and me, it seemed.

On that overcast day
a haze like smoke (it
was smoke) moved about,
gray trails in gray Sunday air,

and into me: do you think
I could forget? I did:
just the memory sometimes
of a room like a cold gray box

where I sat beside Mabel,
enrapt, an arrow in my heart.

Horse-Chestnut Trees and Roses

Twenty-some years ago, I read Graham Stuart Thomas's
"Colour in the Winter Garden." I didn't plant
a winter garden, but the book led on to his
rose books: "The Old Shrub Roses," "Shrub Roses
of Today," and the one about climbers and ramblers.

By the corner of the arbor I planted the splendid
Nevada (a Spanish rose, Pedro Dot) and on the arbor
yellow Lawrence Johnston—I've never known
anyone who made a real success of that. Then
a small flowered rose (like a blackberry in flower),
whose name I forget, and then, oh loveliness, oh
glory, Mme. Alfred Carrière, white, with a faintest
blush of pink, and which will bloom even on a
north wall. I used to shave and gaze down into her—
morning kisses. The day Robert Kennedy died, a
green and evil worm crawled out of a bud. I killed
it, a gardening Sirhan Sirhan.

At the corner of the house Rosa Mutabilis fluttered
its single, changeable wings. My favorite, perhaps.

Then, in the border, along the south side of
the white house, Golden Wings (a patented rose—
did you know you can patent roses? Well, you can);
prickly, purplish Rose de Rescht; Souvenir
de la Malmaison (named by a Russian Grand Duke in
honor of the Empress Joséphine, Empress of Rosarians);
Mabel Morrison, lifting her blowsy white blooms
to the living-room windows.

Then Georg Arends, whose silver-pink petals
uniquely fold into sharp points (or is Georg
my favorite?).

And darkly brooding Prince Camille de Rohan, on
which, out of a cloudless sky, a miraculous rain
once fell. (But I'm forgetting Gloire de Dijon,
Dean Hole's favorite rose.)

Then the smallest, most delicate, delectable
of all, Rose de Meaux. Alas, it pined away.

And elsewhere more: Rosa Gallica, the striped
and the pink, the Pembertons, Persian yellow,
and unforgettable cerise Zéphirine Drouhin.
And a gray rose, Reine des Violettes. Sweet-

brier, Mme. Pierre Oger, Variegata di Bologna,
"like raspberries and cream." And more,
whose names escape me.

I went by there Sunday last and they're gone, all
gone, uprooted, supplanted by a hateful "foundation
planting" of dinky conifers, some pointed, some
squatty roundish. I put a curse on it and them.

On either side of the front walk there towered two
old horse-chestnut trees. I loved their sticky,
unfurling leaves, and when they bore their candles
it was magic, breath-catching, eye-delighting. Cut
down, cut down. What kind of man cuts down trees
that took all those years to grow? I do not
understand.

Oh, well, it's his house now, and I remove the
curse, but not without a hope that Rose de Rescht
and the rugosas gave him a good scratching. He
deserved it.

But oh dear: I forgot the five Old China Monthly
roses, and I always wish I'd planted Félicité
et Perpétue—it's their names I like. And
Climbing Lady Hillingdon.

(But the Garland grown as a fountain seemed
somehow beyond me.)

There are roses and roses, always more roses.
It's the horse-chestnut trees I mind.

Mood Indigo

for David Trinidad

. . . and the curtain rose in that theatre so long ago
and the music is playing
the first song I fell in

love to today so soon
                    is it possible
and there, gigantic, is the face
on the backdrop
of the elegant Duke
                    the song Mood Indigo
unforgettable dragging rhythm
                    his smile
                    the tie
                              the stick pin
enter the dancer
in tights
            darkest blue
she dances sinuously
                          right up to him
                    the elegant smiling Duke
and the stickpin
                    three-dimensional
she lies back upon
      it
        and revolves
                          sexy, I so young
and the rhythm
                    dragged out
enter the man in black
is he her fate?
                    a dangerous destiny
      O infamous race riots
      of Washington, D.C.!
slowly they revolve
                    is she dying?
                    she is dying slowly
and the Duke
the audience so still
                    so rapt
Saturday matinees of vaudeville
      my childhood
already in love today
                    perhaps
they have left the stage
                    and she returns

```
            somehow a different
                              dancer
       and on the tie pin
                         she lies back
  as the curtain descends
                              on a strange love affair
  on the afternoon
                    I first heard
                              Mood Indigo
  everyone claps
               the curtains
                              close
  farewell! dancing madness
                              we will meet again
                         in Harlem
```

Rain

```
quilts the pond and
out from under its plumped-upness
a snapping turtle
pokes its head and
munches a morsel of water-lily leaf.
The sky
falls down in bits and pieces.
Does the face
of the pond
show the level of the water table?
Mebbe yes,
mebbe no.
A girl
no,
an ironwood tree
stands there
so young, so sinewy and slim
as though soft-water rinses were
all it ever wanted.
A branch
```

heavily shifts
its leaves.
Something—
a frog?—
goes plop.
The rough-cut grass,
stuck randomly
with flowers,
accepts the world's shampoo.

Birds

Little Portion
Tuesday, May 10, 1988

start up in gray,
in moist green,
branches laid
across, one call
a ratchet, and
"cooo-cooo,"
a silver spike
thin as a hypodermic
needle: "Just
a little stick."

A congeries of what
once were muddy lanes
shooting, one
into another,
randomly, tangled
as twigs. A round

bed of peonies,
hard in bud,
dark of leaf
and wet, wet:
Long Island Sound
so near, not quite
out of sight.

The birds stop.
The Post Road
shines mutedly,
an asphalt river.
The busy cars
begin to go about
their business.

Time, here, at
Little Portion,
for morning prayer.
Birds join in,
the bell at
the Poor Clares'
convent clangs,
a mourning dove
persists. Soft

morning green
(the longer one
lives, the more
to forget),
budded shapes
of branches
interlaced:
three grays,
sky, road, path.

Shadowy Room

for Brother Thomas Carey
June 27, 1988

". . . tall buildings swayed
in downtown San Francisco.
No reports
            of injuries
                        at present."
Perishable perfection
of Glenn Gould playing

Bach purls on, oblivious
of interruption, building
course on
course, harmonious
in all lights,
all weathers, not unlike
la Rotonda and
so much airier,
spider webs and skeletons
of leaves,
the contiguity
of panes of glass. "No
reports
of injuries at present:
details later."
Mortal music, leading,
leading on,
to San Francisco,
the Golden Gate,
the hands of God.

White Boat, Blue Boat

for Hy Weitzen

Two boats parked
and posing in
the sun-struck
winter landscape:
rough grass, bare
with green washes.
Against self-colored
bark, lithe twigs
end in red buds:
you can't see it,
the red, and when
you do, you can't
not see it, against
a scaling trunk that,
higher than three

men on each
other's shoulders,
becomes more trunks.
Beyond, marsh grass
and reeds scratched
swiftly in.
A woman goes by,
her dog, too,
in short lopes:
a mutt. The day
can't get brighter,
clearer, but it
brightens, brightens,
so much and so
much more under
infinite cloudlessness
and icy spaces
and endless mystery.

Over the hills

the Jersey hills
to grandfather's house
and mother's and father's
(yours, not mine)
and that Morristown cemetery
where they lie
—well, not father:
instantly,
the complexity
of family history
no matter how simple-seeming,
how forthright. A nice,
really a nice
cemetery: rolling somewhat,
like the small clouds
in all the February blue,
and stuck

with admirable trees
and well kept up,
not offensively spruce:
plenty of dead leaves
scurrying about. Few
Roman bank-type
mausoleums. Beckers
abound, and other German names
among the Smiths, the Mellons,
the Courtneys. Your mother called
on her marker,
as she was in life, Sallie:
she hated Sarah Loraine.
A beautiful woman
with a rough side to her tongue,
who always turned
to her father in troublesome times,
and here he is again. When
the other father (yours)
went off to war
he said, "Now you
must take care
of mother." A lot
to lay on a three-year-old!
Of course
he came home,
of course
you were jealous, and
like nearly all
the brokers in Far Hills
he drank.
Oh boy did he drink.
O well,
didn't we all? Life
can be cruel, and
tormented your mother with
one of its cruelest ailments,
long drawn out,
grinding.
But you still were young
and she well

when she took you to see
that Broadway hit whose star
she had such a crush on.
You sat together
in a box by the stage.
The show went on
until
(*and then? and then?*)
Pinza
looked up at Sallie
and sang,
"Some enchanted evening . . ."

A cardinal

in the branches of
the great plane tree
whistles its song:

or is it that mimic
Fairfield
saluting the day

under the branches of
his great plane tree
in his springtime yard?

Ajaccio Violets

Showered, shaved, splashed
(Ajaccio Violets) I
at first light
On Sunday morning go
out to get the *Times* and
by the elevator

393

two girls and a boy
passing a joint:
I
say good morning and
they
look up sullen-eyed and
don't say squat

The vapors of a humid day
and mountainous turds
of black-bagged garbage and
up the street
he comes: the house drunk
too heavily ballasted to leeward
by the *Sunday Times:*

he
ships water, rights himself,
veers past
the harbor buoy
and somehow makes it, maybe:
will he waken
late in the day
and find it, the *Sunday Times,*
that weighty testimonial to
conspicuous consumption,
scattered
beside the bed, unread,
half-read, unreadable
with that head
and those eyes,
those eyes?

Shaker

There was simply
nothing to look at:
a white empty room

with pegs to hang
chairs on: you know

the kind that I mean
the kind that look
like the way that
                    the way that

Teddy Wilson
plays the piano: each
note is so clear

I pointed
the camera down
the hall:
"An Arrangement in White":

the door of the closet
ajar: the lid of
one seat was up:
straight lines:
no curves.

There was a shop: pot
holders, a big bag
of apples: crisp, sharp.

I looked back
at the girl who looked
back
at me: perhaps to be
the last Shaker
at Sabbathday Lake.

Three Gardens

4404 Stanford

On the steep slope by the drive he
built a rock garden: each
different, from schist
to granite to
you name it, sort of a giant hunk
of conglomerate, of
which there was a hunk, purplish,
with bits of crap
caught up in it. Sedum,
maybe some moss pinks:
it was a *rock* garden,
a garden of rocks, but not
Kyoto style.

Erta Canina

Any place else it
was just a yard: but
if it's in Florence,
up above Florence, with some pots
of this-a and that-a
and a giantly ancient cypress
of dark and towering smoke, shut
in on itself, then
it's a garden. One night (in bed,
not yet asleep) from the boughs
of the cypress, a sound
so strange, so old, so new, so piercing
and steady, so clear, so loud (moonlight
in bright bars on the brick floor)
that, yes, of course,
at last:
the nightingale.

396

Chelsea

Petunias, this year,
got the gate and in
the window box that sits
on my balcony, are
three stout plants
of dianthus of an uncertain sort:
two rosy ones
and another a dark, smouldering,
passionate red. They
are more or less at center: in
front, demurely shiny,
green-leaved basil:
at the corners,
sage and rosemary. Drawn by the sun,
woven by the wind, they
intermingle: the herbs flower
unexpectedly with rose-red lights.
Behind,
up the 1880s iron balustrade, twine
a few implacable thin tendrils
of morning glory.

Let's All Hear It For Mildred Bailey!

The men's can at Café Society Uptown
was need I say it? Upstairs
and as I headed for the stairs I
stumbled slightly
not about to fall
and Mildred Bailey
swept by in a nifty outfit:
off-brown velvet
cut in a simple suit-effect
studded with brass nail heads
(her hair dressed with stark simplicity)
"Take it easy, Sonny," she

advised me and passed on to the supper club
(surely no supper was
served at Café you-know-which?)
A star spoke to me
in person! No one
less than Mildred Bailey!

Downstairs I nursed one drink
(cheap is cheap)
and Mildred Bailey got it on
and the boys all stood and shouted
"Mama Won't You Scrap Your Fat?"
a lively number
during the brownout
in war-haunted, death-smeared
NY

Then things got better, greater:
Mildred Bailey sang immortal hits
indelibly
permanently
marked by that voice
with built-in laughter
perfect attack: always
on the note
not behind or above it
and the extra something nice
that was that voice
a quality, a sound she had
on a disc, a waxing
you know it: Mildred Bailey

The night progressed:
a second drunk—oops—drink
(over there, boys, in what seemed
like silence boxcars rolled on
loaded with Jews, gypsies, nameless
forever others: The Final Solution
a dream of
Adolf Hitler:
Satan incarnate)

Mildred Bailey winds up the show
with a bouncy
number: when she gets back
to Brooklyn
from cheapo cruise ship
visitation:
Havana, Cuba
(then the door stood wide
to assorted thrills)
the next one in her life
ain't gonna be no loser, a clerk
oh no
"You can bet that he'll be Latin"

And Mildred Bailey, not
quite alone
in her upstate farmhouse
the rain is falling
she listens to another voice
somehow sadly
it is singing a song:
music
in a world gone wrong

Noon Office

A snowy curtain
slides up the sky.
Across the road,
dead trees whose
tops a hurricane
snapped off, rise
straight and pallid
out of green honey-
suckle nests. That
big tree, nearest
the house, goes
leathery, elephantine,

stands
on one leg.
The blessing—
the bliss—
of one afternoon:
an infestation
of silence. May God
forgive us. To no
one's memory we
erect dead trees.

Simone Signoret

Look, Mitterrand baby, your telegram
of condolence to Yves
Montand tells it like it is
but just once can't some high
placed Frenchman forget about the
gloire de France while the world
stands still a moment and all
voices rise in mourning
a star of stars:
Simone Signoret was and is
immortal
(thanks to seeming permanence
yes the silver screen? *l'écran?*)
Simone Signoret, A.K.A.
Mme Yves Montand, is dead: Let's
re-read Tennyson's "Ode
to the Duke of Wellington"
with subtle emendations:
after all Simone never brought
about deaths by zillions on
a battlefield: no simply adult
entertainment as ambiguous
women beginning
with *Dédée d'Anvers*: Dédée
mixes with the wrong type

waterfront layabouts in
Antwerp and of course
she became some sort of
"star overnight" so let's for-
get about Academy Award
winner *Room at the Top* and
turn full attention to
Casque d'Or meaning
"Golden Helmet" and here
in this still in today's
Times she is wearing
her golden helmet of hair
and musing on the strange
destiny that right at the be-
ginning she does a circular
dance with her soon-to-be
lover (one arm behind back
one arm hangs straight down)
and he's a carpenter (we
find out all about that) and
utterly evil Claude Dauphin
and at the end she watches
from a window his execution—
friend lover, that is, not
well-disposed-of Dauphin—
and she, staring and staring
implacably staring, woman
with mysterious eyes, under
a smooth brushed helmet
of golden hair: I always
remember you like that
and we used to quaff
liquid refreshments in
the same midtown Parisian
bar (Christ, that was long
ago) and I wondered who
the hell is this Simone
Signoret
and what's so great about
Dédée d'Anvers (I still
haven't seen it): Simone

(may I call you Simone
just this once?) tonight
one star in the real sky
the starry firmament
goes out and the rest
the stars, the stars!
shine more brightly for
that star of stars
with almond-eyes
and a well-brushed
helmet of golden hair
and I truly miss you
Simone Signoret

The light within

and the light without: the shade
of a rainy April morning:
subtle shadows
cast backward by lamplight
upon daylight,
soft unforceful daylight,
the essence
of cloud cover
descending mistily into the street:
and the unwhitely
white surround of a curling photograph
models itself
as north light
modeled the face in the photograph:

and against a window
a tree shows
each lightly tinted leaf
another shadowy shade, some
transparently, some
not: and, in the corner
the dark bisected

by the light that falls
from without (created
by its absence)
lies luminous within itself:
the luminous dark within.

Advent

Open my eyes on the welcome
rosy shock of sunshine.

Open the first little door
of my Advent calendar:

a darling hobby horse
on wheels. Open

the window a crack: and
quickly close it against

a knife-like draught. The day
looks warmer than it is.

Six something

on June 5th, '90:
closed shops
and well-washed
bluelessness, and
across the street
a man finishes
his polishing. I
count seedlings:
always counting,
cars, trees, not

infinitudes of
leaves. The Veterans
Building hides all
the Empire State Building
excepting
its antennae
rising in stages
first woven then
slim out of thick
to an ultimate
needle taper pricking
the day: its
point a test
of clarity. And
where is God
in all this?
Asleep? Resting?
and if so, from
what? Eternity
is tireless
surely, like:
rest now forever
blessed tired heart,
wakening otherwhere
in bell-like blue.

Andrew Lord Poems

the flattened shape
the first shape
a bowl

a jug   a vase   a dish

rectangles   cones

lustre glaze
crazed

a fine craze
           hidden
almost
           maple keys
among maple leaves

plunged
hot in water
Chinese ink
rubbed in

———

when is a funerary vase
not funerary?
a vase not a vase?

the shapes of things

tea pot ceramic
vase of bronze vase

trumpet flare
beaker
gu

touching and holding

pressing and holding

———

a random arrangement
changing within itself

      33 pieces   modelling

black
black

          not black
             Wedgwood obsidian
slate
darkening toward black

16 pieces   copper

blue   copper and tin

16 pieces   copper

red   copper and tin
             rouge flambé

———

where light falls
where shade falls
       pressing
       pulling

drunken tea pot
slope-shouldered urn
beauty
of oddity

stoneware clay
matte finish

when is a glaze
not a glaze?

fired
not hot enough
       no silica
       no glass-
       iness
       no shine

flat
matte

———

coiled clay
joined
in three
parts

pretty
       breakable

pretty
       fragile

Sèvres   Meissen

touching and holding

modelling
       hand marks

a knife
      a rolling
pin

———

geometry

age 16
working
with clay
    ceramics

cubist
or
geometric

or
constructivist
angled geometry

1 year
in factory
in Delft

excited
about glazes now
very involved in glazes

finest crackle
see it
hear it

an algebra
of the stars

———

packing up
funeral feast
dishes

wrapping dishes

sending dishes

a platter
shaped
like a peanut

gold drip
on vessel lip

a cup   a basin

fracture
and

```
        durability
a trivet


        ——


always
a shape
   in mind
changes
   each time

freedom
breeds control

elegant
        notebooks

                a handle
twists
        back on itself

dark
     runnels
     over crazing
unwiped
dribbles


        ——


dead-leaf
            tea set
knobbly
   dirtied
   by gold

indescribable
   colors
        of fired
```

metal
favrile
lustrousness

  golden copper
coming forward
  darker
manganese
  coming forward

uncontrollable
            fire
whichever
  it chooses
  to be

———

most beautiful
  glazes
deadliest
  ingredients

lead
manganese dioxide
silver nitrate
copper oxide
tin oxide

glazes with
    darkness
boding through
lights
on the unsmoothedness
bulky
askew

a bowl
with thumb
  drawn lines
another bowl

marked
by thumb nail

here
gold
tries
to come through

Under the Hanger

from Gilbert White's Journals

Wood lark whistles. Hogs carry straw.
Sky lark sings.
Young cucumber swells.
Frogs croak: spawn abounds.
Cold & black. Harsh, hazy day.
Backward apples begin to blow.
Frost, sun, fog, rain, snow. Bunting twitters.
No dew, rain, rain, rain.
Swans flounce & dive.
Chilly & dark.
Dark and spitting. Indian flowers in Dec'r!
Ground very wet. The nightingale sings.
Blackcap sings. The sedge-bird a delicate polyglott.
The titlark begins to sing: a sweet songster!
Turtle coos.
Asparagus begins to sprout.
Cuckoo cries.
No house-martins appear.

Apricots, peaches, & nectarines swell:
sprinkled trees with water, & watered the roots.
Oaks are felled: the bark runs freely.
The leaves of the mulberry trees hardly begin to peep.
Showers, sun & clouds, brisky air.
Much hay spoiled: much not cut.

Put meadow hay in large cock.
Hay well made at last.
Sun, sweet day.

All things in a drowning condition!

First day of winter. Snow on the ground.
Gathered in all the grapes. Snow on the hills.
Full moon.
Rooks resort to their nest-trees.
Grey & sharp.
Earth-worms lie out & copulate.
Great rain. Hops sadly washed.
Ice bears: boys slide.

Rain, rain, rain.

The road in a most dusty, smothering condition.
Full moon. My well is shallow & the water foul.
The grass burns.
A plant of missle-toe grows on a bough of the medlar.
The air is full of insects.
Turkies strut and gobble.
Snow wastes: eaves drip. Cocks crow.
Sun, bright & pleasant.
The boys are playing in their shirts.
Bees thrive. Asparagus abounds.
Dark & chilly, rain. Cold & comfortless.
Mossed the white cucumber bed.
Snow covers the ground.

Planted 12 goose-berry trees, & three monthly roses,
     & three Provence roses.
The voice of the cockow is heard in the hanger.
Grass lamb.
Grey, sprinkling, gleams with thunder.
Wavy, curdled clouds, like the remains of thunder.

Pease are hacked: rye is reaping: turnips thrive &
     are hoing.
Stifling dust.
Sweet moonshine.
Boys slide on the ice!

Dew, bright, showers: thunder, gleam of sun.
Straw-berries, scarlet, cryed about.

Straw-berries dry, & tasteless.
Taw & hop-scotch come in fashion among the boys.
The sun mounts and looks down on the hanger.
Crown Imperials blow, & stink.
Much gossamer.
Moles work, & heave up their hillocks.
Ice within doors.
Rime.
Snow on the ground.
Snow in the night: snow five inches deep. /
Snow on the ground.
Icicles hang in eaves all day.
Snow lies on the hill.

Crocus's make a gaudy show.
Cuculus cuculat: the voice of the cuckoo is heard in
        Blackmoor woods.
The air is filled with floating willow-down.
Fog, sun, pleasant showers, moonshine.
Here & there a wasp.
Black-birds feed on the elder-berries.
Frost, ice, sun pleasant moon-light.
Frost, ice, bright, red even, prodigious white dew.
Thunder, lightening, rain, snow!

Vast damage in various parts!
No frost.
Daffodil blows.

Daffodil blows.
Sweet weather. Mackerel.
Soft wind. The woodpecker laughs.
Cinnamon-roses blow.
Flowers smell well this evening: some dew.
The distant hills look very blue.

Clouds, hail, shower, gleams.
Sharp air, & fire in the parlor.
Sweet day, golden even, red horizon.
Snow-drops, & crocus's shoot.
Vast frost-work on the windows.
Longest day: a cold, harsh solstice!

413   *Last Poems*

Thunder & hail.
Yellow evening.
Potatoes blossom.
Men cut their meadows.
Goose-berries wither on the trees.
The seeds of the lime begin to fall.
Grey, & mild, gleams.
Grey, sun, pleasant, yellow even.
Dark & wet.
Rain, rain, gleams. Venus resplendent.
Showers of hail, sleet. Gleams.
The *Cuckoo* is heard on Greatham common.

Cut the first cucumber.
Pulled the first radish.
Early orange-lilies blow.
Cut *five* cucumbers.
Bright, sun, golden even.
Cut *eight* cucumbers.
Provence roses blow against a wall.
Cut *ten* cucumbers.
Dames violets very fine.

Men wash their sheep.

Yellow Flowers

for William Corbett

Pie-wedge petals
deeply pinked and
the yellow of yellow oranges,
set in a single
layer, ray out
from a pollen shedding tuft:
see the bright dust
on this filing cabinet
enameled the greeny-cream
of the seed-cradling inner flesh
of an avocado

these yellow flowers
on wiry stems, bunched
in a thick gray pitcher:
two bands of washed-out blue,
two transfers in same ("You
don't want
that clunky thing")

and petals fall and tufts
puff up, a brown fuzz ball
with a green frill: the hard
green balls with green frills
of course are buds: and

you plunge your face
in their massed
papery powdery sweetness
and grunt in delight
at their sunset sweetness

it begins with C

yes: coreopsis

Blossoming Oakwood

dead-ends at 19th one
block over from Dolores
(more magisterial, more
of a street
of a street), its houses
not so much quake
resistant as egg crate
concessions to
the possibility of one:
crumple and build again
under the colorlessness
of thickened

Pacific moistened air:
draw in cold breaths
if you can. On Oakwood,
run down, kept up, tinted
San Francisco style,
on Ash Wednesday (early
in February
this year), geraniums—
coarse, weedy, pink—
make a hedge where
there's no room to grow.
One front yard
a delirious garden
jumble sale: a bush
like a sponge
with a myriad small leaves,
jostles a camellia
(blood red, rain fades
a washy orange). Across
a petty scramble
of undergrowth along
an overgrown path,
a window-blocking banana
shredding, thriving, and
trashy, trashy, tropics trashy,
urgent, jubilant, thrashing
on Oakwood Street, on
Ash Wednesday, the day
death begins, and life.

A Chapel

small, just
a room,
the altar
at center,
one wall
all glass,

out in
wet twilight:
by a fence
a tall clump
of calla lilies
(*Zantedeschia aethiopica*
roadside weeds
of Ethiopia),
a camellia
two stories tall,
in full bloom:
they fall
whole and
lie like cow flops
on the grass.
Outdoor stairs:
San Francisco.
". . . and to dust
you shall return"
he imposes
the ashes.

A View

Little Portion
Tuesday, May 10, 1988

How come a thickish tree
casts so thin a shadow
and that sign-supporting pipe
none at all? (here comes Tom)

The road dries off, lighter
and lighter (there goes
Tom, in the red car, after
flour). In the further

distance, a baby-blue camper,
after reeds and dead tree trunks,

peeled and weathered,
and the creosoted phone poles

Closer, on grass, the sunlight
breathes: fades and brightens,
brightens and fades, sparkles
yellow-green on green

Out of nowhere, a breeze
tosses the junk (soon
to be leaves) on twig ends.
Here comes Charlie, the cat.

Closer, window screen and
a six-light window sash
pushed part way up another
makes a fifteen-light window

framed by thick white net.
Closer, a bag says, The Cellar.
Closer, a pair of slippers, and
(khaki canvas) a Maine hiking shoe

invites my foot to go
out there, into the view
of May 10th, 1988
                    Here

comes Tom (he
got the flour) and there
sits Charlie, a white
cat on a green hummock.

This soft October

Monday, October 17, 1988

                    mid-morning
the light, what light
                    there is

that is, comes
from the east
                under the sky
not from it
                more a pulsation
than a glow
            the glow
that on Sunday
                (only
yesterday? was
                it only yesterday?
It was
        it was) shone
from the west
                from
Manhattan
            the train throbbed
on toward
            light tasting
of Chateau Yquem or
                        less grand
more glorious
                the fortified wine
used at the
            sacrament
in communion
                this is the cup
of life
        the blood
of salvation
            light lighting up
the scrub
        in red
and purple
            and gold

On the dresser

that had a swivel
mirror, a swivel
picture frame: greenish-
silvery-grayish:
in it
a photograph (silvery-
grayish) of
a girl, a young
woman: large
soft eyes, hair swept
around her head
and forehead, a filmy
dress over a
silken dress with an
embroidered bodice
flounce. Next
to it,
a matching
(greenish-silvery-grayish)
bud vase
in which once I
put a stem
of freesia: Bernie
liked that
fragrant tribute to
the beautiful
beautiful mother he
never knew. Time
passed and at
the draft board physical
a doctor said, "Wasn't
your mother Hortense
Chittenden? I
used to dance
with her. Now,
then, she died . . ."
". . . of influenza,"
Bernie said. The doctor

frowned, looked
down at the form and
wrote,
"in childbirth."

Princess Di

Intricacies of a devious mind
run amok are explicable
to me who cannot explain:
Helena, you came bravely
into a room I knew was bugged
(outside in the hall
peered and lingered
a literal murderer disguised
as a black man ready to bring
me the ultimate message:
my death:) and bold as brass
but so much prettier in
you came with a flower
wrapped, concealed in
paper and I tried to converse
in the language of the dance:
slipping fingers on fingers
meaning rings, meaning jewels
and the inside of the paper
was white and blank you
laughed to see it and I
saw a message from Korea
holy, mysterious as a stone
a white stone to hold
in hand and meditate to
pray and you smiled and
you left a soft pink rose
on my bed and I went
back of beyond to
the place so far away
where time is eternal and

infinity is grasped not
understood: and when I
came round there was the rose
in a clear plastic container
aslant the petals not yet
curling back and I knew that
the rose was extra special
and you came and I asked
"Who gave me that rose?" You
laughed and you said, "Why
I did: its name is
Princess Di" and each day
as I lay and time slowed
down to its usual shuffle
I watched as the petals
curled back and
came to a point I
exclaimed to myself, "That
point is unique: this
softer, smaller rose
is the hybridized offspring
of Georg Arends!"
silvery, pink
larger with sharply
pointed petals, the only
rose to do so (I thought,
I imagined) what joy
to see it recur in Princess
Di named for we all know
who and the Chinese lady
heard what I said when
she asked and she said,
"Princess Diana the Princess
Diana" and as the days
passed and you came
to escort me home and
the rose I had watched
grown fat and soft
expired as I left
and I thought, "Beautiful
Princess, farewell!"

Haze

hangs heavy
down into trees: dawn
doesn't break today,
the morning
seeps into being, one
bird, maybe
two, chipping
away at it. A white dahlia,
big
as Baby Bumstead's head,
leans
its folded petals
at a window, a lesson
in origami.
Frantically, God
knows what
machine: oh no,
just Maggio's
garbage truck.
Staring
at all the roughage
that hides an estuary,
such urbanity
seems inapt: the endless city
builds on and on
thinning out, here and there,
for the wet green velvet towels
("slight imperfections")
of summer
("moderately priced")
and a hazy morning
in August,
even that
we may grow to love.

INDEX OF TITLES AND FIRST LINES

Printed in Germany
by Amazon Distribution
GmbH, Leipzig